MW01026853

The Personality Disorders Through the Lens of Attachment Theory and the Neurobiologic Development of the Self

A Clinical Integration

The Personality Disorders
Through the Lens of
Attachment Theory
and the Neurobiologic
Development of the Self

A Clinical Integration

Edited by
James F. Masterson, M.D.

Zeig, Tucker & Theisen, Inc.
Phoenix, Arizona

A Word About the Writing Team

In 1986, the Masterson Institute for Psychoanalytic Psychotherapy was established, with part-time postgraduate training programs launched in both New York City and San Francisco. I had spent some 30 years doing the necessary research to develop and refine the theory of the personality disorders, and I felt that the time had come to formally train others.

The training program was a three-year commitment that included three hours of classes a week and one hour of supervision. A successful case-study presentation was a requirement for graduation. From each three-year class, the most likely candidates for the faculty were selected for training with me; that is, two more years of supervision. Thus, all faculty members have had five years of supervision. They have also played a role in our ongoing research and have published in a variety of venues.

The contributors to this breakthrough volume — and to the expansion of the work both on and off paper — are all members of the Institute faculty. Margot Beattie, Ph.D., Barbara Short, Ph.D., and Ken Seider, Ph.D., were in the first class in San Francisco. They graduated in 1989 and joined the faculty in 1991. Steven K. Reed, Ph.D., and Donald Roberts, Ph.D., were in the Spokane class, which graduated in 1992. They joined the faculty in 1994. Joe Farley, M.F.C., graduated in the San Francisco class of 1997, joining the faculty in 1999. Jerry Katz, C.S.W., graduated in the New York class of 1998 and became part of the faculty in 2001. Finally, Judith Pearson, Ph.D., graduated in the first New York class in 1989. She joined the faculty two years later in 1991, and in 2003, was appointed Clinical Director of the New York program.

It is my pleasure to collaborate with this team of excellent researchers, clinicians, and writers to move this latest material from the relative privacy of our own professional domains into a more public sphere so that others may benefit.

— *James F. Masterson, M.D.*

Published by
Zeig, Tucker & Theisen, Inc.
3614 North 24th Street
Phoenix, AZ 85016

Library of Congress Cataloging-in-Publication Data
The personality disorders through the lens of attachment theory and the
neurobiologic development of the self : a clinical integration / edited by
James F. Masterson.
    p. cm.
Includes bibliographical references and index.
ISBN–10: 1-932462-34-1 (alk. paper) / ISBN–13: 978-1-932462-34-2
1. Personality disorders. 2. Attachment behavior. 3. Self. 4. Self psy-
chology. 5. Neurobiology. I. Masterson, James F.
RC554.P472 2005
616.85 '81—dc22   2005044724

Manufactured in the United States of America

10 9 8 7 6 5 4 3 2 1

Table of Contents

Introduction

This book is the culmination of 40 years of clinical research exploring the personality disorders. The journey has taken us past many theoretical way stations, each of which has made its own contribution to the overall theory. Beginning as a descriptive theory, it evolved into a developmental theory, then into a developmental object relations theory, and, finally, into a developmental self and object relations theory.

The recent emergence of attachment theory and the theory of the neurobiologic development of the self has provided the last scientific piece to bring the theory to a successful completion: a scientific statement that describes the origin and development of the personality disorders.

The chapters in this volume illustrate clinically how these two theories have been integrated into, and have completed, the developmental self and object relations theory. Among the subjects covered are transference and countertransference, consciousness, mother–infant attachment, transference and the language of change, from concrete truth to symbolic reality, separation in the countertransference, reproducing the real self, moving from dependence on the false self to a real relationship, the psychotherapy of trauma, and therapeutic neutrality under challenge.

The reader is invited to join us on our journey and to sample the varied ways in which the attachment and neurobiologic theories have influenced and fulfilled our work.

1

Integrating Attachment and Object Relations Theories and the Neurobiologic Development of the Self

JAMES F. MASTERSON, M.D.

The findings of attachment theory and neurobiologic brain research have confirmed and elaborated on a theory I proposed 28 years ago (Masterson, 1976) concerning the role of the mother in the development and psychopathology of the self. As a prelude to discussing the integration of these three approaches, I will briefly review the development of that theory.

REVIEW OF THEORY

Adolescent Turmoil Theory — Psychiatric Dilemma of Adolescence (Masterson, 1967)

The work began in the 1960s when, as a resident, I became interested in the then-prevalent "adolescent turmoil" theory that adolescents who had symptoms did not need treatment because they would grow out of them as such symptoms were attributed to adolescent turmoil. In reviewing the literature, I found no studies supporting this theory, so I decided to do my own follow-up. This led to 12 years of research on two formal follow-up studies — one an inpatient retrospective and the other an outpatient prospective with controls. The conclusion I reached was that they did not "grow out of it."

Five years after their initial evaluation, 50% of the adolescent outpatients were still severely impaired, and what was giving them so much trouble was what we called their pathological character traits, which had not been touched on in their treatment. These findings were published in *The Psychiatric Dilemma of Adolescence* (Masterson, 1967). This led to the next questions: What are these traits? Where do they come from? How does one identify and treat them?

Treatment of the Borderline Adolescent — A Developmental Approach (Masterson, 1972)

To pursue these questions, it was necessary to set up an adolescent inpatient program. The patients' symptomatology consisted predominantly of depression, acting out, truancy, drugs, and the like. At this point, we were able to diagnose them descriptively as Borderline personality disorders. When we controlled their acting out, they became depressed, which led to the first psychodynamic concept that the acting out was a defense against depression.

The next question was: What is the source of this depression? Our initial idea was that it was conflicts related to emancipation. But as we continued to overcome the defenses, the adolescents gradually shifted from talking about current conflicts to focusing on conflicts earlier and earlier in development.

At this time, while looking up developmental research in the library, I came across the work of Bowlby on children's reactions to separation and an article by Margaret Mahler entitled "Autism and Symbiosis — Two Disturbances in the Sense of Entity and Identity." Then I attended a movie presented by Mahler showing normal children's reactions to separation.

This led to a further deepening of the psychodynamic perspective to the effect that the Borderline adolescent's problem was a developmental arrest of the ego, a failure in separation/individuation owing to the mother's difficulty in supporting the adolescent's ego development. This lack of support was experienced as an abandonment depression, which was defended against by forgoing further development, in addition to other defenses. This then led to the adoption of the therapeutic technique of confrontation of the defenses. The findings were published in a book entitled *Treatment of the Borderline Adolescent — A Developmental Approach* (Masterson, 1972).

The success of the treatment was demonstrated by yet another follow-up study five years after discharge, published in *From Borderline Adolescent to Functioning Adult: The Test of Time* (Masterson, 1980).

Psychotherapy of the Borderline Adult —
A Developmental Object Relations Approach
(Masterson, 1976)

The next question related to identifying the link between maternal libidinal unavailability and the developmental arrest of the ego. The answers to this question were found in object relations theory and the notion of intrapsychic structure.

By this time, I was pursuing this question in work with adults in my private practice, which resulted in my focusing on the intrapsychic consequences of maternal libidinal unavailability, that is, the internalization of the mother–child interactions to form the object relations unit. I now added object relations to the developmental approach.

I put together four ideas: (1) maternal libidinal unavailability in the first three years during the separation/individuation phase; (2) object relations theory of intrapsychic structure; (3) Freud's article on two principles of mental functioning; (4) my own clinical observation that as Borderline patients got better, they felt worse, that is, more depressed. This led to the development of a concept called the Borderline triad: self-activation leads to anxiety and depression, which lead to defense. It also led to a broadening concept of its etiology as being attributable to three factors: nature, nurture, and fate. Nature referred to the genetic, nurture to the mother's capacity to support the emerging self, and fate to external separation stresses during the vulnerable phase of separation/individuation (Masterson, 1976).

The Real Self
(Masterson, 1985)

This emphasis on the self in the triad produced an important shift in perspective from the ego and object relations to the recognition that the key pathology was the developmental arrest of the self, along with the ego and object relations, and that the triad was not just Borderline, but also applied to all of the personality disorders, and so it was renamed the Disorders of the Self Triad. Thus, the approach now became a developmental self and object relations approach. The central psychodynamic theme of all of the personality disorders is the Disorder of the Self Triad, and the clinical tasks are (1) to identify the clinical vicissitudes of this triad and (2) to intervene in a way that challenges the defenses so that the self and its abandonment depression can emerge and be worked through, freeing the self to resume its development. A number of publications have demonstrated these findings: *The Real Self* (Masterson, 1985), *The Emerging Self* (Masterson, 1993), and *Psychotherapy of the Disorders of the Self* (Masterson & Klein, 1988).

The theory has taken a journey that lasted over 40 years, from description, to developmental, to developmental object relations, to developmental self and object relations. But there is confirmation of, and additions to, the theory from attachment theory and neurobiologic brain research.

There are two important additions from attachment theory (Hesse, 1999) and neurobiologic brain research on the development of the self: (1) Attachment theory provided a scientifically researched base that confirms and elaborates on the effects of the interactions between the mother and child on the development of the self. (2) Neurobiology (Schore, 1994, 2001) for the first time, took us inside the brain to find the neuronal basis of the development and functions of the self.

MAHLER AND COLLEAGUES (1975), STERN (1985), AND CHILD-OBSERVATION RESEARCH

The clinical observation of the relationship between mother–child interactions and the development of the self during the first three years in normal children provided a dramatic breakthrough in the understanding of the developmental arrest of the personality disorders. I will briefly summarize the work of Mahler and Stern before considering attachment theory and neurobiology.

The child-observation work of Mahler and Stern occupied the center of the psychoanalytic stage, primarily because they made intrapsychic hypotheses from the observation of behavior. Bowlby's (1969, 1973) child-observation work was shunted to the periphery because he limited his perspective to describing the observation of behavior. This difference, which promoted Mahler's and Stern's work initially, was later responsible for Bowlby's work coming to the fore since it formed the basis for scientific research on attachment that could be replicated. It is worthy of note here that I began with Bowlby, then shifted to Mahler's work, which formed one of the pillars of my own work initially, and then led me to the work of Stern, and, finally, back to Bowlby and attachment.

Mahler theorized that the child must separate from a symbiotic relationship with the mother. She made intrapsychic hypotheses based on the observation of child behavior and divided this development into three stages: the autistic (0 to 2 months), the symbiotic (3 to 18 months), and separation/individuation (18 to 36 months). The separation/individuation stage was further divided into the differentiation subphase, the practicing subphase, and rapprochement, on the way to object constancy.

Stern also developed his ideas from intrapsychic hypotheses based on

observing the child's behavior. He concluded that the child was prewired to
see the mother as separate from birth cognitively and that the child was an
active partner in the coregulation of his or her own development, which
occurred in four stages: the emerging self (0 to 2 months), the core self (2 to
6 months), the intersubjective self (7 to 9 months), and the verbal self (15 to
18 months). Sterns emphasized that the child saw the mother as separate
cognitively from the outset. However, he was less clear about emotional
separation. He also suggested that the way in which the mother looked at the
infant and thought about the infant were important.

ATTACHMENT RESEARCH — BOWLBY
(1969, 1973)

Bowlby, approaching the research from a different point of view, hypothesized
that the child at birth had no attachment to the mother, and that in the first
10 months, the task for the child was to establish such an attachment.
   Bowlby's observations initially were addressed to separation research: the
reaction of children separated from their mothers by hospitalization or resi-
dential nurseries. He divided the reactions into three phases: protest and the
wish for reunion, despair, and detachment. The great advantage of Bowlby's
work was that he did not make intrapsychic hypotheses based on his observations, but kept strictly to the level of observation.

ATTACHMENT RESEARCH — AINSWORTH
(AINSWORTH ET AL., 1978; AINSWORTH & EICHBERG, 1991)

Ainsworth took the lead in the second phase of the development of attachment studies. She made naturalistic observations of infant–mother interactions
in the home in Uganda and Maryland. She then developed a laboratory instrument — the strange situation — to study infants' reactions to separation. This
was predicated on the observation of 1-year-old infants' responses to very brief
separation from, and reunions with, a given parent, in order to classify the
organization of its attachment process. Ainsworth discovered that the unfavorable reunion responses previously associated with older toddlers' reactions
to major separations from the parent could appear in nonseparated 12-month-
olds. She rated these reactions as secure or insecure. The insecure were further
divided into avoidant or ambivalent resistant. Later, a fourth category was
added: disorganized, disoriented.

The third stage in the study of attachment, which took place in the mid-1980s, was a move to the level of intrapsychic representation by many follow-up studies demonstrating continuity of the early attachment rating in later years.

THE ADULT ATTACHMENT INTERVIEW

In the mid-1980s, Main and Goldwyn (Main & Goldwyn, 1982–1998; Main, Kaplan & Cassidy, 1985) developed an interview protocol for parents called the adult attachment interview (AAI). It consisted of 18 questions to evaluate the parent's attitude toward attachment. The adult was asked to describe his or her relationship with his or her own parents during childhood, attitudes toward separation, and so on. The analysis of the AAI rested exclusively on the study of the verbatim transcript. The purpose of the attachment interview was to evaluate a parent's state of mind with regard to attachment.

It's important to keep in mind that the evaluation was not of an attachment to any single person, but was an evaluation of the individual differences in state of mind with respect to overall attachment history.

Main and Goldwyn (1982) took as their guide what has been identified as an ideal rational discourse (Grice, 1975), a cooperative principle that required adherence to four maxims: (1) Quality — be truthful and have evidence for what you say. (2) Quantity — be succinct and yet complete. (3) Relevance — let the direction of your conversation be relevant to the topic at hand. (4) Manner — be clear and orderly.

They developed three ratings: secure/autonomous, and insecure. Insecure was further divided into dismissing and preoccupied. Unresolved disorganized was added later. The two outstanding characteristics of the parents of secure infants were a clear valuing of attachment figures in attachment-related experiences, together with an apparent objectivity in the descriptions and evaluations of particular relationships. The dismissing category tended to dismiss the effects of attachment-related experiences. Those in the preoccupied category appeared to be too preoccupied with early relationships with their own parents to describe them clearly and evaluate them. The unresolved/disorganized suffered from unresolved trauma.

The attachment interview evaluations closely correlated with the evaluation of the infant in the strange situation. For example, secure/autonomous was related to the secure infant, dismissing was related to the avoidant infant, and preoccupied with related to the resistant/ambivalent infant. Unresolved/disorganized was related to disoriented/disorganized.

STUDIES OF ATTACHMENT

Many studies of attachment were done using the AAI and strange-situation ratings, all of which showed a close correspondence between the two ratings.

Ainsworth studies children 2 to 6 months after their original attachment classification at 12 months of age. She found an 80% correspondence with the original rating and, particularly, that unorganized attachment in the parent predicted infant disorganization (Ainsworth et al., 1978). In order to examine the question of whether the mother's attachment classification could be influenced by the infant, Fonagy did attachment interviews with 96 mothers before childbirth, and then evaluated the children 12 months after they were born (Fonagy et al., 1991). He found a 75% correspondence between the rating of the mother and the rating of the child. Similar results were found with regard to fathers, and between mothers and adolescent daughters. Beyond that, a high-risk sample of unmarried intercity mothers, whose attachment interview was done before childbirth, demonstrated the same correspondence (Fonagy, Leigh, & Steele, 1996). In essence, 389 dyads studied showed the same correspondence. An impressive array of evidence was amassed that supported the fact that the mother's attachment style is predictive of the child's strange-situation classification.

The research then moved to the clinical scene, with studies of mothers of clinically distressed children and adolescents. The findings were as follows:

Only one of 23 mothers of children hospitalized for failure to thrive was judged secure/autonomous (Benoit, Zeanah, & Barton, 1989). None of 20 mothers of infants with sleep disorders were judged as secure/autonomous (Benoit et al., 1989). Seventeen of 20 mothers of children with behavior problems were insecure (Crowell & Feldman, 1988). Twenty out of 20 mothers of children with developmental delay were insecure. All mothers of children with conduct disorders were insecure. Interestingly enough, only 6 of 10 mothers of children with ADHD were insecure (Crowell & Feldman, 1991). With regard to adolescence: In comparing 12 Borderline adolescents with 12 dysthymic adolescents, all of the Borderlines' mothers were classified as preoccupied — as compared with only one of the mothers of the dysthymic adolescents. Nine of the mothers of the Borderline adolescents reported loss or trauma and were classified as unresolved. Only two mothers of dysthymic adolescents reported loss or trauma, and were classified as unresolved (Patrick et al., 1994).

In 1996, Fonagy studied the mothers of 82 clinically depressed adolescent inpatients and compared them with 85 controls. Most of the mothers of the patients were classified as unresolved/disorganized, whereas most of the mothers of the controls were classified as secure/autonomous.

AAI Classifications and Corresponding Patterns
of Infant Strange Situation Behavior
(Ainsworth et al., 1978; Hesse, 1999; Main & Goldwyn, 1982–1998)

Adult state of mind with respect to attachment	Infant strange situation behavior
Secure/autonomous (F) Coherent, collaborative discourse. Valuing of attachment, but seems objective regarding any particular relationship. Description and evaluation of attachment-related experiences are consistent, whether experiences are favorable or unfavorable. Discourse does not notably violate any of Grice's maxims.	**Secure (B)** Explores room and toys with interest in pre-separation episodes. Shows signs of missing parent during separation, often crying by the second separation. Obvious preference for parent over stranger. Greets parent actively, usually initiating physical contact. Usually some contact maintaining by second reunion, but then settles down and returns to play.
Dismissing (Ds) Not coherent. Dismissing of attachment-related experiences and relationships. Normalizing ("excellent, very normal mother") with generalized representations of history unsupported or actively contradicted by episodes recounted, thus violating Grice's maxim of quality. Transcripts also tend to be excessively brief, violating the maxim of quantity.	**Avoidant (A)** Fails to cry on separation from parent. Actively avoids and ignores parent on reunion (i.e., by moving away, turning away, or leaning out of arms when picked up). Little or no proximity or contact-seeking, no distress, and no anger. Response to parent appears unemotional. Focuses on toys or environment throughout procedure.
Preoccupied (E) Not coherent. Preoccupied with or by past attachment relationships/experiences, speaker appears angry, passive, or fearful. Sentences often long, grammatically entangled, or filled with vague usages ("dadadada" "and that"), thus violating Grice's maxims of manner and relevance. Transcripts often excessively long, violating the maxim of quantity.	**Resistant or ambivalent (C)** May be wary or distressed even prior to separation, with little exploration. Preoccupied with parent throughout procedure; may seem angry or passive. Fails to settle down and takes comfort in parent on reunion, and usually continues to focus on parent and cry. Fails to return to exploration after reunion.
Unresolved/disorganized (U) During discussions of loss or abuse, individual shows striking lapse in the monitoring of reasoning or discourse, i.e., individual may briefly indicate a belief that a dead person is still alive in the physical sense or that this person was killed by a childhood thought. Individual may lapse into prolonged silence or eulogistic speech. The speaker will ordinarily otherwise fit Ds, E, or F categories.	**Disorganized/disoriented (D)** The infant displays disorganized and/or disoriented behaviors in the parent's presence, suggesting a temporary collapse of behavioral strategy, i.e., the infant may freeze with a trance-like expression, hands in the air, may rise at parent's entrance, then fall prone and huddled on the floor, or may cling while crying hard and leaning away with gaze averted. Infant will ordinarily fit the A, B, or C category.

Research has confirmed that those with histories of effective dyadic regulation of arousal and emotion are indeed later characterized by more effective self-regulation. For example, as preschoolers, those with histories of responsive care and secure attachment are judged by teachers and observers to have higher self-esteem, to be more self-reliant, and to be more flexible in the management of their impulses and feelings.

In middle childhood and adolescence, too, those with histories of secure attachment carry forward patterns of effective emotional regulation.

Moreover, throughout childhood and adolescence, research has now established a firm relationship between patterns of early dyadic regulation and later behavior problems and emotional disturbance. At each age assessed, those with secure attachment histories have been found to have fewer emotional problems, whereas those with anxious attachment histories have been found more frequently to have some type of problems. Again, these results often are quite specific. Anxiety disorders, in particular, have been found to be associated with histories of early dysregulation manifested in ambivalent/resistant attachment. Aggression, and conduct disturbances more generally, have been shown to be related to chronic rejection, emotional unavailability, and avoidance attachment. Both resistant and avoidant attachment appear to be related to depression. Finally, disorganized/disoriented attachment, a manifestation of an extreme form of dyadic dysregulation, exhibits the strongest overall relationship to disturbance. The disorganized pattern also is related to dissociative symptoms, that is, to disruptions in orientation to the environment and to the failure to integrate various aspects of emotional and cognitive experience.

The Neurobiology of the Right Brain and the Development of the Self

In medical school, years ago, we were taught that right-brain growth is strictly genetic, and that the brain cannot change after it is fully grown. Now, neurobiologic brain research has demonstrated that both of these propositions were wrong. The growth of the right brain is experience-dependent, and its wiring can change after it is fully grown.

The explosion of knowledge from neurobiologic brain research has been best integrated and articulated by Alan Schore, Ph.D. (1994, 2004), whose work has had a profound influence on the views presented here.

The right brain is the container and regulator of emotion. It is dominant for the first three years of life. The left brain comes on line in the second year. It is cognitive, logical, literate, and linear, and expresses itself in words. The right brain is nonverbal and, in milliseconds, expresses itself unconsciously in facial expressions, tone of voice, and body posture.

In the first years of postnatal life, the brain grows two and a half times its size at birth, mostly through the growth of the cortex. The growth of the human brain starts at least five to six months postnatal, and continues until about 18 to 24 months of age. The major part of the development of the axons and dendrites and their connections that underlie all behavior takes place in early and late infancy. During this time, a center emerges in the right prefrontal orbital cortex in the right brain for the control of emotion and emotional relationships, and is, therefore, a neurobiologic center of the self. Prior to this emergence, the child is unable to regulate his or her own affect, and thus the primary caretaker's interaction with the child becomes the principal regulator of emotion, and also the creator of the background from which the prefrontal orbital cortex will emerge, grow, and mature.

As the infant focuses on the mother's gaze, the mother, in turn, responds with her gaze, thereby providing a potent channel for the transmission of reciprocal mutual influences. The regulation of affect occurs through face-to-face interactions. The mother and the infant synchronize the intensity of their affective behavior within seconds.

In this process of affect synchronicity, the mother finetunes and corrects the intensity and duration of her affective stimulation in order to maintain the child's positive affect state. These mutually attuned synchronized interactions are fundamental to the ongoing affective development of the orbital prefrontal cortex, and, therefore, of the self.

Misattunement inevitably will occur in development, and the primary caregiver must participate in interactive repair to regulate interactively induced stress disruptions. This pattern of disruption and repair of the "good enough" caregiver corrects and, in a timely fashion, reinvokes her psychobiologically attuned regulation of the infant's negative affect state that she has triggered. The key to this is the caregiver's capacity to monitor and regulate her own affect state — especially negative affect. Normally this syncronous interaction is the interactive regulator of emotion.

These attachment experiences of infancy are deeply internalized in the right brain to become unconscious working models of attachment relationships. They are stored as self and object representations and their linking affects, and they function as the internal regulators of affect. Strategies are encoded to use these models for coping with stress. The misattunement are repair process conducted by the mother is internalized and makes an important contribution to the neurologic basis for the child's capacity for resilience, that is, to repair emotional stress. These internal representations are accessed as guides for future interactions, but they remain in implicit memory. The individual is not aware of them, and does not have a language to access them.

The orbital prefrontal cortex is the only cortical structure with direct connections to the hypothalamus, the amygdala, the autonomic nervous system, and the structures in the brain stem that regulate arousal. The right hemisphere contains the most comprehensive and integrated map of the body state available to the brain. It is uniquely situated to process information concerning the external environment, such as visual and auditory stimuli, with subcortical information regarding the internal environment, and the integration of adaptive bodily responses with ongoing emotional and attentional states of the organism.

The prefrontal orbital cortex of the right brain matures in the middle of the second year. The core of the self is thus nonverbal and unconscious, and it lies within patterns of affect regulation. This structural development allows for an internal sense of security and resilience that comes from the intuitive knowledge that one can regulate the flows and shifts of one's bodily based emotional states, either by one's own coping capacities or within a relationship with caring others. The operation of the right prefrontal cortex is integral to autoregulation and interactive regulation.

ATTACHMENT, NEUROBIOLOGIC RESEARCH, AND DISORDERS OF THE SELF

The caregiver whose adult attachment rating is dismissing or preoccupied or unresolved/disorganized does not have the capacity to provide the syncronicity of affect states with the child that is essential to the development of the prefrontal orbital cortex and of the self. Therefore, there is a developmental arrest of this prefrontal cortex and of the self at the neurobiologic level in terms of a wiring defect, which then becomes reflected at the psychological level as a developmental arrest of the self. The right prefrontal cortex develops inefficient patterns of organization, which result in a limited capacity to perceive the emotional states of others and in difficulty with reading facial expressions that are succeeded by difficulties with empathy and relating by projective identification.

The deficit in self-regulation is further manifested in a limited capacity to modulate the intensity and duration of affects, especially biologically primitive affects. Under stress, such individuals can experience, not discrete and differentiated affects, but diffuse, undifferentiated, chaotic states accompanied by overwhelming somatic and visceral sensations, along with the activation of defenses, which leads to a limited capacity for self-reflection.

**Integration of Attachment Theory and Neurobiology
of the Brain with an Object Relations Approach
to Psychoanalytic Psychotherapy**

For years, the developmental self and object relations theory was based on
Mahler's work on early development and on the clinical work with personality
disorders by myself and others. Attachment-theory experiments have provided
further scientific experimental proof of the validity of this theory. Beyond that,
it has made correlations with specific mother and child interactions that describe the channels of interactive behavior that produce problems in connecting with, and separating from, the object. Finally, in its concept of inner
working models, it has demonstrated the origin and development of what we
now call object relations or intrapsychic structure that become the healthy or
pathologic regulators of affect, that is, self and object representations provide
regulation.

NEUROBIOLOGIC BRAIN RESEARCH
AND OBJECT RELATIONS THEORY

Neurobiologic brain research has made an enormous contribution to our
understanding of the neurobiologic basis for affect regulation and its psychopathology, and of therapeutic alliance, transference, and countertransference.

Therapeutic Alliance and Therapeutic Neutrality

We have always know that therapeutic alliance — defined as the real
relationship with the patient — must be more or less positive for psychoanalytic psychotherapy to succeed over the long term. However, now we can
define the issue more precisely. We are dealing here primarily with the attunement functions of the right brain, which communicates its affective state
unconsciously and instantly, not in words (like the left brain), but in facial
expression, tone of voice, and body posture. It's quite possible to receive a
verbal message from the left brain and the opposite message unconsciously
from the right brain. It is vital for the empathic therapist to attune to, and to
resonate appropriately with, the shifting affect states of the patient's right
brain, thus creating a synchronous interaction whereby the clinician helps the
patient to regulate the right brain. As the defenses are overcome, the dyad is
able to hold interactively on-line and to amplify internal affective stimuli long
enough for them to be identified, which leads to the emergence of memory.
The therapist's objective left brain can now help the patient to use the left

brain to co-process subjective right-brain communications. The unconscious pathologic affects that had been locked in implicit procedural memory, and for which there has been no language, now get access to language as they come to awareness to be worked through.

Transference Acting Out, Transference and Countertransference

Nonverbal transference and countertransference interactions that take place at unconscious levels represent right-brain to right-brain communications of fast-acting automatic, regulated, and dysregulated emotional states between the patient and therapist. Transference acting out is the expression of the underlying inner working model or intrapsychic structure, and must be identified and confronted or interpreted. This leads to a therapeutic alliance and transference, which, in turn, must be interpreted.

The verbal formulations of affective states provide a powerful new self-regulatory function. Thus, the therapist functions to establish emotional synchronicity, and to overcome defenses so that affects can emerge with memory, to be processed by the left brain. This allows for the maturation and wiring of the prefrontal cortex, the development of self-regulating functions, and the formation of new inner working models, along with the increase in the capacities for empathy and self-reflection, as old neurologic pathways lose their charge and new neurologic pathways become charged.

Countertransference

Neurobiologic brain research has made an enormous contribution to our understanding of the role of projective identification in countertransference. Projective identification can be defined as a right-brain function whereby the patient's unconscious projects a painful emotion on the therapist, and then, by facial expression, tone of voice, or body posture invokes the therapist to feel it, thereby relieving the pain.

Projective identification used to be thought of as a pathologic mechanism used only by primitive patients. However, it is now redefined as a normal form of communication in the healthy person, beginning with the baby, who co-creates his or her own development by signaling the mother through facial expression, body movement, and so on. It is also now seen as a defense mechanism in the personality disorders. In therapy, it occurs so fast and so unconsciously that the therapist can be caught unaware. As with the mother, it is important for the therapist's right brain to identify and process the negative affect of the projective identification with the left brain, thereby containing it, rather than reacting to it and then returning it to the patient for processing. This process has similarities to the affective synchrony, disruption, and repair that occurs between a mother and her child. The patient's right and left brains can now process it in the service of growth.

Following are some examples of countertransference.

A therapist reported seeing a patient who had been in a local prestigious training group, but had to drop out of the group and out of treatment. Unable to face her feelings of humiliation and embarrassment at her implied inadequacy, the patient started treatment with a new therapist, questioning her ability as a therapist. Did she have the ability to do it for the patient? The therapist identified with this projection, becoming very anxious about whether in fact she did have the capacity to treat this person. In this way, she identified with the patient's feelings of inadequacy and humiliation and embarrassment, rather than reflecting the feelings and interpreting them to her as follows: "Perhaps you were so concerned about my capacity because it was so painful to access the feelings of humiliation and embarrassment you had. Your way of soothing them was to place them on me."

A therapist who appeared Schizoid presented a case of a closet Narcissistic woman who began treatment with flagrant acting out that idealized her. The patient wanted advice, asked to sit next to the therapist, and she made various demands. The more the patient acted out this idealizing, the more the therapist experienced it as a reinforcement of the commanding object's wish for her to be a slave, and the more anxious and angry the therapist became, the more she withdrew and withheld from the patient. The more she withheld, the more the patient felt abandoned, and escalated her acting out. It was necessary to bring the therapist's countertransferential withdrawal to her attention so that she could regain therapeutic neutrality and be able to set the necessary limits for the patient and to interpret the projective identification.

These findings from attachment theory and neurobiologic research have added to and deepened the theory and the therapeutic approach, but they have not essentially changed the treatment approach to achieve the objective. That is, the new understandings have not altered the basic goal to overcome the initial transference acting out defenses to establish a therapeutic alliance and transference to work through the abandonment depression that leads to a repair of the wiring; to the growth of the prefrontal cortex, which is then able to perform more effective self-regulation at the neurobiologic level; and to the growth or transformation of the self from split self and object representations to whole self and object representations at the clinical level.

IMPLICATIONS FOR THE THEORY

The theory, as originally proposed, considered the etiology of the personality disorders to be attributable to a combination of nature, nurture, and fate: Nature referred to possible genetic input, nurture to the mother's difficulty with supporting the emerging self of the child, and fate to separation stresses that took place during the developmental period of separation/individuation.

Attachment theory and neurobiologic brain research have demonstrated a scientific basis for the nurture part of the theory. We also have ample scientific evidence of the separation/individuation stress component from the same source. What remains to be demonstrated is the genetic input.

A case in point demonstrating how the environment and genes interact is a study entitled "Role of Genotype in the Cycle of Violence in Maltreated Children" (Caspi et al., 2002). It addresses why some children who are subjected to chronic physical or emotional abuse grow up to be troubled, violent, abusive, and even criminal, but most become law-abiding and well-adjusted adults.

Researchers from the United States, Great Britain, and New Zealand presented persuasive evidence for why some children are resilient whereas others remain scarred by neglect and abuse: It depends on the child's genetic makeup.

Abused boys who carry one version of a particular gene are more likely to grow up to be violent and antisocial than are those carrying another version.

The gene lies on the X-chromosome and makes monoamine oxidase-A (MAOA), an enzyme that acts like a biochemical garbage disposal, breaking down and metabolizing neurotransmitters, including serotonin and dopamine.

The DNA that determines how much MAOA occurs in the brain comes in two varieties. One produces low gene activity, and thus small amounts of MAOA. Another produces high gene activity and high amounts of MAOA. In mice, the absence of MAOA has been linked to aggression. One study in humans found the same thing. But genetic determination — "gene A causes behavior B" — is too simple an explanation.

In studying 442 white, male New Zealanders who had been followed since their births in 1972, the researchers found that childhood maltreatment was far more likely to lead to adult violence in boys with low-activity MAOA genes than in boys with the high-activity version. The 55 men who have the low-activity form and had been neglected or abused were about twice as likely to have engaged in persistent fighting, bullying, theft, cruelty, and vandalism during adolescence, and also more likely to have been convicted of a violent crime than were men with the high-MAOA form who had been maltreated.

Low MAOA alone produced no increased risk for violence as an adult.

Without abuse, such boys were no likelier to be antisocial or violent adults.

"Genes can moderate children's sensitivity to environmental insults," the study's leader said, which "may partly explain why not all victims of maltreatment grow up to victimize others; some genotypes, for example, high MAOA, may promote resistance to trauma."

Maltreatment seems to cause lasting changes in brain chemistry. However, if MAOA levels are high, it constrains those changes. If low, it can't. Hyperreactivity and the attendant aggression becomes permanent.

POSTSCRIPT

Is it possible that there is a gene that acts in the personality disorders just as the gene in the above study did? If the gene is high, it protects the child exposed to maternal lack of support from becoming prone to a personality disorder; if it is too low, a personality disorder could develop — thus the etiology is a combination of environment and genetics. The frontier of research now focuses on finding the genetic factor.

References

Ainsworth, M. D. S., Blehar, M. C., Waters, E., & Wall, S. (1978). *Patterns of Attachment: A Psychological Study of the Strange Situation.* Hillsdale, NJ: Erlbaum.

Ainsworth, M. D. S., & Eichberg, C. G. (1991). Effects on infant–mother attachment of mother's unresolved loss of an attachment figure or other traumatic experience (pp. 160–183). In P. Marris, J. Stevenson-Hinde, & C. Parks (Eds.), *Attachment Across the Life Cycle.* New York: Routledge.

Benoit, D., Zeanah, C. H., & Barton, M. L. (1989). Maternal attachment disturbances in failure to thrive. *Infant Mental Health Journal, 10,* 185–202.

Benoit, D., Zeanah, C. H., Boucher, C., & Minde, K. K. (1992). Sleep disorders in early childhood: Association with insecure maternal attachment. *Journal of the American Academy of Child and Adolescent Psychiatry, 31,* 86–93.

Bowlby, J. (1969). *Attachment and Loss. Vol. I: Attachment.* London: Hogarth.

Bowlby, J. (1973). *Attachment and Loss. Vol. II: Separation.* New York: Basic Books.

Caspi, A., McClay, J., Moffitt, T., et al. (Aug. 2002). Role of genotype in the cycle of violence in maltreated children. *Science, 297.*

Cassidy, J., & Shaver, P. R. (Eds.) (1999). *Handbook of Attachment Theory, Research, and Clinical Applications.* New York: Guilford.

Crowell, J. A., & Feldman, S. S. (1988). Mothers' internal models of relationships and children's behavioral and developmental status: A study of mother–child interaction. *Child Development, 59,* 1273–1285.

Crowell, J. A., & Feldman, S. S. (1991). Mothers' working models of attachment relationships and mother and child behavior during separation and reunion. *Developmental Psychology, 27*, 597–605.

Fonagy, P., Leigh, T., Steele, M., et al. (1996). The relation of attachment status, psychiatric classification and response to psychotherapy. *Journal of Consulting and Clinical Psychology, 64*, 22–31.

Fonagy, P., Steele, M., Moran, G., et al. (1991). The capacity for understanding mental states: The reflective self in parent and child and its significance for security of attachment. *Infant Mental Health Journal, 13*, 200–216.

Grice, H. P. (1975). Logic and conversation (pp. 41–58). In P. Cole & J. L. Moran (Eds.), *Syntax and Semantics. III. Speech Acts.* New York: Academic.

Hesse, E. (1999). The adult attachment interview (pp. 395–433). In J. Cassidy & P. R. Shaver (Eds.), *Handbook of Attachment Theory, Research, and Clinical Applications.* New York: Guilford.

Mahler, M. S., Pine, F., & Bergman, A. (1975). *The Psychological Birth of the Human Infant.* New York: Basic Books.

Main, M., & Goldwyn, R. (1982–1998). Adult attachment scoring and classification system. Unpublished manuscript, Department of Psychology, University of California at Berkeley.

Main, M., Kaplan, N., & Cassidy, J. (1985). Security in infancy, childhood, and adulthood: A move to the level of representation. In J. Bretherton & E. Waters (Eds.), *Growing Points of Attachment Theory and Research.* Monographs of the Society for Research in Child Development, vol. 50 (1–2), no. 209. Chicago: University of Chicago Press.

Masterson, J. (1967). *The Psychiatric Dilemma of Adolescence.* Boston: Little Brown.

Masterson, J. (1972). *Treatment of the Borderline Adolescent: A Developmental Approach.* New York: Wiley.

Masterson, J. (1976). *Psychotherapy of the Borderline Adult: A Developmental Approach.* New York: Brunner/Mazel.

Masterson, J. (1980). *From Borderline Adolescent to Functioning Adult: The Test of Time.* New York: Brunner/Mazel.

Masterson, J. (1985). *The Real Self — A Developmental, Self, and Object Relations Approach.* New York: Brunner/Mazel.

Masterson, J. (1993). *The Emerging Self — A Developmental, Self, and Object Relations Approach to the Treatment of the Closet Narcissistic Disorder of the Self.* New York: Brunner/Mazel.

Masterson, J., & Klein, R. (Eds.) (1988). *Psychotherapy of the Disorders of the Self: The Masterson Approach.* New York: Brunner/Mazel.

Patrick, M., Hobson, R. P., Castle, D., et al. (1994). Personality disorder and the mental representation of early social experience. *Development and Psychopathology, 6*, 375–388.

Schore, A. N. (1994). *The Role of Affect in the Emergence of the Self*. Hillsdale, NJ: Erlbaum.

Schore, A. N. (2001). Regulation of the right brain: A fundamental mechanism of attachment trauma, dissociation, and psychotherapy. *British Journal of Psychotherapy*, 17(3).

Schore, A.N. (2004). The effects of a secure attachment relationship on right brain development, affect regulation, and infant mental health. *Infant Mental Health Journal*, 22, 201–269.

Stern, D. N. (1985). *The Interpersonal World of the Infant*. New York: Basic Books.

2

Consciousness
and the Personality Disorders:
Developmental and Clinical Perspectives

MARGOT T. BEATTIE, PH.D.

The study of personality disorders invites the study of consciousness, because it is in the early stages of the dawning awareness of self and other, of differentiation leading to separation and individuation, that the seeds of future character pathology are probably sown. Consciousness is usually understood from a subjective perspective. "The term *consciousness* denotes first the actual awareness of experience; second, a subject–object dichotomy; and third, the knowledge of a conscious self, or self-awareness" (DeBerry, 1991). The highest form of consciousness includes the capacity to be aware not only of our own minds, but of the minds of others — awareness that others are aware (Donald, 2001; Hobson, 2002). Finally, this social aspect of consciousness includes a shared awareness with another *about* something else (Cavell, 2003; Hobson, 2002; Rosenfeld, 1992) thus forming the basis for a sense of reality, as will be discussed here. Consciousness is always relational (Fonagy et al., 2002; Hobson, 2002).

The development of character pathology deeply and adversely affects consciousness. The awareness that one is aware (and, therefore, constructs one's own reality), the awareness of others as separate, sentient beings with their own awareness and the capacity to embrace reality — even when it is disagreeable — are all compromised in the patient with a personality disorder. Pathological focus on the object may be seen, in this light as a defense that reflects a deficit in the acceptance of another's autonomous awareness.

THE DEVELOPMENT OF CONSCIOUSNESS

Many theorists have conceptualized triangulation as a necessity for the formation of mental space or consciousness (Hobson, 2002). They are usually referring to self with other and the world at large. James Grotstein (1978) has conceptualized the formation of individual mental space from triangulation based on awareness that one is aware. (See Figure 1.)

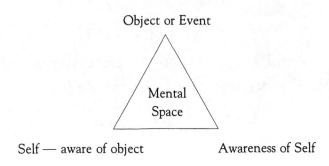

Figure 1

Patients with a personality disorder manifest problems in consciousness on two fronts. First, their disturbance in mentation can be described as a confusional state of consciousness. These patients are prone to confusing their experience of reality with what belongs to their inner psychic world; frequently attributing their internal conflicts to the external world, thus causing themselves great interpersonal difficulty (Masterson, 1988).

Ogden (1990) understood this confusion as a limitation in capacity due to perceptions being unmediated by subjectivity. Fonagy and colleagues (2002) attribute this confusional state to a deficit in mentalization, that is, the awareness that one's experience is mediated by having one's own mind, and they note that it is often a product of trauma:

> Abused and traumatized individuals, unable to conceive of mental states that could explain the actions of the abuser, voluntarily and defensively sacrifice their thinking about internal states ... The abandonment of mentalizing leaves them with an internal reality that is dominated by psychic equivalence (p. 13).

However described, such confusion interferes with taking responsibility for a subjectively constructed sense of reality.

Second, persons with a personality disorder suffer from apparent deficits in mental triangulation, a disturbance of awareness that others are aware, compromising their ability to acknowledge and function in reality. Consciousness is born of a dyadic relationship, but the heart of consciousness, its power of awareness of and communication with others, comes from the triangulation inherent in secondary intersubjectivity (Cavell, 2003; Fonagy et al., 2002; Hobson, 2002).

Expanding triangulated formulation of mental space into a two-person consciousness, the awareness of another as having a *different* perspective, is the basis for conceptualizing reality (Figure 2). When the child and the mother mutually share a focus on an object, for example, a toy, and both find it pleasing, there is no call for substantial awareness beyond that of the mother's being a participant. But if the shared focus is on the street, which looks appealing to the young toddler and is known to be threatening to the mother, the child is forced, through a difference in perspective, into an awareness of something outside the self called reality. As Freud (1911) has taught us, it is through difference, even if it is disagreeable, that we come to embrace the reality principle.

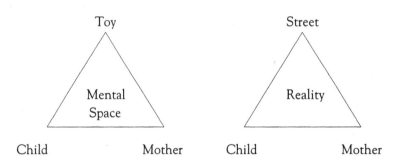

Figure 2: Shared Awareness *About* Something Else — Triangulation

Knowing that "others are minded" (Cavell, 2003), that another person has an individual view of things, is the basis for forming a sense of *reality*. "It is the intersubjective engagements with their different perspectives, and the disagreements to which they often lead, that make room for the idea of a world as something independent of your perspective and mine . . . (p. 809).

In a full sense, consciousness may be thought of as the development of a sense of self (subjectivity) that is in constant relation to a world of others. Consciousness encompasses the *boundary of interaction* between self and other, defining and coloring the space between them. This boundary is in constant formation and flux, continually receding and reforming. Our sense of awareness at any one time is not only entirely subjective, it is transitory. Only the sense of self is continuous (Damasio, 1999). Think about the impact on consciousness then of having an inadequate sense of self. As we know from our clinical work, problems in the early development of a person's sense of self may result in a compromised ability to use his or her mind productively, to take for granted a sense of well-being in the world, and to relate satisfactorily to others (Masterson, 1988, p. 7).

The disturbed mentation characteristic of patients with personality disorders is not the same as that found in psychotic processing. Psychotic mentation may be described as a failure in formal internal–external, self–other differentiation. Character pathology does not reflect a lack of differentiation, but rather a confusional state stemming from an automatic or unconscious attempt to stave off painful feelings by splitting and then attributing the source of subjective experience to the external world, when it is, in fact, internal. Looked at in another way, healthy individuals have an ongoing dialectic between their internal and external worlds and they cross these boundaries with ease. Among patients with personality disorders, defensive maneuvers such as avoidance and denial, as well as repression, bring about a "protective" *detachment between* internal and external reality (Rose, 1978). Once detached, excessive investment is placed on either the external world or the internal world.

Both the growth of healthy consciousness and the developmental progression of character pathology occur within the dyadic mother–infant relationship, and the infant's movement into secondary intersubjectivity, which follows primary person-to-person connectedness. In the primary relationship of the mother and infant, reciprocity sets up a shared world in which meaning is transmitted emotionally. Eventually, the infant, at about 12 months of age, moves into secondary intersubjectivity; that is, becomes conscious of another person's consciousness (Hobson, 2002). Personal relations are not just an exchange of feelings with someone else; they are also a sharing of experience *about something else* (Cavell, 2003, p. 809). Communication is about a third object. "The defining feature of secondary intersubjectivity is that an object or event can become a focus *between* people ... the infant is no longer restricted to a focus either on an object or on a person, but instead may be sensitive to a person's relation to an object" (Hobson, 2002, p. 62). "The essential condition is not merely that infant and caretaker can point to the same object, but that they can observe each other making this reference" (Cavell, 2003, p. 810). "It is intersubjective engagements with their different perspectives, and the disagreements to which they often lead, that make room for the idea of the world as something independent of your perspective and mine" (p. 809), laying the groundwork for knowing reality.

A subjective sense of self is formed out of one's awareness both of one's body in time and space and of the other. The subjective experience of consciousness is the study of one's *relationship* with internal and external reality (DeBerry, 1991). Persons with personality disorders all manifest, in particular diagnostic ways, a difficulty in relating one's self to the outside world, to reality — a conflict between internal and external realities.

More recent work on consciousness greatly affects our understanding of the distorted mentation inherent in character pathology. Viewing patients with personality disorders as having difficulty with the boundary between the self and other, with the space between self and others, is a useful clinical perspective. It allows for a deeper understanding of the use of pathological defenses such as splitting, denial, and repression — all of which protect the ego by deleting stimulus from awareness and thereby "destructively" preserving a sense of self to the impaired ego (Rose, 1978, p. 349) at the cost of future growth. One might say that the boundary of self seemingly is fortified by a turning away from the reality principle. In this light, persons with personality disorders fail to sustain an integration or confluence of internal and external reality.

BRIEF HISTORY OF CONSCIOUSNESS

If we view reality as a correlate of consciousness, we can predict problems inherent in the consciousness of persons with personality disorders. It is, therefore, important to briefly review the history of our understanding of consciousness. The study of consciousness, that aspect of living that makes us most human, until recently has been seriously neglected by psychologists. This has not always been the case. Between 1879 and 1913, structuralists and functionalists fostered an interest in consciousness, thus assigning a central role to the analytic study of the adult normal human mind. Wilhelm Wundt (1832–1920) was the first to shift the focus of interest from the contents of the mind to the processes of the mind; and in the hands of Titchener (1898), consciousness became the center of psychological investigation. Under the influence of Watson's insistence on objective verification, the scientific interest and study of consciousness ended in 1913, and was not picked up again for a good 50 years (Beattie, 1987). Consciousness was deemed inappropriate for study because the methodology of introspection was not amenable to the experimental method.

This dismissive attitude toward consciousness as too elusive to explore contributes even today to the dominance of cognitive–behavioral psychology in America; and to the current emphasis on the brain and neuroscience, sometimes at the expense of interest in the mind. It is only in the last 20 years that the subject of consciousness again became of paramount interest in scientific circles, and only in the last 10 years that a *Journal of Consciousness Studies* became available.

CONTRIBUTIONS OF THEORETICAL PHYSICS

Fortunately, theoretical physics has come to the rescue of psychology. DeBerry (1991) writes:

> The resurrection of consciousness within the "sacred" science of physics is not only paradoxical, but amusing. Psychology still tries to achieve objectivity by eliminating subjectivity, that is, consciousness, as a legitimate variable (p. 67).

DeBerry goes on to say that psychology, in its blind adherence to the experimental method, has tended to exclude the observer as an object of study, whereas physics, both theoretically and mathematically, has accepted the observer as an essential variable in understanding the observed.

Taking into account our own "angle of observation" (Wilson, 2003, pp. 825–855) as clinicians illuminates how we perceive our world, and even how we think theoretically. In his article "Ghosts of Paradigms Past," Wilson describes the dichotomy between two primary angles of observation in current psychoanalytic theory leading to two different visions of how analytic dyads work together. The first, standing "outside the transference," brings the intrapsychic domain most clearly into view. From this positioning of one's self, the clinical dyad of patient and therapist is a "differentiated dyad" (Wilson & Prillaman, 1997, pp. 189–234) and the focus is on unconscious internal conflict. Here the transference is initially unconscious as it emerges from the hold of repression. The second, standing "inside the bidirectional processes," affords one primarily a view of the interpersonal domain, which is based on the centrality of internalization and perceives the analytic interchange within an "attached dyad." The analyst is inside the flux of the bidirectional processes; the patient is seen as struggling to cope with the analyst's presence. In this view, the mind of the therapist and the mind of the patient are seen as less separate.

In addition to the inclusion of the observer in the observation, theoretical physics in both quantum mechanics and chaos theory unfolds for us a constructivist model of the human's relationship to reality — that is, we make our own reality. The relationship between developmental psychology, object relations theory, and physics is heartening and exciting in supporting a view of ourselves and our patients as constructing our experience of reality.

In looking at this integration of physics and psychology in more detail, we see that quantum mechanics has contributed a great deal to our understanding of consciousness (DeBerry, 1991, p. 67). "The theory was devised in the late 1920s to deal with the atom, a tiny entity a thousand times smaller than the wavelength of green light . . . Quantum theory continued, however, to prosper beyond its inventor's wildest dreams, resolving subtle problems of atomic structure, tackling the nucleus some ten thousand times smaller than the atom itself, and extending its reach to the realm of elementary particles (quarks, gluons, leptons) which many believe to be the world's ultimate constituent" (Herbert, 1987, p. 32).

Quantum theory emphasizes the probabilities of connections and events between matter and perhaps between consciousness and matter (DeBerry, 1991, p. 67). In quantum theory, electrons or protons possess no qualities of their own — only a relationship between themselves and their measuring device. From this perspective, there are neither absolute classical realities nor deterministic laws of nature (p. 34). Applied to the development of consciousness and to the clinical hour, the flux and flow of experience become central. We all construct our own reality, and each clinical hour is a creation of the persons who are present.

> A quantum law of motion states that matter must increase and multiply in order to fulfill all possibilities, yet in the act of measurement, only one possibility can occur. In a sense, then through some type of interaction, reality is constantly being constructed, a fact that makes quantum mechanics one of the principle verifiers of constructivism.

From chaos theory we have come to know that consciousness is not linear; that brains tend to organize themselves in modular and parallel fashion. Chaos theory reaffirms psychoanalytic theory in the following ways:

1. The reality of experience is more complex than it seems.
2. In keeping with the Platonic idea of hidden forms, other realities underlie the reality that is being perceived.
3. Phenomena are holistically organized — even though the brain is composed of separate parts, its functioning can only be understood as a whole.
4. Complex phenomena not only are holistic, but also are *dynamic*, especially as espoused in the concept of "flow" [italics added] (pp. 16–17). (I would add to this the concepts of space, shape, change, and motion).

"When we say [that] consciousness is dynamic, we mean [that] consciousness arises from dynamic interrelations of the past, the present, and the body image." As Rosenfeld (1992, p. 84) points out, this interrelation factor is what most scientific theories overlook; we are really only conscious of our body posture in relation to what it was just before the noticing. "At the moment the brain is establishing coherent responses, new stimuli are arising that will alter

them; these dynamic changes will continue as long as we are conscious ...
Awareness is change, not perception of stimuli" (p. 85).

EXPANDED VIEW OF CONSCIOUSNESS
AT IT INFORMS PSYCHOPATHOLOGY

In looking at phenomena — and, in this case, consciousness — through the
lens of quantum mechanics and chaos theory, we are able to expand our view
beyond thinking of consciousness as a "state" or a "mental structure" and
perceive the following core characteristics that illuminate the pathology of
personality disorders:

A. The *dynamic* quality of consciousness is expressed in space and change,
flow and movement, which lead us to understand the subjective experience of
consciousness as the study of one's *dialectic* relationship with internal and external reality. This dialectic is inherent in consciousness. Dialectic describes a
process in which two opposing concepts create, inform, preserve, and negate
one another, each standing in a dynamic, ever-changing, relationship with the
other (Hegel, 1807).

Margaret Mahler and colleagues (1975, p. 3) wrote:

> For the more or less normal adult, the experience of himself as both
> "in," and fully separate from, the "world out there" is taken for
> granted as a given in life. Consciousness of self and absorption with-
> out awareness of self are two polarities *between which he moves* with
> varying ease and with varying degrees of alternation or simultaneity.
> But this is the result of a slowly unfolding process [italics added].

Patients with personality disorders across diagnoses are unable to traverse
internal and external boundaries with ease.

B. Consciousness is also *relational*, between self and object representations,
and in being relative to the figure–ground configuration of time and space (pp.
133–134). This is another way of understanding consciousness as subjective.
The relational nature of consciousness among these patients is impoverished.
Self and object representations have a fixed and static quality, and objects are
often "absented" from the internal world.

C. The *subjectivity* of consciousness derives from the relationship between
a dynamic body image, itself a series of coherent responses, and the dynamic

progression of coherent responses to new stimuli (Rosenfeld, 1992, p. 8). The body image becomes a self and is the frame of reference (pp. 133–134). These self-referential mechanisms are the basis for the feeling of consciousness. This is what patients forget or do not realize — that their consciousness is constructed and subjective. They take their perspectives as fact, and either struggle to make the world conform to their view (Narcissistic personality disorder) or resign themselves to feelings of helplessness and hopelessness in their realizations of the discrepancies between their need and the satisfaction of that need (Borderline and Schizoid personality disorders).

When trauma alters aspects of self-reference, it alters the entire structure of consciousness and exacerbates the challenge of navigating between and integrating internal and external realities.

> Psychological trauma may similarly first wholly absorb many aspects of self-reference (aspects of "self"), after which the brain blocks the pain and limits the mechanisms of self-reference. A part of the self has disappeared, just as a part of the body disappears in the case of physically traumatized patients with alien limbs. Self-reference and the consequent ability to adapt is lost; pain has engulfed a part of the self (pp. 133–134).

Rosenfeld goes on to point out that trauma alters the very dynamic nature of consciousness. "The neurological mechanism of loss is not the pushing of a traumatic memory in the unconscious but rather a reorganization of the ways in which the brain responds to stimuli ... Pain is blocked by eliminating the mechanisms of self-reference, and this, in turn, destroys the notion of the associated space" (pp. 134–135).

D. Consciousness comes about through *self-awareness, an observing* self, also called an observing ego. Being aware that you are aware is a form of "the third," which provides distance from the self. Self-consciousness comes about through feeling — adopting a perspective on oneself. Awareness of self is a vital ingredient of consciousness. But self-awareness comes about not only through body sensations, but through others. Hobson (2002) points out clearly and painstakingly that the child only comes to know his or her self in relation to the world by identifying with others and being affected by their reactions to the world (pp. 105–117).

E. Consciousness *unites* by synthesizing "external" reality into a comprehensible whole. (DeBerry, 1991, p. 59) and in allowing for a dialectic between the internal representations of self and object. Consciousness is, therefore, predicated on separation and individuation; because one cannot bring together something that has not become separate from something else.

ATTACHMENT THEORY

In pursuing an understanding of the dialectic inherent in consciousness that is predicated on separation of the self and object, it behooves us first to consider the role of attachment theory in consciousness. One of the most far-reaching advances in psychoanalytic developmental theory in the last 50 years has been the emphasis on the infant's interactions with real other persons (Cavell, 2003, p. 803). It is within the *relationship* of attachment that the growth of consciousness and the function of language as it relates to separation and individuation develop. The chief interpersonal dynamic of attachment is mother–infant reciprocity, which has been given the name of contingent communication. And it seems likely that it is from failures in reciprocity/ contingent communication within this relationship that later psychopathology becomes manifest in Borderline, Narcissistic, and Schizoid personality disorder (Masterson, 1976).

Cautionary note: It is mentally and clinically tempting to draw conclusions about the specific diagnostic effects on the personality development of maternal misattunement. However, very little is yet known about any *specific* effects of the quality of mother–infant relationship on later personality development. This is so for many reasons, one of which is that such knowledge requires challenging longitudinal research design.

Some of what is known from studies by Fonagy and colleagues, Beebe and Lachmann (1992), and Hobson (2002) is the propensity for a greater frequency of behaviors among children with insecure attachment. A study by Fonagy of children with disorganized attachment, manifest in contradictory and unintegrated behavioral strategies, showed the following: 71% of "disorganized" 18-month-old infants became hostile preschoolers as compared with 12% of those classified as secure in their attachments. Those with both disorganized attachments and a parental rating of difficult temperament were in the 99 percentile for aggressive behaviors.

Hobson did a study of mothers diagnosed with a Borderline personality disorder and their infants and found the following: Mothers with Borderline personality disorders tended to be intrusive and insensitive toward their 12-month-old infants, just as they had been toward their 2-month-old infants. Children in the two groups, those of mothers with a Borderline personality disorder and those of mothers in the control group with no personality-disorder diagnosis, performed at similar levels on nonsocial tasks. But infants of mothers with Borderline personality disorders achieved comparatively low scores when it came to social tasks. They were less likely to refer to another person when needing something or noticing things (pp. 134–135).

ATTACHMENT AND CONSCIOUSNESS

Our understanding of the importance of attachment in human development has expanded. The original definition of attachment refers to a homeostatic process that regulates infant proximity-seeking and contact-maintaining behaviors with one or a few specific individuals who provide physical and psychological safety (Sperling & Berman, 1994, p. 5). Attachment theorists place their emphasis on the behavioral, physiological, innate status of attachment and see attachment as gradually modulated by progressive development (Abrams, 1996). They look to experimental findings based on the study of a single characteristic observed in a group of subjects. Psychoanalysts view attachment within the mother–infant dyad as providing the essential matrix for the development of the infant's mind — the child's consciousness. Attachment provides the soil from which springs the infant's future mental, emotional, and social capacities. Psychoanalytic theory views the propensity of attachment as inborn, but the quality of the attachment as "an *achievement* linked to the provision of physical needs, to affect and to relief from anxiety." Attachment is seen as more complex, not necessarily modulated by subsequent development, but subject to change and reorganization within an individual lifespan (Dowling, 2003). And psychoanalysis relies on clinical findings, seeing attachment styles as part of the larger picture of personality.

In order to activate reunion behaviors (crying, seeking, calling, touching, gazing), the infant must develop "internal working models" of the attachment figure — allowing the infant to recognize the mother on her return and to miss her when she departs (Bowlby, 1988). This model is comparable to the psychoanalytic concept of "object representation," the "schema" or "script" or "personal construct" of cognitive developmental psychology or the "representation of interactions generalized" of Stern. Herein lays the link to consciousness, and here we diverge from the interest in attachment theory with adults as setting either parenting patterns in adult life (Main, Kaplan, & Cassidy, 1985) or romantic patterns in adult life (Shaver, Hazen, & Bradshaw, 1988). As students of character pathology, we are more interested in attachment theory as it serves the development of the infant and adult mind and consciousness (although consciousness does ultimately underlie the considerations of parenting patterns and romantic patterns).

Hobson and Fonagy have both zeroed in on the importance of mother–

infant attachment in the formation of the infant's mind. Fonagy et al. (2002) write that attachment exists in order to produce a representational system to aid in the infant's survival and "the evolutionary function of early object relations is to equip the very young child with an environment within which the understanding of mental states in other and the self can fully develop." Before language can function — which is the primary means of symbolic interaction between individuals — the infant's subjective world must first be organized. Attachment is the means by which the infant organizes himself or herself (p. 5).

Hobson (2002) points out that what sets us apart from animals is not language, but the social foundation of personal relationships that propels us into language. It is emotional links that draw us into thought (p. 2).

Lest we become too comfortable in understanding our own minds, things are changing in psychoanalytic theory; we are in the midst of a quiet revolution. Psychoanalysis has always relied on the concept of psychic representations as a means of conceptualizing the individual's bridging of internal and external worlds. The concept of internal representation relies heavily on the mind's taking something *from* the outside and representing it in some symbolic form *inside* the mind. The concept of a representational world is predicated on the traditional distinction of "what is in me" and "what is out there, in the objective world" (Cavell, 2003). Representations can be thought of as coming from an infant's repeated experiences of the self with the world that are shaped and imprinted into the mind. But Heidegger (1962) rejected this distinction and "advanced the view that the objective world is saturated with emotional qualities, as the perceiver is embedded in the objective world."

According to Edelman and Tononi (2000), current thinking considers that memory may not be representational. "What is stored, coded and retrieved is not a representation, but an ability shaped by selection to 'repeat or suppress a mental or physical act' " (p. 1044). The authors go on to note the challenge this presents to psychoanalytic theory regarding language and representation, but also note that it fits well with the clinical experience that memory is more likely to be enacted than verbalized (acting out). From this perspective, doing precedes understanding, and change precedes insight.

Regarding representations, Fonagy and Target (2003) speak of "procedures," and define them as "patterns of actions, rather than individual experiences, that are retained from infant–caregiver interactions and later come to organize behavior ... procedures are then themselves organized as mental models, better thought of as intricately interlinked sequences of events." What is important here is the emphasis on relationship. The memory is of a relationship that is confined to the unconscious and becomes manifest later in a person's style of relating (Masterson, 1976, pp. 16–17, 27).

EARLY DEVELOPMENT AND CONSCIOUSNESS:
THE ROLE OF SEPARATION AND INDIVIDUATION

Of its older definitions, that of consciousness as the human capacity for *representation*, and ultimately *symbolization*, has been a useful way to understand both normal and pathological thinking. In this light, becoming aware of something is synonymous with capturing it in symbolic form (Donald, 2001). Unlike other animals, our consciousness, evolving into representation, symbolization, and language, enables us *to gain distance* from our raw experience (p. 125). Donald Hebb (1963) identified mental autonomy from one's environment as the single most important attribute of higher consciousness. This ability to gain distance is a useful clinical construct that supports a dialectic perspective of consciousness. Gaining distance from stimuli, in turn, allows for more control over the world, and ushers in the important survival mechanism and social attribute of delayed response — a part of memory, a part of our sense of time and space, and an intricate component of judgment and higher-order thinking. The impulsiveness of patients with personality disorders speaks to the importance of this capacity in social functioning.

In gaining distance, one gains distance from something, and that something is the mother. The primary subjective aspect of consciousness is that of the relationship between oneself and the world. This relationship is, by definition, *dialectic*. With this in mind, consciousness is predicated on the back-and-forth flows between union and separation. Separation is developmentally predicated on prior union of the infant and mother.

Out of union, the experience of *illusion* is the infant's foundation for forming a dialectic experience. Illusion provides an interface between the environment and the psyche, without which there is no relation to reality (Winnicott, 1971, p. 12). Normalcy requires a flexible movement between the poles of self and other, between internal and external realities. Psychopathology, on the other hand, is characterized by a "stuck-ness" in either one or the other pole, with a subsequent lack of malleable space between the self and other that allows for the contributions from each.

The mother's adaptation to the infant's needs, when good enough, gives the infant the *illusion* that an external reality corresponds to the infant's own capacity to create. Repeated experiences of the overlap and convergence of illusion and reality will tend to attach the child positively to external reality (Rycroft, 1985) and to create a sense of agency in the infant. This blissful, illusionary experience fosters what Winnicott (Ogden, 1990, p. 95) called *potential space*, "the intermediate area of experiencing that lies between fantasy and reality," which defines the relationship between internal and external reality, between self and other, and is the interface of boundaries that are inherent in consciousness. Deri (1978) has captured the significance of this experience: "The processes taking place within this intermediate space eliminate the disruption of the life space between the person and his environment" (pp. 45–60). Dr. Melman (2002) has referred to this space between the mother and infant as providing a "background of living," something most of us can take for granted. Patients with personality disorders are, sadly, unable to count on a benign, manageable, and often restful sense of being in the world.

In the formation of the infant self, the mother's job is to support the infant's experience of continuity by responding to the infant's biological rhythms. As time passes, the inevitable imperfection of fit between mother and infant results in the infant's first opportunity for awareness of separateness (Ogden, 1990, p. 95). Along with the undisturbed state of "going on being" (Winnicott, 1992, p. 303), which becomes the "background of living" that is experienced by the cared-for infant, the infant also inevitably experiences wanting and waiting. It is out of this sense of loss and need that the work of differentiation leading to separation begins to take place. Herein lies the groundwork for later symbolization, because symbols are required only when there is desire (wishes) (Ogden, 1990, p. 95).

SYMBOLIC PLAY

Language is the primary mechanism for symbolic interaction. Prior to the development of language, the subjective self first must be organized (Fonagy et al., 2002, p. 5). Part of that organization of self is the building of the dialectic between the internal and external worlds, and comes about through symbolic play. Children deeply engaged in the act of pretending can be called out of play to attend to parental demands and then return to their imaginative roles. For example, a little boy sitting at the front of a row of chairs, playing trains, said to his father, "Please don't kiss the engine, Daddy, or the carriages won't think it's real" (Huizinga, 1955). Pretending is a mental capacity that requires sophisticated self-reflective awareness (Hobson, 2002, p. 77) and represents practicing going back and forth between the dialectic of internal and external reality. This is an enormous accomplishment that requires an ability to take alternating *perspectives* instantaneously and not to lose track of one or the other. This capacity strengthens ego boundaries and facilitates the awareness of other people as separate selves who have their own perspectives.

LANGUAGE

In the development of a subjective conscious self, through separation and in-dividuation, the formation of language serves three important functions in the process of separation and individuation: (1) Language enables the child to gain distance from experience through symbolization; abstraction is necessitated by the separation process and words are necessitated by abstraction (Rosenfeld, 1992, p. 104). (2) Another function of language, *shared focus*, is the fulcrum for triangulation. Reciprocity between the mother and infant over time includes a third object or event and creates a given set of *shared* happenings. (3) Symbolic language serves as a bridge between the internal and external worlds and is the major mechanism of the dialectic mental process. At 18–20 months of age, the child begins to sense the symbolic function of words, no longer assuming that they are part of the objects or people they designate. They begin to grasp that words that have meaning for you have the same meaning for them. Especially in games with another, the infant has the opportunity to "share a common focus of activity. And orienting to a focus is a very basic character-istic of language — the use of words to comment on a topic" (Hobson, 2002, p. 84).

Symbols themselves are devoid of inherent meaning. Their meaning has its anchor elsewhere, down below . . . in what has been called our "deep non-symbolic internal engine." I believe that Donald (2001, p. 156) is referring here to the world of early procedures, interactions between the mother and infant that are laid down in implicit memory.

With this in mind, meaning is always self-referenced, coming from a sub-jective consciousness. I may experience a certain piece of music as moving and am aware that someone else may experience it in the same way as I do, or ex-perience it very differently. As a result, language then carries this conscious subjective experience and meaning of the person talking. "Changes in subjec-tivity, changes in the frame of reference, alter meanings and knowledge in general . . . all spoken language, like all mental acts, has self-reference and the brain mechanisms creating self-reference may, when altered, alter our use of language, just as they may alter our knowledge of our bodies or objects in our surroundings" (Rosenfeld, 1992, pp. 100–101).

Finally, symbols are a go-between, a bridge between one thing and an-other; and symbolizing is an amazing capacity that allows for both connection with and distance between the self and the world, between the thinker and the thought. "What is important about symbols is their double parentage, their derivation from both (external) memory images and (internal) instinctual urges; they connect the outside and the inside" (Deri, 1964, p. 131). Symbols have a Janus face, looking in opposite directions simultaneously. It is no wonder that patients who are in confusion about internal versus external sources of experience, about subjective versus objective realities, have difficulty with language. Rosenfeld (1992) writes, "Language connects, interrelates, and abstracts images; it distances us from the immediate, creating a past, a present, and a future; it enriches our awareness of the myriad ways in which our experience of the world can be organized; and it can create a world of its own" (p. 86).

PSYCHOPATHOLOGY AND LANGUAGE

Misuse of language in the clinical hour is a major manifestation of psychopathology. "When we become conscious of the meaning of a word and understand it, our understanding of the word, our subjective sense of it, is of the relations that constitute its meaning" (p. 99). When words are used concretely, that concrete usage is a manifestation of the loss of the relations that the word usually holds. The pathology of personality disorder runs deep; it is larger than loss of, or absence of, an adequate symbolization capacity. The developmental deficit is more than cognitive or mental; it is an experiential limitation in consciousness. Poor symbolization is caused by one's poor relationship to the world. If the subjective world loses, or lacks, abstract relations to the surroundings, language inevitably loses its abstract meaning. Lack of adequate symbolization is a symptom of a more pervasive loss of capacity for a dialectic relationship between one's self and the world, or between inner and outer realities.

SUMMARY

Persons with character pathology manifest the following distortions in consciousness:

1. *Loss of the dialectic*, as seen in their difficulty with the relationship of the self to the outside world, to reality. This most often takes the form of the patient's not knowing what part of the experience is coming from the inside and what is coming from the outside world. Persons with a personality disorder confuse their experiences of reality with what belongs to their inner psychic world. They are prone to blaming others for their discomfort.

2. *Cognitive rigidity*, which is the most prevalent defense shared among all patients with personality disorders. With the loss of the dialectic, they

tend to become stuck in one or another polarized position. Rigidity manifests as a tenacious adherence to established perceptions and beliefs about oneself and others, an inability to integrate feedback that disconfirms these beliefs, and a lack of oscillation between experiential states of separation and union. Although a sense of a fixed reality is understandably an attribute of the developing child, the healthy adult moves on to increasing complexity and flow in mentation.

3. *Avoidance of dependency* and a hatred of personal need. Clinging is not dependency: dependency requires an acceptance of separation and recognition of the worthiness of others.

4. *Deficits in symbolization* that reflect concrete mental operations and a loss of the dialectic between the internal and external worlds.

5. *Impaired mentalization*, which may be described as a limitation in the gradual realization that having a mind mediates one's experience of the world (Fonagy et al., 2002, p. 5). This amazing achievement occurs as the infant identifies with another's perspectives and attitudes, eventually contributing to both the capacity for empathy and a subjective sense of self.

6. *Disturbed capacity for empathy*. Empathy is part of the early development of consciousness that comes from a dawning awareness of the self with others. For this reason, empathy probably cannot be taught to clinicians to improve their work.

For treatment of patients with personality disorders to be effective in alleviating personal distress and diminishing self-destructive behaviors, the distortions of consciousness listed must be addressed. This is accomplished within the analytic dyadic experience, and depends heavily on the therapist's ability to do three things simultaneously: (1) connect with the patient on an empathic level; (2) remain separate, that is, positioned in reality using the therapeutic frame; (3) choose interventions based on language that the patient can hear and respond to emotionally. The Masterson Approach (Masterson, 2000) is clinically useful and effective in coordinating interventions with the theoretical understanding of psychopathology. Because these patients have different distortions of consciousness and different subjective expectations, based on their internal intrapsychic part self and object relationships, clinical interventions are best integrated by a patient if they speak to the patient's subjective experience.

References

Abrams, S. (1996). Differentiation and integration. *The Psychoanalytic Study of the Child*, 51, 25–34.

Beattie, M. (1987). Attention theory applied to the assessmemt of attention deficits in Alzheimer patients. Unpublished doctoral dissertation, California School of Professional Psychology, Berkeley.

Beebe, B., & Lachmann, F. M. (1992). *Infant Research and Adult Treatment: Co-constructing Interactions*. Hillsdale, NJ: Analytic Press.

Bowlby, J. (1988). Developmental psychiatry comes of age. *American Journal of Psychiatry*, 145, 1–10.

Cavell, M. (2003). The social character of thinking. *Journal of the American Psychoanalytic Association*, 51/3.

Damasio, A. R. (1999). *The Feeling of What Happens: Body and Emotion in the Making of Consciousness*. New York: Harcourt Brace.

DeBerry, S. T. (1991). The externalization of consciousness and the psychopathology of everyday life (no. 17). *Contributions in Psychology*. New York: Greenwood.

Deri, S. (1964). *Symbolization and Creativity*. New York: International Universities Press.

Deri, S. (1978). Transitional phenomena: Vicissitudes of symbolization and creativity (pp. 45–60). In S. A. Groinick, L. Barkin, & W. Muensterberger (Eds), *Between Reality and Fantasy*. New York: Jason Aronson.

Donald, M. (2001). *A Mind So Rare: The Evolution of Human Consciousness*. New York: Norton.

Dowling, S. (2003). Book reviews: Mind and its development. *Journal of the American Psychoanalytic Association*, 51/3, 1034–1043.

Edelman, G. M., & Tononi, G. (2000). *A Universe of Consciousness: How Matter Becomes Imagination*. New York: Basic Books.

Fonagy, P., Gergely, G., Jurist, E., & Target, M. (2002). *Affect Regulation, Mentalization and the Development of the Self*. New York: Other Press.

Fonagy, P., & Target, M. (2003). Book reviews. *Journal of the American Psychoanalytic Association*, 5/13, 1044.

Freud. S. (1911). *Formulations on the Two Principles of Mental Functioning*. Standard Edition, pp. 219–226.

Grotstein, J. (1978). Inner space: Its dimensions and its coordinates. *International Journal of Psychoanalysis*, 4, 55–61.

Hebb, D. (1963). The semiautonomous process: Its nature and nurture. *American Psychologist*, 18, 16–27. (Cited in Donald, 2001)

Hegel, G. W. F. (1807). *Phenomenology of Spirit* (A. V. Miller, trans.). London: Oxford University Press. (Cited in Ogden, 1990)

Heidegger, M. (1962). *Being and Time*. New York: Harper & Row. (Cited in Cavell, 2003, p. 986)

Herbert, N. (1987). *Quantum Reality*. New York: Doubleday. (Cited in DeBerry, 1991, p. 32)

Hobson, P. (2002). *The Cradle of Thought: Explorations in the Origins of Thinking*. New York: Macmillan.

Huizinga (1955). (Cited in Modell, 1990)

Mahler, M., Pine, F., & Bergmann, A. (1975). *The Psychological Birth of the Human Infant: Symbiosis and Individuation*. New York: Basic Books.

Main, M., Kaplan, N., & Cassidy, J. (1985). Security in infancy, childhood and adulthood: A move to the level of representation (pp. 66–104). In I. Bretherton & E. Waters (Eds.), *Growing Points of Attachment Theory and Research*. (Monographs of the Society in Child Development, 50, 1–2)

Masterson, J. F. (1976). *Psychotherapy of the Borderline Adult: A Developmental Approach*. New York: Brunner/Mazel.

Masterson, J. F. (1988). *The Search for the Real Self*. New York: Brunner/Mazel.

Masterson, J. F. (2000). *The Personality Disorders: A New Look at the Developmental Self and Object Relations Approach*. Phoenix: Zeig, Tucker.

Melman, D. (2002). The Mind Object Class. Berkeley, CA: NCSPP.

Modell, A. H. (1990). The roots of creativity and the use of the object (p. 117). In P. L. Giovacchini (Ed.), *Tactics and Techniques in Psychoanalytic Therapy, III: The Implications of Winnicott's Contributions*. New York: Jason Aronson.

Ogden, T. (1990). On potential space (p. 100). In P. L. Giovacchini (Ed.), *Tactics and Techniques in Psychoanalytic Therapy, III: The Implications of Winnicott's Contributions*. New York: Jason Aronson.

Rose, G. (1978). The creativity of everyday life. In S. Groinick, S. Barkin, & W. Meunsterberger (Eds.), *Between Reality and Fantasy: Transitional Objects and Phenomena*. New York: Jason Aronson.

Rosenfeld, I. (1992). *The Strange, Familiar and Forgotten*. New York: Knopf.

Rycroft, C. (1985). *Psychoanalysis and Beyond*. London: Chatto & Windus.

Shaver, P., Hazen, C., & Bradshaw, D. (1988). Love as attachment: The integration of three behavorial systems (pp. 68–69). In R. J. Sternberg & M. L. Barnes (Eds.), *The Psychology of Love*. New Haven, CT: Yale University Press.

Sperling, M., & Berman, W. H. (Eds.) (1994). *Attachment in Adults: Clinical and Development Perspectives*. New York: Guilford.

Tichener, E. B. (1898). The postulates of a structural psychology (pp. 35–47). *Controversial Issues in Psychology*. Boston: Houghton Mifflin. (Reprinted from *Philosophical Review*, 1898, pp. 440–465)

Wilson, A. (2003). Ghosts of paradigms past: The once and future evolution of psychoanalytic thought. *Journal of the American Psychoanalytic Association, 51/3*, 825–855.

Wilson, A., & Prillaman, J. (1997). Early development and disorders of internalization (pp. 189–234). In M. Moskowitz, C. Monk, C. Kaye, & S. Elman (Eds.),

Neurobiological and Developmental Basis for Psychotherapeutic Intervention.
Northvale, NJ: Jason Aronson. (Cited in Wilson, 2003)

Winnicott, D. W. (1971). *Playing and Reality.* London: Routledge.

Winnicott, D. W. (1992). *Through Pediatrics to Psychoanalysis: Collected Papers.* New
York: Brunner/Mazel.

3

Early Development of Personality Disorders — Mother–Infant Dyadic Formation of the Infant Mind: The Psychological Dialectic

MARGOT T. BEATTIE, PH.D.

The purpose of this chapter is to identify and explore the early developmental origins of personality disorders, in particular, problems in the formation and functioning of a psychological dialectic.[1] A psychological dialectic is a developed mental capacity that allows us to "move" back and forth mentally between internal and external reality (Ogden, 1990). The development of a psychological dialectic is fundamental to the development of a subjective self in relation to the outside world. It further is the foundation for the development of self-reflection and movement into secondary intersubjectivity — awareness that others are aware and have minds of their own (Hobson, 2002). The capacity for self-reflection is inherent in the sophisticated achievements of mentalization, symbolization, and self-regulation (Hobson, 2002; Fonagy et al., 2002). A psychological dialectic shapes the infant's relationship to the world and dictates the quality of all future interpersonal relationships. Problems in the formation and functioning of this dialectic are central to the development of personality disorders.

---

[1] I am indebted to James Masterson for his training in the treatment of personality disorders, and to Thomas Ogden for his conceptualization of the psychological dialectic as it relates to Winnicott's concept of potential space.

OVERVIEW

The concept of inner space has been of interest in psychoanalytic study for many years (Spitz, 1957; Winnicott, 1971; Grotstein, 1978). Developmental theory of internal mental space has evolved from the study and appreciation of the mother–infant dyad. Winnicott (1956) and others have emphasized the importance of maternal availability in normal personality development. Masterson (1976), using Mahler's theory of separation and individuation to illuminate the seriousness of adolescent acting-out behavior, was among the first to focus on the long-term adverse effects of maternal "unavailability" in the development of personality disorders.

Masterson identified the child's struggles for separation during the rapprochement subphase of the separation/individuation process as central to the formation of a personality disorder. In pathological development, the responses of the mother, or caretaker, to the toddler's attempts at establishing autonomy interfere with the child's formation of a separate self in relation to the environment. Masterson's theory, which guides the clinical treatment of patients with personality disorders, is based on understanding this pathological development of intrapsychic self and object representations. Such pathological development can be traced to early disturbances in the child's formation of a psychological dialectic — the mental ability to move back and forth between self and other, between internal and external worlds.

RECENT NEUROBIOLOGIC RESEARCH

Attachment and neurobiology research now has given a resounding endorsement to Masterson's early research on the evolution of personality disorders and his emphasis on the centrality of the mother–infant relationship. Mother–infant interaction, already the domain of attachment research, has become the focus of infant development research in social biofeedback theory (Fonagy et al., 2002), in co-constructed dyadic systems for interactive organization theory (Beebe & Lachmann, 1992), in the role of the dyadic unit in the development of thought (Hobson, 2002), in affect-based theory of mental development (Damasio, 1999), and in the neurobiologic theories of early brain development (Schore, 2003).

The developmental process of the infant's acquiring a sense of self in relation to the outside world is complex, intriguing, and fortunately, increasingly available to understanding. Given genetic and temperament considerations, it is now well established that the infant's personality development emanates from the mother–infant dyad and that the adult personality reflects the integrity of that early dyadic relationship. It is also known that the primary purpose of attachment, beyond safety and survival, is the development of the infant mind through an interactive relationship with the mother (Fonagy et al., 2002), and that the quality of the infant–mother attachment — secure, insecure, or disorganized — has a far-reaching impact on later adult mental and emotional functioning (Masterson, 1976).

IMPLICIT LEARNING

Developmentally, the infant's early experience and learning are nonverbal, or what Stern (1998) has referred to as "implicit relational knowledge." Whereas whole-brain functioning is involved in all human endeavors, recent neurobiologic research has demonstrated the dominance of early right-hemisphere development for implicit learning, nonverbal processing, and emotionally related interactions between the mother and the infant (Schore, 2003). More specifically, the right prefrontal orbital cortex is the area of the brain particularly involved in infant–mother attachment functions. The innate propensity toward attachment is activated and protected through synchrony with the infant on the part of the mother. Most of this synchronous relationship for both the mother and infant takes place on the implicit level of experience.

A knowledge of implicit experience is important both developmentally and clinically. Developmentally, implicit experience can be described as a gathering up of sensory and somatic experience for registration into what becomes subjectivity. However, implicit experience does not belong only to the domain of infancy. Because implicit experience unites the boundaries of what is felt into what is known (Damasio, 1999), it is the seat of abstraction, a necessary foundation for the later capacity for symbolization (Aragno, 1997).

At first, the infant learns by way of implicit processing, or what used to be called primary processing — the world of feeling and image. Primary processing occurs on the psychic path between sensory and motor boundaries, along which instinctual drives travel under the pleasure principle (Glover, 1956). In writing of dreaming, Freud described primary processing as "residues of the phase of development in which they were the only kind of mental processes; that in laying aside our mental acquisitions in sleep we approach remarkably close to the situation which began life." Using the mother, the infant experiences an implicit dawning awareness of self that must develop into a mind capable of *bridging* this internal sense of self to the external world. One of the least recognized developmental milestones for a healthy personality is the achievement of a *flexible* psychological dialectic — the capacity that enables the mind automatically to traverse back and forth between inner and outer realities.

Self-development originates from instinctual id impulses and implicit learning within the dyadic relationship with the mother. This complex achievement follows from the very early development of internal mental space, leading to the development of a psychological dialectic. A psychological dialectic not only provides a framework within which an individual moves back and forth between inner and outer realities, but it represents a form of dual consciousness. Winnicott (1971) wrote:

> Why is it that the *ordinary healthy* person has at one and the same time a feeling of the realness of the world, and of the realness of what is imaginative and personal? [*italics added*]

Winnicott's question points to the early development of a normal, constant, and ever-changing relationship between internal and external reality. We tend to take for granted our capacity to live in both inner and outer reality because of the early formation of a psychological dialectic.

"A dialectic is a process in which two opposing concepts each creates, informs, preserves, and negates the other, each standing in a dynamic (ever-changing) relationship with the other" (Hegel, 1807). Living among others requires us unknowingly to move back and forth between subjective experience and the "objective" world. But we are not temporary visitors traversing interior and exterior landscapes; we construct our sense of self out of our relationship, first to the mother, and always to the world. We are continually assimilating aspects of the larger world, as well as finding aspects of ourselves in the world, so that the unfamiliar is not necessarily foreign (Milner, 1957). We both endure and flourish in "the perpetual human task of keeping inner and outer reality separate yet inter-related" (Winnicott, 1958). Mannoni (1999) writes:

> . . . the most elemental ordeals of the disturbed child are at the same time the ongoing challenge of human experience. Just as the differentiation of inside and outside is perpetual, the task of locating oneself in relation to one's hidden desires in order to act upon them or not and the task of separating oneself from the demands or desires of another in order to respond to them or not are the always unfinished ordeal of human autonomy.

DEVELOPMENTAL SIGNIFICANCE OF A
PSYCHOLOGICAL DIALECTIC

Development of a Self

The study of the subjective experience of consciousness is the study of ones relationship with internal and external reality (DeBerry, 1991). The infant's early experience of illusion lays the foundation for a dialectic between internal and external worlds that, over time, formulates individual subjectivity in relation to reality.

"The dialectical process is centrally involved in the creation of subjectivity" (Ogden, 1990). The differentiation of "me" from "not me" within the mother–infant dyad allows the infant to accentuate the "me," while holding onto and relating to the "not me," thus carving out an awareness of self by means of, and in the form of, a dialectic. It is the eventual "I" that "does the moving" back and forth between internal and external worlds. "Subjectivity is related to, but not the same as, consciousness. The experience of consciousness (and unconsciousness) follows from the achievement of subjectivity. Subjectivity is a reflection of the differentiation of symbol, symbolized, and interpreting subject (Ogden, 1990). The differentiation of mother, infant, and infant as interpreter creates "the possibility of triangularity within which space is created."

The achievement of a psychological dialectic comes from the development of space between internal experience and external reality, at the interface of the boundary of self and other. Winnicott called this "potential space." Inner space is not only a chief determinant of self-development in the early months of life; as adults, it is where we live, where we rest, and where we recover from the arduous and worthy struggle for separation (Winnicott, 1971). The development of potential/inner space is bound up with the infant's psychological experience of illusion, with sensory experience and with the infant's physical experience of a skin boundary.

People with balanced and flexible psychological dialectics, those able to move freely back and forth between internal and external realities, are able to self-activate by expressing themselves in giving to and taking from the world. Self-esteem accrues from reciprocity that acknowledges the world of others and facilitates the cumulative experience of getting along well interpersonally. The presence and exercise of a psychological dialectic are fundamental to living a relational, productive life, and are strikingly deficient in patients with personality disorders. In fact, deficiency in the functioning of a psychological dialectic is characteristic of all patients with personality disorders and is the source of serious interpersonal difficulty.

Patients who have had problems in the formation and functioning of potential space leading to a psychological dialectic are familiar to (if not identified by) clinicians. Clinical symptoms of cognitive deficiency, including perceptual rigidity, concretization of thought, and impoverished language (stunted symbolization capacity), as well as symptoms of emotional duress, including feelings of confusion, alienation, and superiority, are all indications of a troubled personal relationship to reality (Masterson, 1985) that is attributable to developmental problems in the formation of inner space and a psychological dialectic. Across Axis II diagnoses, patients show deficits in vitality and resourcefulness of inner space and its offspring, a flexible psychological dialectic. Clinically, we can often observe the results of the collapse of the dialectic; it is more difficult to see the underlying incompleteness and/or the inflexibility of the dialectic in the patient's mental and emotional functioning.

Perhaps Winnicott's (1971) chief contribution to psychoanalytic theory is his understanding of the importance of the mother–infant relationship in the formation of the infant mind.

> From birth . . . the human being is concerned with the problem of the relationship between what is objectively perceived and what is subjectively conceived of, and in the solution of this problem there is no health for the human being who has not been started off well enough by the mother (p. 11).

It is the purpose of this chapter to review and explore those aspects of the mother–infant dyad that are particularly pertinent to the infant's development of potential space and to the growth of a psychological dialectic. The dyadic developmental components, each one germinating the next, include the infant's union with the mother, the infant's experience of illusion, and the mother's capacity for separation seen in her introduction of disillusionment and formation in the infant of potential space, allowing for a psychological dialectic.

UNION WITH THE MOTHER

Paradoxically, the acquisition of the ability to move back and forth between one's own thoughts and the world of others is predicated developmentally on the infant's sense of a seamless union with the mother (Winnicott, 1956). This psychological union, called maternal preoccupation or maternal synchrony

(Schore, 2003), provides the infant with the opportunity for *continuity of being*, a primary internal building block for developing a sense of self. "The mother knows, instinctively as people say, what need is just about to become pressing. She presents the world to the infant in the only way that does not spell chaos, by the meeting of needs as they arise" (Winnicott, 1957). The most important biological impetus "in developing from a simple core self to an elaborate auto-biographical self is *stability* because of all kinds of self, one notion commands center stage: a single individual who changes ever so gently across time but, somehow, seems to stay the same" (Damasio, 1999).

The mother holds the infant physically; and for an infant, that which is physical is also psychological. The infant's slow integration into personhood and the development of a separate sense of self emerges out of physical care by the mother. According to Winnicott (1958):

> The tendency to integrate is helped by two sets of experiences: the technique of infant care whereby an infant is kept warm, handled and bathed and rocked and named, and also the acute instinctual experiences which tend to gather the personality together from within (p. 150).

In the early months of life, the function of the good-enough mother is to help the infant to establish, and then protect, the infant's continuity of existence. "For this purpose, the mother's empathic ability to treat the baby in harmony with his own biological rhythm is crucial" (Deri, 1978).

The mother's attunement to her infant's biological rhythms is accomplished primarily in three ways. First, she feeds the infant in a timely fashion, thus preventing the infant's hunger from reaching levels of unbearable tension that disrupt the infant's sense of unity and continuity. Second, she engages in appropriate tactile/kinesthetic communication in the holding of her infant. The infant's skin is the first concrete boundary or interface between himself or herself and the world. "The rhythm, the intensity and the indefinable ways of communicating love through touching and holding will determine whether this skin boundary is felt as good (as a source of pleasure) or as bad (as a source of discomfort)." A primary source of self-integration for the infant is the establishment over time of an early awareness of a skin boundary.

> I believe the capacity to experience space is a primary apparatus of ego autonomy in Hartmann's terms (1939), which seems to have emerged from the inchoate sensations upon the fetal skin at birth, thereby "awakening" the skin with its sense receptors into its functions as a surface, as a boundary between self and non-self, and as a container of self (Grotstein, 1978, pp. 55–61).

"A libidinally cathected skin surface pleasantly delineates the inside from the outside. Communication between two areas lying on either side of a boundary will be felt to be desirable" (Deri, 1978). These early sensory experiences come into play in the development of later complex mental capacities. As Deri points out, it is worth noting that symbolization is, by definition, a communication across a boundary.

Third, through mutual gaze, the mother reflects the infant's emotional experience back to him or her. Mirroring allows the infant to register the essential phenomena of being known by another, fostering the categorization of experience necessary to a sense of separateness. The infant sees himself or herself in the mother's eyes. In Winnicott's (1971) words: "The mother is looking at the baby and *what she looks like is related to what she sees there.*" The infant sees and formulates his or her own subjective emotional experience in the mother's reaction — this is the subjective object. He or she sees the object imbued with some of himself or herself. Seeing oneself in the other is also the basis for the later capacity for empathy. "If too precociously, it is the face of the mother/object that he perceives, he cannot form the subjective object but will prematurely evolve the object objectively perceived. The result is that he must organize a false self, as an image conforming to the mother's desire" (Green, 1978). This is the false defensive self formed by the personality-disordered patient (Masterson, 1985).

Fonagy points out that in mirroring, the mother is not actually mirroring exactly her infant. She instead shows the child the feelings she assumes that the child has, thus demonstrating her capacity to move in the same affective direction. Beebe and Lachmann (1992) speak of a "moment of meeting." Perhaps even more important, she provides the experience and a space, a "meeting ground," where the outside meets the inside.

In neurobiologic terms, the gaze of the mother and infant is important for the development of brain structure. In this interactive system of reciprocal stimulation, "both members of the dyad enter into a symbiotic state of heightened positive affect essential in the imprinting of the right hemisphere, thereby enabling maturation of the limbic areas of the cortex involved in emotional functions (Schore, 2003). Gaze cutoff, one of the infant's only forms of arousal control, also facilitates the developing sense of the infant as subject and agent, able to exert some control over inner experience.

For the patient with a personality disorder, weakness in the ego structure and the continual presence of anxiety in the self structure suggest that deficiencies in these basic dyadic biological and psychological experiences have set awry personality development from a very early age. These patients have difficulty with personal continuity; they repeatedly lose and regain their emotional equilibrium. Emotional volatility, or the opposite, stagnation, is the hallmark of character pathology. These patients have difficulty with waiting, because they do not believe in a rewarding environment. Under conditions of frustration and disappointment, they often collapse into preemptive resignation and helplessness. Without adequate early mirroring from the mother, they are likely to become seekers in relationships, trying to find themselves in the object's eyes, often moving from one "unsatisfying" partner to the next. Taken together, these internal hardships make up what we call characterlogic depression. Although these individuals are often highly functioning professionally, they live with pervasive inner sorrow and anxiety.

ILLUSION

Continuity of being experiences, in turn, provide the infant with an opportunity for the mental experience of illusion. Illusion may be described as the attribution of one's experience to one's own creation, and it provides the infant with the gratifying feeling of omniscience.

> The mother, at the beginning, by almost 100 percent adaptation, affords the infant the opportunity for the *illusion* that her breast is part of the infant. It is, as it were, under the baby's magical control ... Omnipotence is nearly a fact of experience (Winnicott, 1971, p. 11).

Illusionary experience is fundamental to the development of consciousness under the governance of the pleasure principle (Ogden, 1990). But the experience of illusion also has far-reaching effects on adult mental capacity. It is the beginning of a bridge between subjective and objective reality that will always be a mixture of inner experience and outer circumstances. Illusionary experience is made possible by maternal synchrony when the infant is separating "me" from "not-me," and is a necessary prerequisite for developing a sense of self with a positive attitude of anticipation. Illusionary experience is the dawn of an autonomous self *with a sense of agency*.

EARLY DEVELOPMENT OF ILLUSION

As Ogden (1990) wrote of Winnicott's concept of illusion, "Here the experience of oneness with the mother and separateness from her coexist in a dialectical opposition." Illusion is the means by which the infant both holds on to, and moves out of, union with the mother.

Early on, the fortunate infant with an attuned mother is allowed to believe that he or she creates the satisfying experience of oral gratification.

> The mother's adaptation to the infant's needs, when good enough, gives the infant the *illusion* that there is an external reality that corresponds to the infant's capacity to create. In other words, there is an overlap between what the mother supplies and what the child might conceive of (Winnicott, 1971, p. 12).

The mother's love and her close identification with her infant make her aware of the infant's needs to the extent that she provides something . . . in the right place at the right time (Winnicott, 1958). Repeated experiences of satisfaction at the breast bring about memory, and these memories cluster in the preconscious. The memory–image becomes an expectation of the breast. A meeting ground has been found for the inside experience and the outside provision.

ILLUSION IN THE ADULT PERSONALITY

Winnicott taught us that without this experience of a "primary illusion" of omnipotence, the infant, the growing child, and the eventual adult do not enjoy reality. The mother's willingness to allow the infant to attribute experience to his or her own creation "offers up the world as a friendly place" (Deri, 1978) and engenders a love of reality. As Modell (1990) summarized, "The capacity to mediate experience through illusioning provides a sense that life is worth living . . . Those individuals who retain . . . a capacity to perceive the world uniquely and thus to transform reality, will be able to modify and soften their harsh relation to reality. Frustration can teach individuals to perceive and adapt — often defensively, to reality, but only the experience of fulfillment, coming from the outside but magically created by a wish, can foster a true love of reality.

For the adult, the early experience of illusion provides the following core mental capacities: (1) The capacity to wish — because needs have to be met. Being alive is experienced positively, and so is wishing. The infant begins with an optimistic attitude toward life. "The way the mother hands over the world to the child determines whether the child will form an optimistic attitude toward living or be caught in the arid anhedonic world of personality disorder." (2) Internalization of a fulfilling mother leads to a sense of agency. When maternal giving is poorly synchronized with the infant's wishes, the result is a disruption between the internal self and external reality, with accompanying feelings of longing, anger, and alienation. (3) The illusion of creating gratification during interactive regulation is a powerful impetus for developing self-regulation. (4) Illusionary experience anchors the core self in an emotional life of implicit imagery and feeling, later to be expressed in imagination and creativity.

The seeming contradiction between illusion's playing an essential role in relation to reality is resolved by understanding that what in the infant was a more total illusionary relation to reality, in the adult, refers not to the total relationship, but to the *erotic* component of the relationship to reality — the enjoyment, the hope, "those parts that are concerned, even if only nascently, with love (Rycroft, 1968). In the adult, "the development of a healthy erotic relation to (external) reality involves that at the moment of consummation of a wish, there should be a convergence and merging of this hallucinated image (and its cathexis) with the image of the available object ... Failure to fuse these imagos leads to a divorce between the imaginative and the intellectual functions, that is, in principle at least, unnecessary. Successful fusion, on the other hand, leads to freedom from the belief that desire and reality are in inevitable opposition to one another.

DEFICITS IN THE EXPERIENCE OF ILLUSION

Patients with a personality disorder not only find it difficult to "love" reality, but they commonly struggle to perceive and accept it. Their struggle becomes manifest clinically in a lack of awareness of the role that psychic reality plays in their emotional experiences. This struggle is prevalent in all patients with personality disorders. It is at this interface between self and others that patients with personality disorders are most impaired. They fail to identify their emotional experience as imbued with their own psychic reality. In understanding character pathology, this one symptom — difficulty in integrating and keeping separate internal and external reality — points us to the early developmental stage when the infant is separating the self from other and using the emerging intermediate area between the two, potential space, to do so. Personality disorders are also called "Disorders of the Self" because it is the awareness of being an autonomous, but not omnipotent, self that fails to develop (Masterson & Klein, 1989). Reasons for this failure can be traced to disturbances in the infant's experience of union, illusion, and disillusionment with the mother — all necessary in forming a psychological dialectic.

Early disturbances in illusion formation are manifest clinically in patients with personality disorders. Failing to have seen themselves in their mother's eyes, they are forever seeking to find themselves in the eyes of the object, and when they are unable to do so, they resort to idealization of the object. Their developmentally understandable, but inappropriate, search for a mirroring object relegates them to the pain of short-lived love relationships and endless seeking. These patients lack the feeling and awareness that they can create that which they need in their lives (coming originally from a primary illusion of omnipotence), and, therefore, fail to develop a sense of self as agent. Passivity is among the most common destructive defenses of individuals with personality disorders.

Early disturbance in illusion formation sets in motion a lifetime of difficulty with interpersonal relationships. The inability to know what belongs "inside" and what belongs "outside" (that is, what to attribute to oneself and what to attribute to others) creates turbulence among friends and lovers. Borderline, Narcissistic, and Schizoid patients tend to see the object as a (needed, but unavailable) savior, and/or blame the object for their discomfort. This destructive perspective can be traced to problems in illusion formation within attachment dynamics. A primary function of attachment is to provide the infant with an environment within which an *understanding of mental states* in self and others can develop. Fonagy et al. (2002) refer to this as mentalizing, the realization that having a mind mediates experience. Masterson's description of personality pathology in terms of the patient's "focus on the object" is a description of underdeveloped mentalization.

Patients who cannot understand the mental and emotional dynamics of themselves and others cannot sustain rewarding personal relationships over time, and, therefore, suffer feelings of emptiness and isolation, often reacting with passivity or inappropriate aggression in their interactions. The capacity to understand one's own and others' mental states begins with the experience of illusion during self and other differentiation, and develops into mental flexibility in the form of a psychological dialectic. A psychological dialectic is inherent in mentalization, and is the guardian of sane subjectivity: a sense of self built out of an integration of the inside with the outside, a little of each in the other. That which is internal is seen and found in the world, while a little of the world is taken in and made one's own (Winnicott, 1971).

DISILLUSIONMENT

The power of early illusionary experience will sustain the infant, even through the painful arrival of illusionment. The infant must survive the dawning awareness that he or she did not create the mother and still tolerate an intense need for her. Being unable to create a mother is balanced by being unable to destroy the mother. In Kleinian terms, the infant's realization that objects survive the infant's aggression is paramount in the infant's acceptance of the separation of self and mother, of reality. Personal agency then is not perceived as dangerous.

The child's growing sense of agency depends on the experience of disillusionment following a healthy dosing of illusion. Disillusionment ushers in more defined reciprocity with the mother, and lessens the immediacy of her synchrony. Later, taking turns at rolling a ball, being both giver and receiver, the child is arriving at the painful, but exciting, insight that he or she is not the center of the universe (Hobson, 2002). The world is not just what the infant makes it out to be on his or her own. Now one's self exists primarily in relation to others. In the adult, earlier successful disillusionment results in the ability to hold the capacity for creativity without giving in to the impulse for control. Disillusionment in the adult will still be used to make separation less painful through artistic and intellectual achievements and in cultural interests. It will translate into personal characteristics of agency — perseverance, confidence, and, equally important, humility.

> Even the best external reality is disappointing because it is not also imaginary, and although perhaps to some extent it can be manipulated, it is not under magical control. One of the chief tasks before those who care for a little child is to give help in the *painful transition from illusion to disillusion*, by simplifying as far as possible the problem immediately in front of a child at any one moment (Winnicott, 1957, p. 104).

For the fortunate child, disillusion will be confined to belief in the omnipotent control of reality, not reality itself (Rycroft, 1968). When illusionment is too rapid, or there is too great a gap between the child's libidinal expectation and fulfillment, the child will withdraw personal investment from real, external objects and resort to internal idealization. Idealization is a common substitute for a healthy illusionary relationship to reality. But the purpose of idealization as opposed to illusion is to enable the ego to deny feelings of hopelessness and emptiness and to evade the necessity of feeling ambivalent that accompanies experiences of being let down and disappointment.

Treatment Issues

Masterson has based his theory of the development of personality disorders on the difficulty these patients have with embracing the reality principle. Establishment of the reality principle in the mind of the child comes about through appropriate management of disillusionment.

There is no possibility whatever for an infant to proceed from the pleasure principle to the reality principle toward and beyond primary identification [see Freud, 1923], unless there is a good-enough mother (Winnicott, 1971, p. 10).

Winnicott goes on to describe the good-enough mother as one with the ability to move from synchrony to reciprocity *based on* the infant's ability to wait and to tolerate frustration. As clinicians, we provide a frame that both "holds" the patients and requires them to participate in reality. The reality of treatment is not only a dyadic reality (although it is that), but it also is an intersubjective reality in which different minds are respected and in which observation of the patient by the patient is an expectation.

POTENTIAL SPACE

As the infant separates out of union with the mother, the infant's experience of illusion is held within what Winnicott (1971) called "potential space." Potential space refers to the space between the infant and the mother, between internal subjective experience and external reality, at the interface of the boundary between self and other. "Potential space is an intermediate area of *experiencing* to which inner reality and external life both contribute. It is an area that ... shall exist as a resting place for the individual engaged in the perpetual task of keeping inner and outer reality separate yet interrelated" (p. 2) ... "It belongs neither entirely to the subjective inner world nor to objective external reality; it represents the subject's creative transformation of the external world" (Modell, 1990).

Thomas Ogden (1990) explored Winnicott's concept of potential space in terms of the developing psychological dialectic. Potential space that begins as space between the mother and infant as the infant differentiates out of union later includes transitional phenomena, play space, the analytic space, the area of cultural experience, and the mind's area of creativity. Potential space varies greatly among individuals according to the quality of their experiences with their mothers. Infants, who, because of initial maternal synchrony, and later, maternal reciprocity, are able to build trust in the environment, separate themselves from the original mother–infant union. The infant in such an environment does not have to continually reestablish safety, but can proceed to the increasingly complex overlapping of internal and external experiences.

Potential Space in Adulthood

Potential space, beginning as physical and mental space between the infant and the mother, grows to become central to all of us throughout life. Because potential space is made up of both inside and outside, but resides in neither and is not fixed, it is that "place, using the word in the abstract sense, where we most of the time are when we are experiencing life (Winnicott, 1971). This space becomes a "complex relation between what is inside and what is outside, continues throughout the individual's life and is the *main relationship we each have to the world* — a relationship even more important than either object relating or instinct gratification (Winnicott, 1986).

Potential space not only facilitates separation, but it provides space for union. "It is par excellence the dimension of connectedness or, even better, or mutual immanence" (Deri, 1978). Potential space gives rise to our capacity to enjoy the richness inherent in symbolization. "Steady experiences in relationships (allow) for the development of intermediate areas in which transitional or play phenomena can be established for that particular child, established so that the child may enjoy all that is to be derived from the use of the symbol, for the symbol gives wider scope for human experience than union itself (Winnicott, 1957).

Potential space in adult life provides us with a state of mind allowing for a dialectic between our subjective internal world and reality.

> Life is difficult for everyone from the beginning. From what do difficulties arise? First, from the mental clash of two kinds of reality, that of the external world, which can be shared by everyone, and that of each child's personal inner world of feelings, ideas, imagination . . . Throughout life there must always be distress in connection with this essential dilemma (Winnicott, 1971).

Relief comes from an intermediate area of experience (cf. Winnicott & Riviere, 1936) and from the use of transitional phenomena. The creation of this intermediate area, potential mental space, comes over time to constitute what has been called the *"background"* of living — that is, taking for granted a benign interpersonal world, an entitlement to some measure of contentment, all growing out of maternal attunement to the infant's needs and the infant's reciprocal response.

Deficits in Potential Space: Patients with Personality Disorders

It is becoming increasingly apparent that disturbances in the very early stages of development underlie the formation of a personality disorder. At the interface of self and other, the healthy personality learns to oscillate between internal wishes and external reality, between union and separation; whereas the patient with a personality disorder tends to become overwhelmed and frozen — unable to move within a psychological dialectic.

> The potential space between baby and mother, between child and family, between individual and society of the world . . . can be looked upon as *sacred* to the individual in that it is here that the individual experiences creative living. By contrast, exploitation of this area leads to a pathological condition in which the individual is cluttered up with persecutory elements of which he has no means of ridding himself (Winnicott & Riviere, 1936, p. 17).

The pathological condition to which Winnicott refers is that of a personality disorder. Persecutory elements are formed early in the individual who fails to experience illusion and the healthy formation of a psychological dialectic. The dialectic serves to continually alter internal psychic representations according to ongoing experience. Patients with personality disorders have a worldview anchored in fixed expectations formed in past interpersonal experiences. So wedded are these patients to subjective internal reality, so limited are they in the use of potential mental space, that they are not generally receptive to disconfirming evidence countering their perceptions.

Owing to restricted internal mental space and the lack of mental flexibility, patients with a personality disorder sadly lack access to their creative mind (self), which we all use to temper the harshness and disappointments of reality. They also lack access to the peace of mind that comes from a lifetime of seeking and finding refuge internally with oneself. Potential space allows us to withstand separation. For the healthy child and adult, separation is managed, or in Winnicott's words "avoided," "by the filling in of the potential space with creative playing, with the use of symbols, and with all that eventually adds up to a cultural life." For patients with a personality disorder, diminished potential space imprisons them in fears of being either too alone or too close to others, abandoned or engulfed (Masterson, 1976). The psychological dialectic that enables us to move back and forth internally to adjust to psychic comfort is underdeveloped in these patients.

PSYCHOLOGICAL DIALECTIC

From Synchrony to Reciprocity

Synchrony between the mother and infant, now called "contingent communication" (Beebe & Lachmann, 1992), is the chief dynamic for self-organization and building psyche structure. Contingent responding means that the mother's behavior meets the infant's need and the infant's needs precipitate the mother's behavior. Contingent communication sets up a shared world in which meaning can be transmitted emotional and is, therefore, the main interactive mechanism of attachment.

As the infant matures and separates out of union, signaling becomes a more overt action on his or her part, and ushers in a more interactive, verbal, reciprocal process with the mother. The infant now engages in self-expression in the form of signaling that contributes more actively to the dyadic process. Giving a signal to the mother and experiencing the consequences of her attention is the beginning of a dialectic in practice, which, with predictability and stability, can be trusted and internalized.

A psychological dialectic is established and practiced by the infant through the use of transitional objects and by the young child through playing. The transitional object symbolizes the interplay between separation and object (Modell, 1990).

> The appearance of a relationship with a transitional object is not simply a milestone in the process of separation/individuation. The relationship with the transitional object is as significantly a reflection of the development of the capacity to maintain a psychological dialectical process (Ogden, 1990, p. 97).

One of Winnicott's (1971) great gifts to us was his taking notice that children at play are going back and forth mentally between internal and external worlds. "The thing about playing is always the precariousness of the interplay of personal psychic reality and the experience of control of actual objects. This is the precariousness of magic itself, magic that arises in intimacy, in a relationship that is found to be reliable (one offering illusion) [*parentheses added*].

A mother interrupted the play of Tom, a 4-year-old boy, dressed in mask and cape, by asking him to pick up his toys. He stopped mid-stance, looked at her seriously, and replied, "Batman doesn't pick up toys! Tom will do it later." This child held two worlds in his mind at once. He was able to hold on to pretending and to answer to reality, a sophisticated psychological and mental achievement, born out of the child's much earlier experience of illusion and potential space. These experiences, plus an ongoing internal push to the child to continue to self-differentiate, make room for potential space, an intermediate area — all fundamental to the development of a separate autonomous self.

Children at play are practicing what a healthy personality takes for granted; that is, fluidity is traversing the boundaries between subjective feelings and external reality. This mental flexibility lends itself to the automatic capacity to be alternately self-absorbed and unaware of self when in the world (Mahler et al., 1975). The capacity to move freely mentally between internal and external worlds is necessary for the mature corresponding accurate capacity for attributing emotional experience. We can become aware of what internal pressures we bring to any particular situation. This capacity for self-reflection is an advanced form of self-awareness.

Deficits in a Psychological Dialectic

Deficits in the formation of a psychological dialectic result in at least three forms of pathological intrapsychic development seen in three separate diagnoses of a personality disorder. Narcissistic and Schizoid patients, with quite different clinical presentations, seem to suffer more from deficits in the actual formation of a psychological dialectic, whereas those with Borderline disorders seem to suffer from deficiencies in the functioning of the dialectic.

The Narcissistic personality disorder, whether exhibiting or closet, lives by perceptions that do not regularly register the separate reality of others. This apparent lack of a psychological dialectic seems to originate in the early stages of mental development, when the infant's readiness to take on more of a role in the dyadic relationship is ignored by the mother. With the onset of more overt signaling and the quest for reciprocity, the infant "no longer expects the condition in which there is almost magical understanding of need. The mother seems to know that the infant has a new capacity, that of giving a signal so that she can be guided towards meeting the infant's needs. It could now be said that if she knows too well what the infant needs, this is magic and forms no basis for an object relationship" (Winnicott, 1965).

A deficit in the development of a dynamic for real object relating describes the pathology of the Narcissistic personality disorder. The disorder develops not so much from a failure of the mother to provide disillusionment in the infant, but from her failure to allow *space between them* in order for the infant to assume part of a relationship by signaling. A mother who "automatically" meets an infant's needs without waiting for expression from the infant is robbing him or her of self-development, of participation in a dyadic relationship, of inclusion in the process of give-and-take with the external world, and of creating a dialectic between the mother and infant that becomes an internal psychological dialectic between the self and the world. From the infant's point of view, it must seem that the mother needs merging forever. The Narcissistic patient later will approach others in the same way, with little regard for their opinion, their inputs, or their separate existences.

In current language, these mothers' responses are overly contingent. Their responses are not sensitive to continuous modification by the simultaneously changing actions of their partners. Beebe and Lachmann (1992) report a number of studies that show that infants who are later found to be insecure/avoidant in attachment have mothers who are overstimulating, intrusive, highly intense, noncontingent, or *overly contingent* [italics added].

Patients with Schizoid disorders also suffer from the deficient formation of a psychological dialectic. It is likely that noncontingent responding by the mother leaves the child too much alone and results in the development of Schizoid disorders. Schizoid patients do not assume the presence of others in the world (Klein, 1996). These patients, instead of experiencing a bridge between themselves and others, feel a *gap* between themselves and the world, leaving them with feelings of alienation, loneliness, futility, and depression. They have not been fortunate enough to experience what Susan Deri (1978) describes (p. 58):

> If ... the infant is allowed the experience of magical creativity by a mother in tune with the infant's biological rhythms, then with appropriate dosing of the delay, the infant can discover how to *mend the gap* in his life space that is produced by the absence of the mother. [*italics added*]

Schizoid patients manifest, instead, excessive reliance on the internal world of fantasy for gratification, and attribute to the world "out there" painful perceptions emanating from within. They also appear to have missed the fruits of early illusionary experience leading to the creation of potential space and a psychological dialectic — prerequisites for later separation and individuation in the development of an autonomous self in a world of others.

SUMMARY

The clinical treatment of personality disorders is greatly improved when the clinician has an awareness of the role played by illusion, potential space, and a psychological dialectic in personality formation. The patient originally does not have the words to describe the painful mental limitations laid down early in implicit learning. A difficulty on the part of the patient in considering alternative viewpoints can be met with some patience and understanding of the enormous task at hand, that is, providing the patient the analytic space in which to move from dependency to autonomy by way of self-creation.

Clinically, it is the task of the psychoanalytic therapist to struggle to understand and symbolize the implicit level of the patient's living. For patients with character disorders, the implicit process carries the therapeutic leverage. These patients, with certain kinds of distress and disturbance, at first use only the analytic space on their way to being able to use the therapeutic process or the transference relationship (Kahn, 1990).

In psychoanalytic treatment, "the universe of discourse appropriate to the analytic experience is not that of language, but that of image." In analytic treatment, the patient is placed in a situation in which desire — the real self — is required to speak to the exclusion of defensive satisfaction, as well as to the exclusion of slipping into acting out. In other words, psychoanalysis only knows desire as what can be said. This demand is not a problem; it is the source of self-activation. To quote Ricoeur (1978): "Requirement of findings words is not an amputation of the human experience reduced to discourse. On the contrary, it extends the semiotic sphere to the obscure confines of mute desire antecedent to language. Psychoanalysis rejoins preverbal experience — language is extended beyond the logical plane of rational discourse to the alogical regions of life — it makes that part of us speak that is not so much dumb as it is constrained to silence.

Because Masterson's (2003) treatment of personality disorders is based on an understanding of development, interventions serve to "free up" the growth of the patient's real self. In calling the patient's attention to his or her own destructive defenses, "treatment is like removing stones that obstruct the flow of the stream that is the real self." But the patient will only move in this direction within an atmosphere of trust created by the provision of analytic space. Analytic space is created from a *consistent and stable* therapeutic frame of time, place, and expected interactions with the therapist. Such space, mutually created with a therapist who makes room for the patient's self-expression, is the basic requirement for renewed psychological growth. Growth of the real self will include reigniting the capacity for illusion, revisiting the pain of disillusionment, and forming a more flexible psychological dialectic.

References

Aragno, A. (1997). *Symbolization: Proposing a Developmental Paradigm for a New Psychoanalytic Theory of Mind*. New York: International Universities Press.

Beebe, B. M., & Lachmann, F. M. (1992). *Infant Research and Adult Treatment: Co-constructing Interactions.* Hillsdale, NJ: Analytic Press.

Damasio, A. R. (1999). *The Feeling of What Happens: Body and Emotion in the Making of Consciousness.* New York: Harcourt Brace.

DeBerry, S. T. (1991). *The Externalization of Consciousness and the Psychopathology of Everyday Life. Vol. 17, Contributions in Psychology.* New York: Greenwood Press.

Deri, S. (1964). *Symbolization and Creativity.* New York: International Universities Press.

Deri, S. (1978). Vicissitudes of symbolization and creativity (p. 48). In Grolnick & Barkin (Eds.), *Between Reality and Fantasy.* Northvale, NJ: Jason Aronson.

Fonagy, P., Gergely, G., Jurist, E., & Target, M. (2002). *Affect Regulation, Mentalization, and the Development of the Self.* New York: Other Press.

Glover, E. (1956). *On Early Development of Mind.* New York: International Universities Press.

Green, A. (1978). The object in the setting. *Between Reality and Fantasy.* Northvale, NJ: Jason Aronson.

Grotstein, J. (1978). Inner space: its dimensions and its coordinates. *International Journal of Psychoanalysis, 4,* 55–61.

Hegel, G. W. F. (1807/1977). *Phenomenology of Spirit.* (A. V. Miller, trans.) London: Oxford University Press. (Cited in Ogden, 1990)

Hobson, P. (2002). *The Cradle of Thought: Explorations in the Origins of Thinking.* New York: Macmillan.

Klein, R. (1996). The self-in-exile: a developmental, self and object relations approach to the Schizoid Disorder of the Self (p. 48). In J. F. Masterson & R. Klein (Eds.), *Disorders of the Self: New Therapeutic Horizons.* New York: Brunner/Mazel.

Mahler, M. S., Pine, F., & Bergman, A. (1975). *The Psychological Birth of the Human Infant: Symbiosis and Individuation.* New York: Basic Books.

Mannoni, M. (1999). *Separation and Creativity.* (S. Fairfield, trans.) London: Other Press.

Masterson, J. F. (1976). *Psychotherapy of the Borderline Adult: A Developmental Approach.* New York: Brunner/Mazel.

Masterson, J. F. (1985). *The Real Self, a Developmental Self, and Object Relations Approach.* New York: Brunner/Mazel.

Masterson, J. F. (2003). Conference presentation, San Francisco.

Masterson, J. F., & Klein, R. (Eds.) (1989). *Psychotherapy of the Disorders of the Self: The Masterson Approach.* New York: Brunner/Mazel.

Milner, M. (1957). *On Not Being Able to Paint* (rev.). London: Heinemann. (Cited in Winnicott, 1971)

Modell, A. (1990). The roots of creativity (p. 115). In P. L. Giovacchini (Ed.), *Tac-*

tics and Techniques in Psychoanalytic Therapy. III, The Implications of Winnicott's Contributions. Northvale, NJ: Jason Aronson.

Ogden, T. (1990). On potential space (p. 94). In P. I. Giovacchini (Ed.), Tactics and Techniques in Psychoanalytic Theory, III. The Implications of Winnicott's Contributions. Northvale, NJ: Jason Aronson.

Ricoeur, P. (1978). Image and language in psychoanalysis (p. 295). In J. Smith (Ed.), Psychoanalysis and Language. New Haven, CT: Yale University Press.

Rycroft, C. (1968). Imagination and Reality. New York: International Universities Press.

Schore, A. (2003). Affect Dysregulation and Disorders of the Self. New York: Norton.

Spitz, R. A. (1957). No and Yes. New York: International Universities Press.

Stern, D. N., Bruschweiler-Stern, N., Harrison, A. M., et al. (1998). The process of therapeutic change involving Implicit knowledge. Infant Mental Health Journal, 19, 300–308.

Winnicott, D. W. (1957a). The Child and the Outside World. London: Tavistock.

Winnicott, D. W. (1957b). The Child and the Family: First Relationships. London: Tavistock.

Winnicott, D. W. (1958). Through Paediatrics to Psychoanalysis: Collected Papers. New York: Brunner/Mazel.

Winnicott, D. W. (1960). The Theory of the Parent–Infant Relationship. The Maturational Processes and the Facilitating Environment. Madison, CT: International Universities Press.

Winnicott, D. W. (1965). The Maturational Processes and the Facilitating Environment. (p. 51). Madison, CT: International Universities Press.

Winnicott, D. W. (1971). Playing and Reality. London: Routledge.

Winnicott, D. W. (1986). Home Is Where We Start From. New York: Norton.

Winnicott, D. W., & Riviere, J. (1936). On the genesis of psychical conflict in earliest infancy. International Journal of Psychoanalysis, 17.

4

From Concrete Truth to Symbolic Reality — Transference and the Language of Change

BARBARA L. SHORT, PH.D.

TRANSFERENCE AND TRANFERENCE ACTING OUT

History of the Transference

When Freud struggled with the failure of his analysis of an adolescent patient he called Dora in his prophetic "Postscript" to an earlier article entitled "Fragment of an Analysis," he puzzled about her inability, or unwillingness, to use the information he had provided to "unravel her true thoughts and feelings." His conclusion was portentous; Dora had transferred onto him a "whole series of psychological experiences . . . not as belonging to the past, but as applying to the person of the physician at the present moment." Dora reacted to Freud's interpretations of her difficulties as stemming from her oedipal sexual conflicts with indignation and withdrawal — not once, but twice (Freud, 1905, p. 116; in Ellman, 1991, pp. 12–17).

Later, Freud rather wistfully referred to his pretransference treatment as a "smooth and pleasing course of events." On the other hand, he came to regard treatment of the transference as arduous, a perpetual struggle, a difficult passage, and a troublesome undertaking that the analyst faced "almost without assistance and with only the slightest clues to go upon." Nevertheless, Freud reluctantly concluded that working in the transference cannot be evaded, because, as he came to believe, only after the transference has been resolved will the patient accept the new understandings arrived at during treatment (Freud, 1905, pp. 116–117; in Ellman, 1991, pp. 17–20).

In a more optimistic vein, Freud recognized that the transference could become a realm of fantasy within which the analyst and the patient could engage in a transforming alchemy of mind. Transference, which Freud understood to be an expression of the patient's compulsion to repeat (although many now understand the compulsion to repeat quite differently), is "rendered harmless, and even made use of . . . , by according it the right to assert itself within certain limits. We admit it into the transference as into a *playground*, in which it is allowed to let itself go in almost complete freedom and is required to display all the pathogenic impulses hidden in the depths of the patient's mind. . . . The transference thus forms a kind of intermediary realm between illness and real life, through which the journey from the one to the other must be made" (Freud, 1914, p. 374; in Ellman, 1991, p. 32). Freud's use of the terms "playground" and "intermediary realm" were suggestive of directions in working with the transference that we are only now coming to understand.

Untreatable or Unbearable: Dumplings, Gruel, and Concrete

Freud described several types of transference. In this context, I shall focus on three. The first is the so-called unobjectionable or conscious transference, which Freud believed could be analyzed because these patients, in his words, could form a libidinal cathexis of the analyst — an early version of what we now call the therapeutic alliance. This alliance, he believed, helped patients to endure the disconfirmation of their transference onto the analyst, and the corresponding emotional distress caused by the loss that inevitably must occur when the transference is interpreted. In other words, they could more readily understand their transference — fantasies, meanings, beliefs — in a symbolic realm, which was amenable to change through verbal interpretation of the transference.

However, patients with an impulsive erotic or paranoid or Narcissistic transference were described as putting up a powerful resistance to entering this symbolic realm of the playground, the intermediary realm, and tolerating disconfirming interpretations. For these patients, what the therapist called transference was concrete truth. Analytic interventions disconfirming this truth were reacted to with defensive maneuvering that defeated even the most skillful interpretations. Regarding Narcissistic patients, Freud observed, "We have good reason to recognize and to dread in the amount of his narcissism a barrier against the possibility of being influenced by even the best analytic technique (Freud, 1916–1917, p. 446; in Ellman, 1991, p. 29). Regarding erotic patients, Freud grumbled that they were amenable only to the "logic of gruel and the argument of dumplings" — in other words, only to *doing*, to concrete action, and not to symbolic understanding (Freud, 1915, pp. 377–391; in Ellman, 1991, p. 75). Freud appears never to have departed from his stand that transference was primarily effective as a tool to recover pathogenic memories. Contemporary attachment, neurobiology, and clinical research suggest that appropriate use of the transference can extend the treatment of patients with a character disorder much farther into this playground or intermediary realm, to an arena in which therapeutic experience can reshape the very structure and process of mind.

Most of Freud's Narcissistic, paranoid, and impulsive erotic patients (and possibly some of the neurotic ones) are now thought to have been suffering from what came to be called preoedipal, or character, disorders. And, since patients with these disorders were not amenable to treatment based on the standard analytic techniques available through the 1950s, they were regarded as being untreatable.

Although this diagnostic deadlock prevailed for decades, a shift in treatment technique gradually began to emerge through the accumulation of clinical evidence from therapists and analysts such as Sandor Frenczi, Wilhelm Reich, Alexander, and French, the analysts of the British middle school and object relations analysts, and many therapists and analysts working with veterans of two world wars, coupled with the groundbreaking research of Rene Spitz, Harry Harlow, and such analysts as Margaret Mahler and John Bolby. The confluence of this information provided the foundation for a revolution in the treatment of character-disordered patients. These revolutionary theory-building therapists and analysts — Masterson, Kernberg, Kohut, Searls, and Giovacchini, among others — broke out of this "concrete" definition of "concrete" disorders, and began working effectively in dynamic psychotherapy with patients suffering from character disorders. I believe it is impossible to overstate the significance of this transition for our profession, for our patients, and for ourselves. However, it is a revolution still in the making.

Transference Acting Out:
A Treatment Revolution

The Masterson Approach is one of the enduring clinical methods for treating outpatients with character disorders that developed during this analytic revolution. In developing this approach, Masterson combined key features of the standard analytic technique of ego psychology with object relations psychology, self psychology, Bolby's attachment theory, and Mahler's research, to create a unique clinical method. It was a revolutionary approach in which interventions were tailored to fit the level of the patient's developmental arrest, early pathological attachment history, and preoedipal intrapsychic structure.

Masterson understood that early developmental problems could set the stage for a malformation of the intrapsychic structure. This structure, when surviving into adulthood, became the "character disorder" that was virtually impossible to treat with interpretations of standard analytic techniques. The rigid pathological structure of the character disorder, which Masterson called the false self, was seen as a protective adaptation to severe neglect. As such, the intransigence of this structure was believed to arise not only out of developmental arrests in successfully navigating passages such as the oedipal conflict, but perhaps more important, out of the protection it afforded against the overwhelmingly painful emotions and meanings resulting from early neglect and/or abuse — the abandonment depression. Therefore, Masterson found that the treatment of these disorders must first focus on dissolving defenses of the pathological intrapsychic structure using interventions appropriate to the level of the developmental arrest and maladaptive attachment contract. The repeated and empathic use of these interventions in a stable and safe environment, protected by a firm therapeutic frame, can clear the path for the patient's nascent real self to emerge and assume its appropriate place at the center of the patient's identity.

Masterson points out that most patients with a character disorder do not enter therapy to discover or recover their real selves. For these patients, problems are external, as are solutions. Any interventions suggesting the opposite may be, as Freud ruefully acknowledged, responded to with anger, withdrawal, and/or renewed efforts to get the therapist to see the "true" truth. Initially in treatment, the fundamental meaning system supporting this structure is not available to be thought about, talked about, or changed. For the patient, their meanings are truth, out of awareness, and appear in the transference through the doing of things rather than through self-reflection and understanding.

Freud had little hope of working in the transference with the Narcissistic or erotic "concrete" patient. Masterson agrees. However, this is not the end of the story. It is the beginning. These patients are not untreatable. Rather, they require a treatment designed to address the nonsymbolic, concrete nature of their (representational) part self and object structures. The therapist does not work in the transference. The therapist works with the transference acting out to turn it into transference. In this process, the concrete, ego-syntonic defense system (the entire false defensive self) becomes ego dystonic; the patient endures the loss of the concrete, compensatory part object and its static, fixed attachment relationship with the part self; and emerges into whole self and object representations with the attendant mental and affective maturity.

The initial phase of treatment — the testing phase — is exclusively devoted to transforming transference acting out into transference and therapeutic alliance. This is the phase that accomplishes what for decades was thought to be the impossible, and it may last for years. In the language of the existentialists, the patient moves from being into becoming. Patients move from the hopelessness (and, paradoxically, the omnipotence) of being concrete truth to the potential of creative becoming — of living in adaptive and creative interaction with reality.

The second phase of this treatment revolution is now under way, providing psychoanalytic psychotherapists with new understandings to bring to treatment refinements in interventions that can facilitate the transition to full transference.

DEVELOPMENT OF SYMBOLIZATION

A Hierarchy of Symbolization and the Developmental Continuum

In one sense, "everything we perceive and [everything] our sense organs process is constantly being transformed into symbols — these constructed vehicles of meaning are our elementary ideas. This transformational process, which constitutes mind, is symbolization" (Aragno, 1992, pp. 146–147). However, the concept of "symbol" itself is complex. Psychodynamic researchers and philosophers writing in this area differentiate among three types of symbols: the sign, the signal, and the true symbol. They point out that "the road to the construction of a true symbol is gradual and proceeds hand in hand with ... the differentiation–individuation process of early childhood." The entire nature of subjective experience changes as one moves through the process of increasing differentiation and loss from sign, to signal to the true symbol (Aragno, 1992, p. 160).

The true symbol is a vehicle of thought; symbols are not the same as what they stand for, but represent a concept or idea of what that means. Symbols are tools for thinking that can be mentally manipulated and changed. Signs, on the other hand, signify an act or an event — they announce their object. Signals indicate, they command action. Both signs and signals are immediate, still tied to the senses. Signs and signals have a concrete, one-to-one correspondence between the sign or signal and what it indicates. The true symbol does not have this one-to-one correspondence. It is an instrument of thought. The meaning of the true symbol can be thought about and changed. Words are signs before they are symbols, and acquire the status of true symbol only through the process of separation and individuation. The object, and the hope of being or possessing the object, must be relinquished before it can be represented by a true symbol in memory. As Freud said, "The ego is a precipitate of lost objects," and, "The point of departure for the human ego is object loss.

The symbol results from separation — it transcends loss" (Aragno, 1992, pp. 160–161).

Transitional objects, amulets, tokens, fetishes, and the like, are equivalents, or stand-ins *for*, not symbols *of*, what they stand for. A sign may be a substitute for an object. A symbol evokes the object, but never replaces it. "What is renounced by the senses becomes mind. This is a gradual process occurring throughout the life span. . . . It is mediated by language, and constitutes a basic principle of human development" (Aragno, 1992, p. 161). It is clear that in this sense, patients with character disorders have not been able to relinquish the part object representations as signs that substitute for the object. Rather, they hold them in static, concrete truth rather than endure the abandonment depression that would follow their loss.

In addition, we are now coming to understand that the formation and use of symbolic thought may have functional areas of specialization governed by the affective salience of the object's being symbolized (Fonagy et al., 2002, p. 374). Patients who have difficulty symbolizing their experience of self and other may be able to symbolize in other arenas with great skill and facility. For example, we are all familiar with patients who have intellectual gifts and accomplishments, but who cannot tolerate disappointments or disconfirmations in relationships. In fact, it is likely that for some of these patients, the affects that disrupt mentalization are those specifically related to the attachment contracts created in the early development of self and object representations. When these affects are quiescent (when attachment issues are not active), symbolization in arenas not related to these contracts may not be severely disrupted. On the other hand, for patients whose every thought, feeling, and activity are under constant scrutiny and/or attack by a critical part object, it is likely that no mental arena is immune to frequent and ongoing traumatic affect.

In this context, I will focus on the development of the capacity to symbolize with regard to self-object representations.

Concrete, Symbolic, and Analytic Interpretation with the Personality Disorders

Margaret Mahler's (Mahler et al., 1975) research on early development charted the fate of infants and toddlers making their way through the early months of development. Her research left little doubt about the daunting challenges that must be successfully negotiated before the child emerges into the possibility of engaging in healthy human relationships and true symbolic thought about them. Toddlers who experience undue neglect during the separation and individuation phases may developmentally remain near the entry point (differentiation) or stay poised at the exit point (rapprochement). In later adulthood, the intrapsychic structure and dynamics these unlucky toddlers develop will reflect not only this point of arrest, but also the kind of attachment contract they had to negotiate to get needs met. Without significant corrective intervention, they will remain in some state of arrested emotional, cognitive, social, and, in severe instances, intellectual arrest for the remainder of their lives.

Masterson locates the origin of the various character disorders in this developmental arena, and believes that interventions must be directed to the developmental tasks and attachment contract that are specific to the point of arrest. The task of these interventions is at once singular and threefold. The singular intent is integration and ego repair. Regarding the first, research in neurobiology supports Masterson's insistence that in work with patients who suffer from character disorders, interventions must focus, focus, focus, and focus again on the patient's connection with the real self — a focus that will inevitably evoke intense, archaic, unverbalized affects.

These patients are believed to have missed early experiences of this kind of focus, which would have fostered the development of left-hemisphere (verbal) processing of right-hemisphere (affective, relational) experience that is the basis for symbolic thought and affect mentalization in this functional realm. In treatment, the use of an unrelenting focus of these interventions on the real self and appropriate responses to the evoked affect will enable this process (and its neurologic substrate) to be developed. As a corollary, the divided, weakened ego of a patient with a character disorder cannot perform tasks of real self-reflection, activation, and accurate assessment of reality, especially in the realm of emotionally charged relationships. Moves in this direction activate the affects of the abandonment depression that the weakened ego cannot process in symbolic thought. Therefore, initial interventions must perform this function for the patient so the patient's ego can come to undertake it on its own.

The threefold task determines the structure of the interventions. First, interventions call the patient's attention to a specific defense of the false self. Second, they implicitly, or explicitly, identify the general purpose of the defense — protection from painful feelings of the abandonment depression associated with activation of the real self. This is the first move in transforming the experience of these affects from concrete reality (as if the traumatizing event were occurring in the present) into symbolic experience that can be thought about as belonging to the past. Third, these interventions implicitly or explicitly identify the cost of the defense to the "real self." This is a call to the "real self" to move toward expression and reality. If successful, it creates a potential space for the needs, talents, and abilities of the real self to find expression, and a safe container for the nearly intolerable affects that will accompany this rediscovery. The implicit or explicit suggestion is that such defenses might indeed be useful in protecting the patient from these terribly painful feelings in the immediate present, but the cost of using them is lifelong suffering, which need not continue.

The use or misuse of traditional interpretations with these patients is still a debatable issue in the analytic literature. In 1997, analyst Alan Bass wrote that there is a "large group of apparently analyzable, nonpsychotic patients who cannot make use of interpretation" (Bass, 1997, p. 642). He refers to a 1957 paper by Edith Jacobson in which she described patients who would "present projected fantasy material, but who would reject any interpretation that implied that . . . [they were] not simply seeing things as they are." Jacobson, he continued, "proposed that such patients tend to 'handle intrapsychic conflicts as though they were conflicts with reality.' They can do so, she said, via regression to a "concretistic' infantile stage where the child, though already aware of the difference between internal and external worlds, between the self and objects, still treats them both in the same manner. . . . [This] infantile concretization of psychic reality . . . permits persons who employ this defense to treat their psychic strivings as if they were concrete objects" (Bass, 1997, p. 643).

Interpreting always implies that one thing might mean another. In a sense, this is analogous to Piaget's formal operational stage. Typically, psychoanalytic psychotherapists use interpretation to call the patient's attention to unconscious conflicts that distort reality and underlie troubling behavior. The use of this sophisticated intervention requires the patient to engage in thinking at the symbolic level. In other words, "To use interpretation therapeutically, psychic organization has to be not unduly threatened by the possibility that one might be different from what one consciously thinks oneself to be. . . . Persistent 'concreteness' is the result of complicated defenses against the possibility of differentiation itself" (Bass, 1997, p. 645). The patient who believes that his or her experience must correspond to reality — that the symbol is the same as what it stands for — cannot consider alternative views.

Bass concluded that the therapist working at this "concrete" level with a patient must focus on process, not on content, on *how* a patient "thinks" rather than the patient's compelling "magic of action," and communicate to the patient his or her understanding of that process. In other words, in constructing interventions, Bass recommends that the therapist focus more on the *level* of the patient's mental functioning than on its content.

Bass, like many analysts struggling to retain the interpretative mode, suggests that greater attention be paid to the patient's level of functioning. More recent findings from both neurobiology and attachment research suggest that even further accommodations must be made, and that, in some cases (or at some times during treatment), the interpretative mode must be suspended altogether.

NEUROBIOLOGY, IMPLICIT MEMORY,
AND TRAUMA

Trauma

In 1991, Lenore Terr redefined childhood trauma as the "mental result of one sudden, external blow (Type I) or a series of blows (Type II), rendering the young person temporarily helpless and breaking past ordinary coping and defensive operations" (Terr, 1991, p. 11). She went on to broaden the "concept of trauma to include not only those conditions marked by intense surprise, but also those marked by prolonged" accumulation of events that render the child helpless and break past ordinary coping mechanisms, and are never resolved by adult intervention. Since that time, neurobiology and attachment research has added immeasurably to our understanding of the effects of early trauma on adult personality. For the purpose of this chapter, I will focus on the effect of long-term (Type II) early trauma on the early development of the ability to symbolize in the realm of self and object representations and relationships.

Transference, Implicit and Explicit Memory,
and the Effect of Trauma on the Developing Brain

Transference, described as the activation of mental models and states of mind from relationships with important figures in the past, is a ubiquitous human experience. It is not whether or not we experience transference, but how fixed or concrete the meanings of the experience are to us as the perceivers. The work of neurobiology has provided us with new knowledge about the ways in which concrete meanings of transference are established, and thereby gives us a better understanding of how to treat them.

Repeated defensive experiences are ingrained in the circuits of the brain as states of mind. When chronic, these states can become character traits of the individual. In this way, lives can become shaped by the effects of memories formed during the first year or so of life — memories we now know as implicit memories. These form the basic foundation of the meaning structure of one's life. In later life, these implicit memories operate to generate an experience of what "is," rather than to provide a sense that something is being recalled. One simply enters these ingrained states and experiences them as the reality of the present (Siegel, 1999, p. 33).

The onset of the development of explicit memory is delayed until the second year of life. It requires focal attention for its encoding, and produces the subjective sense of "something being recalled," eventually in verbal recall as belonging to the past. Explicit memory includes two major forms: semantic (factual) and episodic (autobiographical). The latter has the unique sense of self-awareness, and a sense of self and time. If the trauma of neglect and/or abuse occurs during the early years of childhood, and is unresolved owing to a lack of appropriate repair and collaborative communication, the memory of the trauma will not be integrated and consolidated in verbally mediated explicit memory. Therefore, it will not be available to symbolic, verbal recall as happening to the self in the past, and when evoked, will retain its original emotional state of "happening in the present."

In this way, implicit elements of major, and perhaps even minor, traumatic events may continue to shape the individual's life without conscious awareness. This may impair the creation of life stories that would otherwise allow for emotionally significant events to be permanently consolidated in explicit memory. In this way, unresolved traumatic memories seem to *remain in an unstable state of potential implicit activations, which tend to intrude on the survivor's internal experiences and interpersonal relationships.* In addition, implicit memory is the source of emotional "anticipation," alerting the brain about the meaning of events to come. These implicit elements of memory torment the individual's internal subjective world, and permit the intrusion of past meanings into the present context of interpersonal relationships.

ATTACHMENT STYLES, TRAUMA, AND CONCRETE IMPLICIT MEMORY

The Attachment and Development of Mentalization

Contemporary attachment research is focusing on the self and its mental development. Fonagy and his associates state that introspective, self-reflective, self-aware mentalization is a hard-won developmental acquisition. The development of a mind or a psychological self depends on interactions with more mature minds that can be appropriately attuned emotionally to the mind of the developing infant, and are capable of benign, reflective thought. In other words, the self arises out of being experienced by the other, and the healthy self experiences caretaker responses that are attuned and appropriately contingent on their own initiating gestures (Fonagy et al., 2002, pp. 4–8).

These researchers suggest that there are five sequential levels of agency of the self, forming a developmental hierarchy that the infant acquires in stepwise progression if appropriate experiences with other minds are available. The most important stage for the purpose of this chapter, the fifth and final or *representational stage*, occurs during the third, fourth, and fifth years. This stage has three substates, roughly one for each year. The 3-year-old is functioning in a stage of *psychic equivalence*. In this stage, which overlaps with Mahler's stage of separation/individuation, many important building blocks for understanding the nature of psychic reality are already in place. The normal 3-year-old has already developed the capacity to distinguish between dream images, thoughts, and real things, to play pretend games, and to understand someone else's intention to pretend. However, his or her psychic reality has a dual character. At times, when this child is in the mode of "psychic equivalence," ideas are not felt to be representations, but to be direct replicas of reality, and, consequently, always true. At other times, the child uses a "pretend" mode in which ideas are felt to be representations, but their correspondence with reality is not examined.

Normal children of this age sometimes behave as though their own and others' thoughts faithfully mirror the real world (Fonagy, et al., 2002, p. 257) and, at other times, in the "pretend" mode, they can think about thoughts as thoughts because they are stripped of their connection to the real world. The child may be able to do this only if an adult is there to provide a necessary frame and to insulate the child from the compelling character of external reality. The very young child does not yet have the capacity to appreciate the merely representational nature of ideas and feelings. Therefore, play can become frightening. The young child who is not yet able to mentalize or to reflect on his or her beliefs is forced to believe that they inevitably and correctly mirror the real world.

The 4- to 5-year-old child who has successfully negotiated earlier stages can now begin to attribute intentional mental states — goals, desires, and beliefs — to himself or herself, or others, as an explanation for actions. This child knows that what he or she thinks or believes about something does not necessarily reflect reality. The child knows that the self is a representational agent, and that his or her actions are caused by his or her intentional mental states [desires and beliefs] that are representational. This child can understand intentional mind states of the self, and has the representational capacity to relate the memories of the self's intentional activities and experiences to a coherent understanding of causation and temporal organization. The healthy child at this stage has successfully moved into the realm of whole self and object representations. This complex ability to mentalize leads to the establishment of the "proper" self, or the *autobiographical self* (paraphrased from Fonagy, 2002, pp. 205–206, 248, 263).

Focus on Disorganized Attachment and Personality Disorders

As described above, secure attachment appears to underlie effective and satisfying functioning in the social world. Insecure attachment signals a limitation of mentalizing skills in the two fundamental realms of affect and cognitive functioning. Finally, disorganized attachment not only is the basis for these limitations, but also is the lifelong debilitating experience of an absence of mentalizing capacity under stress — often even a very minor stress can evoke a loss of mentalizing capacity and a retreat to early, primitive cognitive and affective experiences of concrete one-to-one correspondence between internal and external reality.

Abusive caregivers often show an inability to be attuned to the infant's mind or to make contingent responses to the overtures of infants and toddlers. This repeated experience may lead to disorganization in the child's self-development, and the development of a tendency to dissociate, accompanied by *preoccupation* with perfect contingencies in the attachment context. It is almost as if the adult with this early history seeks to "make up" for the missing contingent response experience in every new relationship he or she forms. When these individuals fail to find themselves in the contingent response of the other in emotionally loaded adult relationships, it can create reactivation of early cumulative trauma states and corresponding acting out of powerful, even violent, reactions (Fonagy, 2002, pp. 249–250).

When a relationship is emotionally salient, these individuals not only may require perfect contingent responses, but, when the contingency is missing, will regress to the state of psychic equivalence, in which they will experience the external object as the cause of traumatic experiences evoked from the past. For these individuals, the experience is not memory, but a subjective experience as real as that of a physical object. In this mode of psychic equivalence, there is no potential space, no playground, and no transforming fantasy.

Treatment: Adjusting Interventions for
Arrested Mentalization in Personality Disorders

As we have seen, for decades, patients with character disorders were believed to be untreatable because they did not respond insightfully to analytic interpretations. Sometimes the root cause was seen as arising out of early environmental distress, but more often it was attributed to genetic or constitutional factors that permanently sealed the fate of these patients.

In the late 1960s, sufficient research and clinical data had accumulated to support the position that a major "cause" of character disorders was the neglect these patients had experienced in their early years of life. Based on this evidence and an abundance of information from other sources, Masterson recommended using interventions that positioned the therapist-as-auxiliary-ego at the leading edge of the range of arrest, so interventions would implicitly say to the patient, "This is next, there's nothing here you can't do. Why would you stay in this terrible (intrapsychic) place if you didn't have to?" These interventions were transforming for therapists and patients alike. Therapists felt that they at last had something effective to offer their patients, and patients at last could begin to move into genuine emotional connection with their own real self and others.

However, the passage from concrete to symbolic, from transference acting out to transference, is often difficult. The pathological structure of this disorder can be seen as a stable survival structure that both contains and wards off the painful affects experienced as a result of the mother's libidinal unavailability. At some points in treatment, attempts to dismantle this structure will inevitably evoke the implicit memory of reexperiencing these affects. (Many therapists are now referring to this phenomenon as an "enactment" that includes the therapist's countertransference participation.)

This experience, may, in turn, evoke in the patient an extreme intensification of several profound, primitive defenses, including more active and aggressive splitting, projective identification, avoidance, denial, and acting out in the form of withdrawal. At this time, the unmetabolized past experience blocks, or severely impairs, the ability of the patient's mind to integrate material into the verbal sphere where the event and the emotion it evoked can be thought about and experienced symbolically. The leading edge of the range in which the developmental arrest occurred is far away at these times, and the patient has returned to an earlier stage of concreteness in which there is no bridge to representational reality. Interventions directed to this leading edge of the arrest may be difficult for the patient to hear. At best, the patient may experience these interventions as failures of the therapist to understand the patient's experience.

When patients reexperience the painful affect, they probably will have entered a state of "psychic equivalence," in which they believe that their internal experiences are identical to external reality. In this state, body states, rather than language, convey mood. The patient enacts with the body, not with thought and language. This is experienced as concrete truth, rather than as symbolic reality. In this way, the patient experiences real anxiety, real anger, and real confusion, rather than being able to describe these internal states in language. However, in this state, any symbolic capacity the patient had begun to develop will be temporarily lost.

At these times, the absence of the skill of mentalizing affectivity is most striking. If the first task of affect regulation — through being experienced by the object — was not accomplished, the second remains virtually unknown. In this second phase, affects can be used internally and symbolically to regulate the self. This level of mentalized affectivity, in which the individual no longer requires a "self-regulating other," enables one to discover, think about, and arrive at a reality-based meaning of affective states. This capacity remains a distant possibility for patients functioning at the level of psychic equivalence.

Attempts to reassure patients verbally or to continue with interventions evoking these experiences will be seen as further evidence of the therapist's malfeasance. There often is enormous emotional pressure on the therapist to do something "real," rather than remain in the realm of understanding, empathy, language, and a focus on the patient's mind — the patient's experience of his or her thoughts and feelings.

At these times, the therapist needs the ability and willingness to understand and mentally or symbolically hold the mental representation of the patient's psychic equivalence — the concrete truth — in his or her mind. After sorting out countertransference information, the therapist can find ways to express empathically his or her understanding in body language, tone, and words. This experience, during or immediately after a psychic equivalent interaction, can begin to provide the patient with an internal mental representation of these unbearable affects — through being experienced and understood in the other's mind. This is the unfinished business of contingent communication and the stage of psychic equivalence, and it allows the patient to feel felt, to feel known, and to know that his or her mind can be understood by the mind of another.

The exact construction of interventions at this level, however, is more difficult. One clue is provided by attachment data about the development of affect regulation. In infancy, the infant looks to the caretaker to regulate his or her affect. In fact, this can be thought of as a kind of regulation of affect states through the perceived response of the other. For the infant, the image of the caregiver's mirroring the child's internal experience comes to organize the infant's emotional experience. But this is not understood to be true "mirroring." In fact, Fonagy makes the point that responses must be "analogous" mirroring, in which the parent "marks" the contingent response as an understanding, rather than as an exact replica. In fact, an exact replica of the infant's state may be experienced as traumatic. Certainly, at this stage of development, a lack of contingent responses and analogous mirroring will be traumatic. However, for the adult patient reexperiencing the disorganizing affects of the abandonment depression in a clinical setting, neither analogous mirroring nor contingent responses alone will provide the reorganizing bridge to symbolic thought and more adaptive behavior. These factors may be helpful, even necessary, but they are not sufficient.

Another necessary part of this bridge is therapeutic containment. The therapist must "contain and regulate" a patient's projective identification, provide a safe, stable frame on which patients can rely, and not violate therapeutic neutrality. Bending or breaking the frame in an effort to help the patient will, in the long run, be a detriment to treatment. The patient experiencing the abandonment depression needs consistency and containment. Adjustments of the frame may simply confirm the reality of their experience, and detract from the power of this opportunity to reach a transforming outcome. Similarly, reassuring the patient about the safety of the therapist or the therapeutic setting may have the opposite outcome. Reassurance is a common response that adults make to children in emotional distress, including children who are being neglected and abused. Reassurance can be a recreation of the experience of being told that they should not have the feelings they do — that their experience is unwelcome and unreasonable.

Finding the words — the tools for mentalization — is extremely difficult. In addition to providing emotional containment through his or her empathy, neutrality, and attunement, the therapist must also verbalize his or her understanding of the patient's experience in this concrete state of psychic equivalence. At this juncture, a patient is most likely to be able to hear a simple verbal acknowledgment of his or her experience of psychic equivalence, that is, a simple description of the precipitating event (most likely something the therapist did or said) and the patient's subsequent experience of that event. Any attempt to try to talk about more symbolic features or to discuss an interpretation of the defenses (probably intensification of splitting and projective identification) has a high probability of being experienced as another assault on the patient's truth. In the heat of archaic reactivity, the therapist's descriptive statement that "when I did X, you felt (or believed) I meant (or did) Y" establishes the therapist's awareness of the patient's psychic equivalence, observes the requirement of contingent communication, and allows the patient to experience the therapist's calm acknowledgment (without retaliation, validation, or other frame violations) of his or her experience. After the patient has been able to integrate the experience of being understood in this particular way, the use of leading-edge interventions can be resumed.

BRIEF CASE PRESENTATION
OF A PATIENT WITH A
CLOSET NARCISSISTIC PERSONALITY DISORDER AND
SEVERE EARLY TRAUMA

Presenting Complaint and History

Ms. B entered once-a-week treatment with me in late 1999. She was a 61-year-old modestly successful businesswoman who had entered therapy because, as she put it, her life was meaningless and empty. She reported that she had been in therapy once before, when her husband died, and thought that it might have helped somewhat. At any rate, she was dissatisfied with her occupation, and angry that a satisfying relationship with a man was "impossible," so she thought that therapy might help. She had just broken off a relationship with a man she had been seeing for two years, and more or less felt that it was "good riddance to bad rubbish."

She had three children, one daughter and two sons. All are married, with children, and living reasonably successful and productive lives. Ms. B visits them or talks with them frequently, and, with the exception of one daughter-in-law, she seems to be on good terms with all three families. She has an active social life, and seems to have friends. However, she reports frequent instances of hurt feelings and injuries by friends that leave her angry and frustrated. In her words, "It's not worth it to keep trying. Everyone lets you down eventually."

Ms. B was born in an Eastern European nation that was occupied first by the Germans during World War II, and then by the Soviet Union. At the time of her birth, her family was still living in a semifeudal society. Her mother had some distant claim to being a descendent of pre-World War I aristocracy, and her father was the only son in a wealthy banking family. Through the mother's family, they "owned" a village that the father managed until he was sent to a concentration camp at the beginning of the occupation. He did not survive his internment. She was very young when he was sent away, and sadly recounted at one point in her treatment that she believed that her life would have been very different "if she had had a father."

Ms. B's mother seems to have spent her days longing for better times — real or imagined — during which she was a privileged star, and paid little attention to Ms. B or her two brothers. For all intents and purposes, Ms. B and her brothers were raised by a moderately well-educated, devoutly Catholic woman from a nearby town who remained with the children and their mother through the end of the war and into the Soviet occupation. Ms. B described the woman as cruel and abusive, with a heart of ice, who terrified her and her brothers with threats of God's enduring wrath. Ms. B adored her mother, whom she perceived as beautiful, talented, and unattainable. She reported that she never felt she could get her mother's attention or approval, no matter how hard she tried.

During the Soviet years, Ms. B and her brothers were denied an education because of their privileged background. However, she married an educated man, and together they escaped to the United States when she was in her early 20s. As she recounted this experience, she expressed no regret about leaving her mother. But later in treatment, she showed intense grief about never seeing her again, and wondered whether she should have tried harder to get her mother to leave with her. She recounted their harrowing escape in the middle of the night, jumping off a train and running across the frozen fields to the line of trees demarking the border they had to cross. She observed that people who had jumped off the other side of the train "did not make it." At that time, she was five months pregnant with her first child.

It was not until she escaped to the United States that she could begin her schooling. While she was bearing, and raising, her children, she was able to complete her education, including an advanced degree. Her husband did not progress in his profession owing to his "weakness," as she described it, and he spent increasing amounts of time away from home, using alcohol and the company of other women to console himself. Ms. B felt she had sacrificed for her husband and their marriage, and his betrayals left her feeling victimized and enraged.

Intrapsychic Structure and Diagnosis

I diagnosed Ms. B as having a closet Narcissistic Disorder of the Self. She initially formed a superficial idealizing transference to me, which alternated at various times with devaluations of my profession, my degree, my title, my fees, my ability, and my frame. Her one joy in life, she reported, came from serving others. Joy in serving, however, would deteriorate into anger, and then rage, if expected responses were not forthcoming. She looked to others to regulate her affect and her sense of self, and worked untiringly to get this desired regulation, shifting her focus from one to another as disappointing responses accumulated. Her rage was withering — laced with contempt, and driven home with devaluation. At these times, she became quite formidable, and it was difficult to withstand her attacks.

It appeared that Ms. B's self and object representations consisted of a fused harsh, attacking object/empty self, and a fused omnipotent object/grandiose self between which she alternated with little or no awareness of the swiftness of her reversals.

Treatment

Ms. B's focus on the object was unrelenting. Initially, my attempts to point out this focus, to mirror the possible cause, and to suggest its effect of diminished awareness of her own self were greeted with interest. Her other therapist, she observed, had not talked to her this way. It seemed that he had agreed that others had wronged her, and had tried to help her to find ways to keep these people from taking advantage of her. She blandly noted that while she appreciated this, she felt that the other therapist did not know what he was doing.

However, as I continued to call her attention to her focus on others, Ms. B responded to my mirroring interpretations with less and less interest. Instead, she would fall silent, change the subject, resume her prior story, or use other deflections. When I suggested that she had responded in these ways to stay further away from the pain of focusing on herself, she would initially resume her deflecting responses, and finally become hurt and then angry, saying that I was blaming her or accusing her of some wrongdoing. If I attended to her angry focus on me, understanding it as a disappointment in me that left her feeling vulnerable and/or in pain, and that it seemed she moved away from this pain by focusing on her anger at me, she would become more convinced that I was accusing her, not just of wrongdoing, but of being wrong and bad, and respond with greater anger.

This cycle defined our work together. But, somehow, she always came back. She often left slamming my office door, storming and muttering, but she came back. There were times when Ms. B could integrate my mirroring interpretations, connect with herself, and talk with genuine feeling about her pain and emptiness. But she almost inevitably returned for the next session in a rage, believing I had mocked and ridiculed her, and left her feeling worthless — a slide that would end in her devaluing me, her therapy, and therapy in general, and with threats to end this ridiculous waste of money.

This cycle became more intense as the months passed, and I decided to try to interrupt her defenses in a different way — by using an unexpected intervention of simply describing the beginning of the cycle. That is, I pointed out that when I suggested that she focused on others to keep from feeling the pain of focusing on herself, she believed that I was telling her that she was wrong and bad. She replied, "Absolutely! I tell you I'm vulnerable, and you slam me with something. I don't get a break. . . . I get suckered in, and then you whack me. I'm vulnerable and I get whacked. You can't stand my vulnerability. There's something wrong with you. Just when I'm vulnerable, you accuse me of something. You're afraid of vulnerability. When I'm needy and vulnerable, you whack me. I'm innocent. I feel so open-hearted and trusting, and when I least expect it, you attack me." As this rush of angry accusations wound down, Ms. B grew silent; then she began to cry. After several minutes, she said, "I feel like I'm horrible. I'm worthless, empty, and my life is meaningless, and when I'm in this place, anything you say about my trying to stay away from it sounds like a condemnation. You are blaming me, and it's a confirmation of my badness. It's a dungeon."

Eventually, Ms. B was able to integrate the mirroring interpretations and use them effectively to bring her focus to herself and her terribly painful feelings of abandonment. I found, however, that the most effective way to interrupt the concrete reality of her fusion, of her projective identification, of her transference acting out at junctures of intensely traumatic affect, was simply to describe the sequence of events leading to that affect. This acknowledgment seemed to permit her to recover and resume her treatment, and to pave the way for a more effective integration of the mirroring interpretations.

Termination

Ms. B has not used threats of termination for over a year, and I believe we have forged a strong therapeutic alliance.

References

Aragno, A. (1992). *Symbolization: Proposing a Developmental Paradigm for a New Psychoanalytic Theory of Mind*. Madison, CT: International Universities Press.

Bass, A. (1997). The problem of concreteness. *Psychoanalytic Quarterly*, 66, 642–682.

Ellman, S. J. (1991). *Freud's Technique Papers: A Contemporary Analysis*. Northvale, NJ: Jason Aronson.

Fonagy, P., Gergely, G., Jurist, E. L., & Target, M. (2002). *Affect Regulation, Mentalization, and the Development of the Self*. New York: Other Press.

Freud, S. (1905). Fragment of an analysis of a case of hysteria. *Standard Edition*, 7, 7–122.

Freud, S. (1914). Further recommendations in the technique of psychoanalysis—recollection, repetition, and working through (pp. 366–376). In *Collected Papers, Vol. 2*. New York: Basic Books.

Freud, S. (1915). Further recommendations in the technique of psychoanalysis—observations on transference love (pp. 366–370). In *Collected Papers, Vol. 3*. New York: Basic Books.

Freud, S. (1916/1917). Introductory lectures in psychoanalysis. *Standard Edition*, 15/16, 446.

Mahler, M., Pine, F., & Bergmann, A. (1975). *The Psychological Birth of the Human Infant: Symbiosis and Individuation*. New York: Basic Books.

Masterson, J. F. (1981). *The Narcissistic and Borderline Disorders: An Integrated Developmental Approach*. New York: Brunner/Mazel.

Siegel, D. J. (1999). *The Developing Mind: Toward a Neurobiology of Interpersonal Experience*. New York: Guilford.

Terr, L. C. (1991). Childhood traumas: An outline and overview. *American Journal of Psychiatry*, 148, 1, 10–20.

5

Ownership of Mind:
Separation in the Countertransference

BARBARA L. SHORT, PH.D.

TRANSFERENCE, COUNTERTRANSFERENCE,
AND ACTION: A BRIEF REVIEW

Freud and Psychic Reality,
the Unconscious, Transference, and
Untreatable Patients

One of the most significant and troubling phenomena discovered by Freud was the difference between psychic (or subjective) reality and material (or external) reality — however troublesome or difficult the latter is to define. During his difficult reevaluation of *Studies on Hysteria* (Breuer & Freud, 1895), Freud found that although patient's reports of events from their past contained elements of actual experience, much of it was woven into a kind of complex memory that patients believed to be an absolutely accurate reflection of external reality. This fantasy/memory is largely unconscious, and is typically saturated with emotion. It contains not only the kernel of truth, but also amalgams of drives, wishes, desires, compromise formations, and the defenses produced by frustration, deprivation, and trauma. This is psychic reality. It is through this filter that one perceives (interprets) external or material reality. The understanding of psychic reality has been refined and deepened since Freud's first formulation, but it remains essentially unchanged.

Descartes codified for Western philosophy the "belief" or truth that one's

perception of external reality is "truth" — that there is a one-to-one correspondence between internal perception (innate memory) and external reality.
Freud, more in the empirical tradition of Locke, came to understand that perception is an amalgam of meanings accrued over a lifetime, and that different
minds have different amalgams and will ascribe different meanings to the same
stimulus. However, Descartes' perspective toward subjective perception prevails
in the Western mind, and, as members of this intellectual culture, we tend to
believe that we "accurately" perceive external reality. Freud's early patients
presented dramatic illustrations of this perceptual conundrum, and nearly
brought analytic theory to an early and untimely conclusion.

After the disastrous outcome of his treatment of the teenage patient, Dora
(Freud, 1905), who twice slammed out of his office in anger, Freud came to
understand that not only transference, but also the concreteness of a patient's
psychic reality expressed in the transference, would determine whether the
patient would be able to respond to treatment. A patient, he believed, would
be available to treatment only insofar as they were capable of a libidinal
cathexis of the object. In part, this libidinal cathexis was revealed through the
ability of patients to accept interpretations of their psychic reality with curiosity and interest rather than its' causing them to redouble their efforts to get
needs met or to escape the impact of the therapist's intervention.

If patients were unable to accept the possibility of alternative interpretations of their psychic realities, they would not be able to consider the analyst's
interventions. In Freud's words, "We have reason to dread in the amount of
narcissism a barrier against the possibility of being influenced even by the best
analytic technique" (Freud, 1916/1917, p. 446). Concerning another group of
patients who also demanded gratification from the therapist, Freud grumbled
that they were amenable only to the "logic of gruel and the argument of
dumplings" (Freud, 1915, p. 371) — in other words, only to doing, only to
concrete action, not to symbolic interpretation. Freud observed that the therapist's refusal to respond as these patients wish often causes them to feel hu-
miliated and/or frustrated beyond their abilities to tolerate. They respond with
rage and resentment, and, like Dora, may feel that they have no option other
than to destroy the treatment.

Freud cautioned that analytic therapists must engage in a "perpetual struggle with the patient to keep all impulses which he would like to carry into
action within the boundaries of his mind, and when it is possible, to divert
into the work of recollection any impulses which the patient wants discharge
in action" (Freud, 1914, p. 371). However, the rules of classical analysis, such
as abstinence, free association, and classical interpretation, made analytic treatment largely unusable for patients whom we now understand as having probably suffered from personality disorders or Disorders of the Self.

Ferenczi and the Language of Gesture

Ferenczi and Rank (1925) made many significant contributions to the analytic understanding of patients whom we now think of as having Disorders of the Self. However, for this chapter, I want to consider just one proposal they made that appears to have been in direct contradiction to Freud's conclusion regarding transference — that patients' wishes for gratification must be interpreted verbally.

Ferenczi and Rank's solution to difficulties in using free association, interpretation, and abstinence with these patients was to conclude that once patients had regressed to the level of primitive needs, they should be treated with actions, or the "language of gesture" — that is, the rule of abstinence should be suspended — because their developmental arrests were preverbal. Balint (1968) was later to observe that this might work under some circumstances, but that in many cases, it tended to produce what he viewed as a malignant regression. Under these conditions, patients did not experience the language of gesture as repairing early damage or making up for early deprivation. Rather, they seemed encouraged to demand ever more gratification and greater efforts from their therapists, with no sign that these heroic efforts had any benefit. In fact, it seemed to embed patients even further in their quest to get from the environment the means to satisfy their needs.

Symbolism and Concrete Thinking

Although traditional analytic interventions were not effective with these patients, it was decades before clinical and experimental research generated the understanding necessary to allow modification of analytic technique. Part of this understanding arose through analysis of the interface of symbolism and psychic reality.

Freud initially recognized that "the ego is the precipitate of lost (relinquished from identifications) objects," and that "the point of departure for the human ego is object loss" (Aragno, 1992, pp. 160–161). Through mourning, the lost object is relinquished. In melancholia, the lost object is retained intrapsychically — is never relinquished, and remains a fixed, concrete, unconscious part of the internal self structure.

A symbol results from separation — it follows and transcends loss. "What is renounced by the senses becomes mind. This is a gradual process occurring throughout the life span . . . It is mediated by language, and constitutes a basic principle of human development" (Aragno, 1992, p. 161). The object, and the hope of being or possessing the object, must be relinquished before it can be remembered — before it can be represented by a true symbol in memory.

Patients who have not been able to move through full loss and transformation of the object, who have not been helped to mentalize the separate existence of mind and affect in the object, will not be able to maintain a distinction between perception and memory. Alan Bass (1997, p. 661) observed of these patients that "one is always impressed by the tenacity of concreteness, by the typical way in which concrete patients will stay in treatment, but not be able to use the analyst's interpretations." He quotes Edith Jacobson, who noted that such patients "handle intrapsychic conflicts as though they were conflicts with reality." [They do so via regression] "to a 'concretistic' infantile stage where the child, though already aware of the difference between internal and external worlds, between the self and object, still treats them both in the same manner. . . . [This] infantile concretization of psychic reality . . . permits persons who employ this defense to treat their psychic strivings as if they were concrete objects perceived" (Bass, 1997, pp. 642–643).

Patients with Disorders of the Self, character disorders, personality disorders, early disorganized attachment, and the like, are very likely to experience the therapist as being the concrete embodiment of their externalized fantasy objects (or part-objects, part-selves). The intensity and concreteness of this projection might vary from time to time, but at the very least, it is always present in the background. If the therapist is acting out the countertransference, the therapist too will experience it as reality and will find himself or herself justifying and rationalizing the acting out by referring to the patient's past needs and deprivation. This fantasy is tenaciously maintained, because it provides a relatively stable position that wards off loss and the creation of memory (experience of truth) that the patient unconsciously experiences as unbearable. If the therapist attempts to interpret this conscious content as having another meaning, the patient will very likely deny, avoid, and/or distort the interpretation, or simply engage in an all-out power struggle.

Transference, Countertransference, Therapeutic Alliance, and Acting Out (Masterson, 1981, pp. 146–181)

Transference

Transference is the unconscious process of using the therapist as a displaced (fantasy) object upon whom is projected unresolved infantile fantasies, and the fate of their expression is memorialized in implicit memory. If a patient is capable of transference, the therapist can use interpretations directed to explore the content of the patient's communication. A therapist is quiet after a patient arrives late, and the patient asserts, "I know you're angry with me for being late." The therapist might reply, "I wonder why you believed I would be angry with you for being late." Or, "Perhaps it is so painful for you to focus on yourself and wonder about how *you* feel about being late that you turn to focusing on me and how I feel. But then, you leave your own feelings out, as if they didn't count." A patient in transference can genuinely consider this question, and wonder, "Yes, why do I jump to that conclusion? That's not like [him or] her at all." In this case, the patient is not likely to take it as an accusation, a pretense, a manipulation, a trick, a seduction, or any one of a number of meanings that patients will impute to the therapist if they are not in transference. Masterson expresses it eloquently and simply: The patient in transference has the capacity for whole object relations. He or she can recognize the independent existence of the object, and can consider the possibility that he or she is displacing feelings, thoughts, and motives onto the therapist.

Therapeutic Alliance
Is a real object relationship based on an implicit agreement that patients are in treatment to change themselves. The therapist is perceived as an ally of the real self, and of the reality ego. The patient's psychic reality is not experienced as concrete truth, but as hypotheses available for the process that will allow the integration of experiences with the therapist to become part of his or her ongoing perceptual understanding of himself or herself and of others. The patient can understand that he or she and the therapist are working together to help the patient mature through insight, progressive understanding, and control.

Transference Acting Out
This is an unconscious process in which a patient projects early needs and related fantasies onto the therapist when there is at best a brittle and fragile therapeutic alliance. Patients with personality disorders do not enter therapy in alliance with the therapists. They enter therapy to feel better, not, as Masterson says, to get better. In early childhood, these patients developed a "false self" defensive structure in order to cope with neglect and/or abuse. If they relinquish their defenses, and the related search for sources that will make them feel better, affects of the real self — the abandonment depression — will begin to emerge. However, the Masterson Approach defines this as the central goal of treatment. Therefore, the initial goal of therapy is to establish, strengthen, and maintain a therapeutic alliance, not through making the patient "feel" better, but by providing appropriate interventions that the patient can use to get better. The initial alliance will inevitably and repetitively break down whenever the patient is exposed to sufficient separation anxiety (especially disagreements about the frame and interventions that differ from defenses of the false self). If these breakdowns are properly managed, one by one, over the minute-by-minute challenges to the therapist's separateness, the patient

will come to understand and "master" the separation/individuation problem. To paraphrase Freud, only by living the resistances through (working them through) can patients become conscious of their existence and power.

Gabbard and Lester (1995, p. 70) quote Lawrence Friedman as observing that "the psychoanalytic situation involves an element of seduction. "The patient is misled by the analyst to expect love, whereas the analyst tends to provide an ill-defined substitute for love." Friedman acknowledged the fact that the exact nature of that substitute remains "difficult to define."

Although it is true that patients may "feel" seduced, it is the therapist's job to provide a patient with a safe opportunity in which to explore this "feeling" (which will be experienced by the patient as "truth"), and verbally and nonverbally provide understandings that will build a bridge to connections with the internal needs generating this projection — this "feeling." But if the therapist has, in fact, led the patient to "expect love" — this is quite another matter, and would be a conscious collusion with the patient's belief that supplies missing from the distant past can be obtained in the present from the therapist. On the other hand, if the therapist believes he or she has "seduced" the patient into expecting love in spite of his or her relatively successful efforts to hold the frame and provide appropriate therapeutic experiences, this belief — that the therapist has unwittingly generated this expectation in the patient — is more likely to be an unconscious collusion with the patient's projective identification.

Masterson provides an understanding that is very different from Friedman's. In the Masterson Approach, there is no substitute, and no seduction. Rather, the therapist is expected to be present with interest, concern, understanding, curiosity, boundaries, empathy, and diagnosis-appropriate interventions in order gradually to provide a patient with a foundation on which to begin to understand and explore his or her self-destructive search for love "in all the wrong places." This step-by-step process gradually enables the patient to relinquish defenses against his or her own internal truth, and to live a life not defined by an endless, fruitless search for the one true love, the one person, substance, or action that will "make up" for everything.

If patients are seduced by easy gratification, given what they ask for, they do not have to put deeper needs into words, and this keeps them out of treatment. If they are kept out of treatment, these needs will continue to press for expression in the everyday activities of their lives. False-self defenses will reappear, or appear in another form, to protect them from directly experiencing their basic needs and the affects they evoke; for example, if a patient is late and asks the therapist to make up the time at the end of the hour, to "go over," and the therapist does, it may seem like a small thing — much too small to make it an issue. Or the therapist may tell himself or herself that he or she is doing something nice for the patient, who has little enough "niceness" in life. Besides, the therapist rationalizes, it will illustrate to the patient that people can be "nice." However, this patient cannot use information in this way. The information becomes another experience of too little, too late, and appears to have no impact on the ceaseless expression of the part-self for a part-object who will provide missing supplies in ways dictated by dysfunctional attachment experiences of the early, primary relationships.

Through such seemingly small gratifications, the patient misses essential opportunities to build the *basic trust* necessary for a therapeutic alliance. The reality ego has once again been abandoned, this time by the therapist, and the patient will know it in these ways. First, he or she misses the modeling of boundaried behavior. A therapist is only a therapist, not a friend, not a parent, not a coach, not a counselor, not a healer, not a priest or a magician — not anything else, just a therapist. The moment a therapist stops being just a therapist, the therapist has lost the boundaries, and the patient will lose trust in the therapist's ability to hold the line. Second, the therapist misses the opportunity to experience and verbally express his or her reactions to the frustrations of reality with someone who will understand and interpret them, rather than retaliate, relinquish, or retreat. Third, and most important, the therapist misses the opportunity to verbalize about needs expressed as wanting; wanting to be special, wanting to be wanted, wanting someone to *want* to want him or her, wanting that unconditional love that is an ingredient only of fortunate early infant–maternal bliss. It is these verbal expressions, and the corresponding therapeutic containment and empathetic verbal understanding of these needs and wants and their emotional meanings, that will bring the truth of the abandonment depression into the realm of awareness.

For patients who have personality disorders, these experiences may be almost unbearably painful, and the therapist must be able to be empathically present while these needs and affects are being experienced and expressed. For this reason, the present-moment experience of these needs and their associated pain is kept largely unconscious — guarded by the defenses of the false self. However, these needs "leak" into everyday behavior in distorted or compromised forms, and can cause great damage to a patient's life. When the therapist can hold the line, explore and interpret the needs (wishes) as they are progressively deepened and revealed, the defenses of the false self can be relinquished, and the truth of what happened when these needs were first experienced can be known. The patient, as with all humankind, was helpless, dependent, and at the edge of non-being for a very long time. It is a potentially terrifying experience, and to ask patients to reenter this state in which their very being may seem to be in jeopardy requires a very firm grip on one's own reality.

However, it is in this way, step by step, that these defenses are dissolved — the resistances lived through. This is the experience Freud described as being arduous, a perpetual struggle, a difficult passage, which the therapist faces almost without assistance and with only the slightest clues to go on. Freud reluctantly concluded that working in the transference cannot be evaded, because "only through resolving the transference will the patient accept the new understandings arrived at during treatment." Freud called the transference an "intermediary realm," a "playground" on which the patient's compulsion to repeat is allowed to let itself go in almost complete freedom — as long as it is in words. The playground is the realm within which the meaning structure of archaic fantasy can come into consciousness and be verbalized, and the patient can allow a new structure of meaning to take its place (Freud, 1914).

Most contemporary psychoanalytic therapists will make more explicit Freud's implied dictum that the patient's experience of, and with, the therapist is a vital part of these "new understandings." Developmental and attachment research has underscored the importance of this added emphasis. Masterson included these understandings in the basic framework of his model (long before the rest of the analytic community did). He asserted that an essential part of the experience the patient must have is the moment-by-moment differentiation, individuation, and separation inherent in the therapeutic enterprise. Patients, especially those with Disorders of the Self, must traverse this difficult and arduous passage. Interventions must be titrated by diagnosis, and held with understanding and commitment, often for long periods with only the "slightest clues to go on."

DISORDERS OF THE SELF:
A BRIEF REVIEW

Development: Spitz, Bowlby, Mahler

The field research of Rene Spitz (1965), followed by Margaret Mahler's (1975) studies of mother–child interaction and John Bowlby's (1969, 1973, 1980) exhaustive treatise on attachment, changed forever the analytic understanding of human development and motivation. For Freud, the maternal object was simply the target of instinctual impulses through which instinctual tension is discharged — a need-gratifying object. Freud believed early competent caretakers to be interchangeable, and that early loss of the mother produces no great psychic trauma or mourning. Spitz found that having a libidinal object is both a developmental necessity and a developmental achievement — a selective, very personal attachment. Spitz's libidinal object is not simply a means to an end, a drive discharge, or the consequence of defensive internalization, but is fundamentally important in its own right. For Spitz, the libidinal object provides the essential human connectedness within which all psychological development occurs.

Bowlby argued that the child's attachment to the mother is instinctual, is not acquired, and is not derivative of the mother's need-gratifying activities. He used extensive surveys of separation and loss in both animals and humans to show that early loss results in true mourning.

Bowlby's concept of attachment, closely related to Fairbairn's (1952/1954) notion of libido as object seeking, was the linchpin of his reformulation of all the central features of personality development and psychopathology. "Emotional security is a reflection of confidence in the availability of attachment figures, which is built up gradually through early childhood experiences. Different kinds of anxiety are rooted in a basic anxiety concerning separation from the object of attachment; anger is, most fundamentally, a response to, and a protest against, separation. At the root of all defenses, Bowlby suggested, is detachment, a deactivation of the fundamental and central need for attachment, around which emotional experience is organized" (Mitchell & Black, 1996, pp. 136–137). Edith Jacobson and other analysts disagree with this formulation of anger and aggression, noting that libido and aggression are indispensable counterbalances to each other, that appropriate aggression is necessary for separation, and that both are necessary for a stable identity and healthy ego function (Bass, 1997, p. 645).

Mahler provided psychoanalytic psychotherapists with the evidence needed to reevaluate whether patients who did not respond to traditional analytic interventions could be treated within an adapted analytic mode. The new evidence suggested that the primary factor creating these disorders might not be libidinal withdrawal. Rather, the evidence overwhelmingly pointed to a failure in the basic formation of the self owing to specific kinds of difficulties in early experiences with the primary caregiver. Through her research, Mahler documented these difficulties, and the fatal consequences for the developing self.

Mahler found that there was a complex interplay among physical and cognitive maturation, psychological evolution, and the function of the caregiver in the child's evolving self. Mahler's research allowed her to identify the overarching process she called separation/individuation, and the subphases, each with its essential steps so crucial for the successful birth of the psychological self. "In breaking down the developmental journey through successive states of psychic organization, Mahler enabled clinicians to understand more deeply, and treat more effectively, children and adults who came to be officially diagnosed as Borderline patients" (Mitchell & Black, 1996, p. 47).

Contemporary Attachment Research: Peter Fonagy

Peter Fonagy et al. (2002) place the self at the center of their new understanding of development, psychological disorder, and clinical treatment based on decades of attachment and infant research. They observe that "the self is an experience of the other," that introspection, self-reflection, self-awareness, and mentalization are hard-won developmental achievements, dependent on years of appropriate experience with a caregiver who possesses a mature mind that is both benign and reflective.

Fonagy further observes that significant and prolonged early childhood maltreatment can result in an individual's capacity to behave with any degree of flexibility becoming severely compromised. In these cases, there appears to be an intensified need on the part of individuals to demand closer-to-perfect contingent responses from those with whom they have emotionally loaded relationships. It is as if these relationships trigger the need to rediscover the self in the response of the other, and, therefore, reactivate the need for high levels of contingent responsiveness.

In therapy, when an event is highly salient emotionally, a patient may enter into a state of psychic equivalence — characteristic of an early developmental stage in which there was no distinction between internal and external reality. In this state, the patient experiences transference, not as a fantasy, but as a subjective experience as real as a physical object in the room.

If the therapist can hold the emotional/mental representation of the patient's experience of this psychic equivalence in mind and find ways to express this holding in words, conveying an empathic understanding of the patient's experience, the patient can begin to observe the therapist's mental representation of the transference "truth" state in action. In this way, a patient may slowly become able to develop a tentatively held image of his or her own needs, desires, wishes, and fantasies as they are expressed in the transference (acting out), and begin to see them as his or her archaic needs and wishes rather than as requirements for objective truth located somewhere in the outside world.

Neurophysiology: Allan Schore and Daniel Siegel

Out of the now vast compilation of research discussed by both Allan Schore (2003a, 2003b, 2003c) and Daniel Siegel (1999), I will select only one piece to use in this context: the nature and function of implicit memory and how it differs from explicit memory.

When explicit memory is retrieved, it requires focal attention for its encoding, and has the subjective sense of "I am recalling something." Explicit memory has two major forms: semantic or factual, and episodic or autobiographical. The latter has the unique feature of providing a sense of self and time. Brain imaging studies suggest that episodic memory is mediated by a number of regions, such as the hippocampus, which do not come on line as a system until after the first year of life. The maturation (synapse formation and myelination) of this and related parts of the prefrontal cortex occurs during preschool years, and appears to be the neurobiologic basis for the emergence and development of autobiographical memory and self-awareness during this period of childhood and beyond.

The neurologic substrate for implicit memory appears to be on line at birth. The circuitry does not require focal attention for encoding, nor does it include or provide a sense of "I am recalling something" when retrieval occurs. Implicit memory afforded the schematas or mental models of self in experience — the truths of meaning beyond words, beyond thought. They simply are.

When the early caretaker experience does not provide appropriate attachment experiences, infants may suffer an impairment in the process of consolidation and integration of implicit memories — especially the resolution of excessive affective arousal. In later years, this lack of integration can make the individual vulnerable to entering inflexible, reactive states of heightened emotion that lack self-reflection. These experiences have been described as "incoherent narratives and intrusive implicit elements of memory that torment an individual's internal subjective world and interpersonal relationships." In other words, implicit memory intrudes into, and defines, the present moment — it becomes the "truthful" meaning from the past defining what is happening in the present in ways so compelling that it is beyond question.

Attachment research proposes that the transition from nonverbal to verbal knowing is mediated by caretakers; the infant or toddler looks to the caretaker for congruent, contingent, attuned, marked verbal and affective interpretation of his or her experience.

OWNERSHIP OF MIND

Recruitment: Robert Caper

Caper's (1999) position is that the most important tool the therapist has for learning about the patient's unconscious, psychic reality is the transference. The past material reality of the patient is unknowable in absolute terms, and can only be understood by what happens in the patient's behavior in the present. Caper quotes Strachey (1934/1969), noting that the therapist becomes "an external phantasy object" for the patient. However, because the patient is in treatment to "feel better rather than to get better," as Dr. Masterson reminds us, the patient must "recruit" the therapist in reality into playing this role of the "external phantasy object." All of this is unconscious and ego syntonic — it is transference acting out to invoke countertransference acting out. "This recruitment consists of the patient using his (largely unconscious but often highly intelligent) ability to perceive, assess and play on the nuances of the analyst's personality to stimulate in him a state of mind that corresponds to the role he is meant to play. He does this using both verbal and non-verbal means, the way a director might prepare an actor for a part in a play (if he could do so without the actor knowing that he was doing it). This activity is part of what we mean by the term projective identification, and the state of mind stimulated in the analyst is one of countertransference. . . . When under the influence of the patient's projective identifications, the analyst . . . actually experiences the powerful emotions connected to this role as belonging entirely to himself, and having nothing to do with the patient's psychological impact on him" (Caper, 1999, p. 34).

"By working to extricate himself from the feeling that his emotions are justified entirely by objective realities — what Bion (1962) called the 'numbing feeling of reality' that is produced by projective identification — the . . . [therapist] is gradually able to recognize the patient's contribution to his countertransference. This places him in a position to treat the patient's projective identification as a communication which can be brought into the therapist's conscious awareness and in a way and at a time the patient can bear it, returned to the patient in a verbal interpretation" (Caper, 1999, p. 34).

Caper observes that just as the therapist is about to make such an interpretation, he or she will be vulnerable to believing that he/she is about to do something to harm the patient or to jeopardize the therapeutic relationship. In this case, the therapist has shifted from functioning as the patient's auxiliary ego to something closer to representing an identification with a part-object — with the split absolute good and bad of the archaic superego. But here the therapist shifts from representing a realistic ego to representing (or fearing) a moralistic (archaic) superego. In the latter instance, everything that happens is felt somehow to be deliberate, and, therefore, someone deserves the blame or credit. The perspective of the ego is realistic, concerned with seeing things as they are. The absolute good or bad of the archaic superego is constantly on a search-and-destroy mission for fixing fault and blame, and when the therapist resonates with that projection, he or she will be unable to remain aware of his or her reality.

Colonizing: Roy Schafer

Roy Schafer (2003) describes patients who live primarily in the Paranoid–Schizoid position as attempting to "colonize" the mind of the therapist. He describes these patients as being characterized by unreflective or concrete thinking and being unable to move independently toward the pain of the depressive position (similar to the Masterson understanding of whole self and object representation).

Schafer observes that as long as the therapist retains his or her own mind, he or she can maintain enough distance and perspective to keep trying to develop a collaboration — a therapeutic alliance. Once colonized, however, the therapist cannot remember to persist in thinking about the patient's mind, the patient's self. In Schafer's words, the therapist does not "persist in understanding . . . what the patient is up to each moment defensively" because the therapist has been "blinded by the patient's shows of helplessness, hopelessness, suffering, and, most of all, failure." In other words, an appreciation of the patient's power and strength is no longer available to the therapist.

"The idea of colonizing implies that projective identification has played a paramount role in the attacks on the analyst's capacity to remember autonomously" (Schafer, 2003, pp. 37–48).

Projective Identification

Klein's original idea about projective identification held that it served the defensive function of projecting unwanted aspects of the self onto the object, which the object would be induced to experience as his or her own through the behavior of the person engaging in the projection. Bion (1962/1988) extended this theory to define another type of projective identification as a realistic, normal, preverbal form of communication between the mother and infant. Mitrani (2001, p. 1085), building on this, speculated that if a mother and child are adjusted to each other, projective identification plays a major role in communication. The infant is able to arouse feelings in the mother that will evoke appropriate caretaking behavior, and the responsive behavior generates a sense of self-agency in the infant. In other words, it is a normal, preverbal form of communication between the mother and the infant. However, if the mother cannot tolerate these projections through much of her infant's early development, there are severe long-term consequences for the normal development of thoughts and thinking — what Fonagy would call mentalization. Mitrani believes this is the kind of misattunement that later will produce nearly unresolvable impasses between the therapist and patient. The therapist's ability to contain and interpret the patient's primitive communication will rest on the ability to translate just this kind of projective identification.

A patient's "realistic projective identification" — the experience of truth — is the patient's attempt to communicate "something about the deepest level of her most troublesome state of mind as it is experienced in the immediacy of the session." The therapist's ability to contain and appropriately translate this communication — not to gratify, but to understand and translate — is the royal road to integration.

FOCUS ON THE REAL SELF:
A REVOLUTIONARY IDEA

A Clinical Perspective from the Masterson Model

In his work on countertransference (Masterson, 1983, pp. 8–12), Masterson asks therapist A, whom he is supervising, "What do you mean by 'I gave her a lot of support?.' . . . You evidently became her [the patient's] savior, the essence of the rewarding unit she's been searching for all her life but has never been able to find. . . . You must convey to her, 'We are here to work on your problems, why are you focusing on me?' "

Masterson asks therapists to work in treatment to focus on the patient's self, the patient's real self, the defenses against the patient's real self, and nothing else. Keep the work in words, not in action. The patient is not in treatment to change the world. The therapist is not in business to change the patient's world. The feelings and/or behavior of the spouse, children, boss, employees, neighbors, or friends are not in play. In Dr. Masterson's words, "we are here to work on your problems," and they are not located in someone else's mind.

Patients diagnosed with Disorders of the Self undoubtedly experienced terrible deprivations and/or traumas at the hands of their parents. These experiences leave patients stranded in adulthood with a massive handicap: They have little access to the needs, emotions, guidance, and gifts of their real selves. The real self is saturated or associated with unconscious or implicit memory (affect and meanings) about what happened in childhood (the abandonment depression); leaving the patient to live in or "to be" a false self — developed to fend off these affects and to obtain survival supplies from the environment. The combination of these forces largely forecloses the possibility of the patient's spontaneously forming connections with the real self (or real connections with other real selves) in adulthood.

However, in order for the patients to get better (rather than temporarily to feel better), they have to be able to face these real-self feelings and work them through. In Dr. Masterson's words, the therapist empathically requires by his or her interventions that patients can and must do this work. The therapist cannot (and must not try to) do it for them. If a therapist does anything resembling reparenting, it occurs (1) only through empathic interest, understanding, curiosity, steadiness, confidence, and expectation that the patient can do the work of focusing on and developing connections with his or her real self; (2) through the therapist's experiencing and expressing an unrelenting empathic interest in wanting to understand the patient's real self; and (3) through holding an equally unrelenting interest in providing the opportunity and tools for the patient to understand, and want to understand, his or her own mind — his or her own real self. To paraphrase Dr. Masterson, the therapist's job is to remove the boulders from the stream bed; the therapist doesn't tell the water where or how to flow.

Dr. Masterson asks therapists to confront and/or interpret their patients' lack of interest and concern about their real selves — about what's happening in their minds to produce the very problems that make their lives so difficult.

Often our patients' lives are painful, disorganized, and disordered, with the same disastrous outcomes occurring over and over again (Freud's original description of the repetition compulsion). If the therapist maintains his or her focus on a patient's real self, and intervenes appropriately to identify defenses against activation of the real self, the patient will inevitably begin to integrate these interventions into his or her mental life. The therapist focuses on the real self so that the patient can focus on the real self. It's that simple, and it's that difficult.

When this happens, the course of the patient's life will smooth out, the repetition of exciting, urgent, enthralling, and disastrous outcomes will begin to diminish, and the patient will begin to feel the affects of the abandonment depression. At this juncture, the patient is likely to turn back to some defense. This is the triad. Self-activation evokes depression, which evokes defense. The patient will resume acting in or acting out. He or she will withdraw, or attack the therapist, or return to overeating, overdrinking, overworking, or whatever, or attack the self with accusations that he or she is stupid, boring, pitiful, disgusting, pathetic, a weenie, a sucker, empty — anything to move away from the affects of the abandonment depression.

The therapist can empathically describe these events to the patient, wonder why they are occurring (Borderline cluster of disorders), or point out that it moves the patient away from pain (Narcissistic cluster of disorders), or that it must not be safe to reveal so much (Schizoid cluster of disorders). (In the Masterson Approach, each major diagnostic category represents a cluster of several related DSM personality disorders, depending on the nature of the intrapsychic structure rather than on observable symptoms.) Through interventions, the therapist verbally identifies the defenses of the false self, notes the damage they do to the patient's life, and observes that they occur whenever the patient seems to have had some kind of activation of the real self, including an internal awareness of, or "connection" with, the real self. These interventions place the problem inside the patient — in the patient's mind. Once this is understood, the patient can begin to do it for himself or herself. Any other response places the difficulty and the solution outside the patient's mind, and there is no reason for that patient to do anything differently, no reason to begin to develop the real self in order to live his or her own life.

The Cost of Rewarding (Gratifying)

Initially, both the patient and the therapist may miss the old, acting-out ways and days. (Perhaps much like Freud missed the "smooth and pleasing course" of pretransference treatment.) A patient's stories often are dramatic, fascinating, and engrossing, and seem to call for immediate and urgent action on the part of both the patient and the therapist. Over and over again, every day, perhaps every session, therapists lose their minds to these stories. They lose their focus, they get recruited, colonized, induced, and pulled into becoming fascinated and involved with the patient's ever-renewable drama, and respond to the urgent call to use their "magic," which both therapist and patient may secretly believe will make the pain and problems disappear. They note Dr. Masterson's injunction not to intervene without a reason. And there is only one reason: The patient is in defense and cannot return to activating the real self without assistance. The only assistance is through identifying the defense, and, when the patient cannot, identifying the cause (the immediate, intrapsychic cause) and the cost of the defense to the patient's life.

In Masterson's words, anything else is rewarding. Therapists reward not only by yielding to a patient's demands to change the treatment frame for them, but also by directing, pushing, advising, suggesting, recommending, educating, cajoling, informing, questioning, and just giving their opinion. "Rewarding is moving in and taking over the responsibility for what happens [in her feelings] in the session, and trying to push [the patient . . .] one way or another" (Masterson, 1981, p. 22). "I always say, 'Don't verbally reassure patients.' However, enormous reassurance and strength are conveyed by the quiet assumption: 'We are here to work on your problems' " (1981, p. 12). Not someone else's problems, technically not the patient's problems with someone else, but the patient's problems with his or her real self.

Focusing on the patient's real self, and identifying the defenses against it does not allow therapists to engage in reassuring patients by offering them the curative power of the therapist's love and tenderness. When a therapist tells a patient, "you have a right to feel love," Dr. Masterson observes, "Oh my God, where did that come from?" (Masterson, 1981, p. 23).

When patients question whether the therapist likes or loves them, they are not focused on their real selves. The patient is inducing, seducing, recruiting, colonizing, and deflecting — he or she is in defense. Patients using this defense are trying yet one more time to "get" from the world supplies they have been missing for years, sometimes decades. There is a vital distinction between talking about feelings related to the leftover need for "unconditional love" and acting out old programs to try to "get it" from the most available object. If patients can talk directly about their *need* for love, and then explore the need and related feelings, they face a terrible grief that comes alive through their conscious realization that they were helpless to prevent what happened, that what was done cannot be undone, and that their best chance at a better life is through feeling this need (and all the archaic needs of the real self), experiencing their grief, anguish, despair, terror, rage, and helplessness, and expressing them at and with their therapist.

The therapist's job is to interpret and/or confront the patient's pull to get the therapist to act, to reassure, to deliver the goods. The therapist's job is to understand, to contain, to be present and empathic, and to help patients work through the nearly unbearable feelings that accompany activation of the real self — the affects of the abandonment depression. If therapists reassure patients that they are loveable or loved, or engage in other actions to "meet" their archaic needs overtly rather than to work toward bringing their expression into consciousness and verbal expression, patients are robbed of the opportunity to work through. In other words, if therapists craft appropriate interventions *over the course of treatment* and *focus on the needs and affects of the real self, the patients will integrate the interventions and do their work.* If the therapist has been gratifying over the course of treatment, there is a high probability that a moment will arrive when the patient will demand what the therapist will feel is *too much* gratification, love, or special treatment. At this point, when the therapist attempts to hold the frame or set limits, it will quite probably produce an impasse of unresolvable proportions.

When the patient asks the therapist to act, from making exceptions with the frame to declaring special care and/or love, it is a deflection and defense. These may be the most difficult defenses for therapists to handle. And they may be the most important.

Note: In the following section, excerpts of sessions with three different patients are presented with commentary. Identifying characteristics of, and statements by, these patients have been changed to ensure the patients' anonymity.

CLINICAL EXAMPLES

(S indicates silence of less than five minutes;
LS indicates silence of five minutes or more.)

Patient at the Edge of
Therapeutic Alliance and Transference

A woman patient in her 20s who has a clinging Borderline disorder and who has been in twice-a-week treatment with me for about 14 months recently asked me if I really cared about her. I said:

THERAPIST: Your focus on me and how I feel really takes you away from your self. A few minutes ago, you were feeling a lot of sadness and regret about not staying in school. Now you are focused on my feelings about you. What happened to *your* feelings about you?

PATIENT: Yes, but you're trying to get out of answering my question. You're being evasive, and that means you don't care. If you did, you'd just say so. I can't be here if I can't trust that you care about me.

THERAPIST: I don't understand. I wonder why you are focusing on me and my feelings about you right now. Nothing has changed in what I'm doing. I'm doing the same thing I've been doing all along. I'm listening, taking notes, understanding, or trying to understand, what is happening here. Yet right now, you are very urgent about focusing on my feelings about you rather than returning to your feelings about why you turned your back on yourself.

PATIENT: You're just trying to evade my question; you're trying to trick me.

THERAPIST: I wonder if the real evasion, the real trick, doesn't happen when you deflect your attention from yourself, from trying to get a handle on your life. Right here, you evade yourself, you turn your back on understanding why you quit school — something you said was really important to you.

PATIENT: (Angry) You're just like (X — the stepmother). She didn't give a damn about me either. All she cared about was whether I did things her way. (S) [Patient begins to tear.] (S) You just sit there and take your damn notes. Fuck you. (LS, different voice) I don't know why I quit school. It's the same thing I always do. ... (She continued with her work, for the moment.)

Patient Over the Edge Into
Therapeutic Alliance and Transference,
But Teetering

Another woman patient, this one in her 30s, who has a clinging Border-line disorder and who has been in three-times-a-week therapy for about three years, began to cry toward the end of a particularly difficult session, saying:

PATIENT: I guess I want from you now what I wanted then. I want someone to love me. (S) You're you, and I think you care about me, but you don't love me. (S) I don't know. I don't feel like you're even listening to me. (Anger)
THERAPIST: Maybe when I don't say what you want to hear, you get angry.
PATIENT: You never say what I want to hear. (End of session. Patient leaves, slamming the door.)

This patient is struggling with real self feelings and needs that she has been able to touch on previously, and is on the verge of beginning to explore again. If I move in to reassure her (which I feel powerfully pulled to do), I believe I rob her of the opportunity to connect with her real self's needs and feelings, and to experience and express them in her own words. At the beginning of the next session, the patient picked up where she had left off at the previous session, continuing:

PATIENT: I feel like I shouldn't have to do this. (S) I don't belong anywhere and no one wants me. (S) I feel like an outsider. I used to feel I could come here and that this was a place where I could find a kind of home. Now I'm not feeling that, and I'm really angry. Like you've misled me, you've tricked me. I don't know what to do. I don't know where I can go. (S) I'm really angry at you and I really hate you and I don't even know why. I guess Monday was . . . , it's something about because you won't fix it. . . . I lose sight of how it happens. Of what happens to this place inside me. I just hurt. . . . so badly [sobbing]. I just want not to feel like this [sobbing]. I don't know what to do any more. (S) What's going to happen? I don't know what to think. Nothing, I guess. I guess if I don't think you can fix it, I don't think it can be fixed. I guess that's not exactly true. I don't mean like it never happened. I mean so there can be some part of me that . . . [deep sobbing]. I guess realizing that you're not going to fix it was a big shock. It sent me into a desperate place. (LS)
THERAPIST: I wonder if that desperate wish to get someone to fix it isn't what this part of you feels all the time, and . . . [patient interrupts].

PATIENT: It's a huge need that can't be met! [sobbing]. I guess I feel like it's wrong to be feeling this because I feel I won't get comforted. Those feelings keep being there. I don't want to know about them. I don't want to know about needs that aren't going to be met. (S) (Anger) Somebody's starving and you see it and you just sit there and you say, "Well, I feel how hungry you are. Sorry. You just have to feel it". . . . So tell me that's not what's happening.

THERAPIST: I wonder if that isn't your hunger for your own self — your own truth, and you're beginning to realize that your effort to feed it substitutes just keeps you hungry.

PATIENT: Maybe there isn't food, so why do I have to do this? I hate you because you bring bad news. The bad news is, I'm not going to get someone to love me the way I wanted to be loved. I don't understand what's going to reach me. I don't understand what there is. Being understood doesn't feel like enough. It feels like you say, "Oh, I have compassion for you," while I starve to death [sobbing]. I want you to *do* something. I just don't understand. I'm going around and around, and you don't help me.

THERAPIST: You hoped that if you got someone — me — to love you just the right way, it would solve the problems.

PATIENT: (S) Yes. Now I know it doesn't work, and I hate you. [sobbing] It feels like such a loss. [sobbing] I just feel like I want to die.

I have to trust that our work together has built the foundation for her to do this. I am trusting that the reliability of the treatment, my genuine interest in her and her previous ability to use relatively well attuned, empathic interventions have built a sufficiently resilient container within which she can do her work. If not, we just have more foundation to build.

If I step in and reassure her, I become just another fool (fooled by her facade) or another liar. This patient "knows" she's not lovable, in that unassailable, implicit place of hidden truths inside her, and no amount of reassurance will change that truth. She has received countless reassurances from others during her brief adult life. They do not touch this place. She is a bright, talented, attractive, woman who is trapped in a clinging defense against depression. My reassurance or my indulgence of her demands will not be the magic that releases her from her prison.

When she can experience her longing to be loved with and by me, and perhaps hate me for not giving it to her while "knowing" the truth about what happened and what is happening, she has the opportunity to safely experience her needs and release her grief. Only then will she be able to accept the truth about her helplessness and about coming to believe that her real self was unlovable and "unwantable" in order to get what supplies were available, and to "explain" to herself — to make sense out of — *what really happened*. Only then will she be free of her insatiable hungers for food, for what passes for love, for drugs, for fame, for extreme self-reliance, for anything that might fill the emptiness and assuage her pain. This is the transference playground of which Freud spoke; the possibility of a transforming experience.

Patient C: Proof of Love — Accept My Gift. On the Edge of Therapeutic Alliance and Tranference with a Patient Who Has a Distancing Borderline Disorder and Marked Dissociation as a Result of Posttraumatic Stress Disorder (PTSD)

The last patient, a well-educated, unmarried woman in her late 20s, in treatment three times a week for four years, has a distancing Borderline disorder with PTSD and dissociative defenses. During the middle of a session, the patient began to be more in contact with herself, and then to dissociate.

PATIENT: Now I'm in that place. Oh, I was in that place. I was talking about something outside. Where do I go from here? (S) Remember that book we talked about, with the father at the end. Did you read it? (S) The passage at the end was really sad. At the end, I started to cry. I know, I know, oh, I thought about your talking to me. I heard your voice, and I cried so hard I was choking. Frank [the boyfriend] got scared, and I told him it was about therapy. (LS) I thought I wanted to bring you a copy. Maybe it's not ethical? (S) I just think about it a lot. (S) [Thick voice] I'm in the white space. I don't know, I don't know.

[Patient told a story about a friend who was also very moved by the book, then there was a long silence, and she continued]

PATIENT: I feel very emotional right now. I know when I come in, there's something deeper I want to talk about, but I can't. I want to tell you, to talk — it happens every time. (S)

THERAPIST: Seems like you were just beginning to touch on something deeper that you often want to talk about, then you stopped. Did you jump away?

PATIENT: [Thick voice, mumbling] Uh-huh. Any time ... I don't know ... I'm gone.

THERAPIST: You were reaching for something you wanted to talk about, and something happened, some part of you took you away.

PATIENT: Oh, yeah, quick thoughts of rejection. Yeah. Oh, she's not interested in that book. I was trying to do something — to give you something, and you didn't say, "Oh yeah, I would like to read it." You didn't say Yes or No about wanting the book. Something said, "She's not interested in that."

THERAPIST: When I'm quiet and listening, you believe I'm not interested.

PATIENT: It's not a thought [voice is thick], it feels like a push-away.

THERAPIST: It's not a thought. It's an experience. Like it really happened.

PATIENT: Yeah. It just feels like it. It's gauzy. I just acknowledge it and move on.

THERAPIST: It sounds like it feels like a truth — like it really happened. And some part of you says you have to just acknowledge the truth of it and get on with things.

PATIENT: Yeah. It feels like the truth. It doesn't need to be considered. It shouldn't be considered, actually. [Patient's voice is very thick and she mumbles] I'm gone.

THERAPIST: It seems like some part of you forbids your knowing about this process of creating these truths. (S)

THERAPIST: Are you gone?

PATIENT: Yeah.

THERAPIST: You feel that dazed place?

PATIENT: Yeah. (S) [Patient told a story about a movie, focusing on a violent segment in which several people were "blown up."]

THERAPIST: Seems like you might feel like part of you has been blown up, and part of you saw it happen, and you're saying, "I'm not going to see it or talk about it. I'm going to go away."

PATIENT: [Very long silence, voice less thick:] I wish I wasn't like this. I wish I didn't jump away so much. I didn't realize it. I didn't know I did this. I used to not believe you. (LS) I'm thinking about the book. I'm thinking, "She's not here." I put out a little feeler — do you want the book? I wanted to hear something, and when I didn't, I left. (S) Right now, I feel like I'm floating.

THERAPIST: You wanted me to read the book, but maybe more, you wanted me to want to read just what you read, so maybe I'd just know what was so important to you. Then you wouldn't have to tell me — to put it into words. I think you were starting to find the words when you said you used to not believe me.

PATIENT: I don't know. (LS) I feel really gauzy.

THERAPIST: But part of you is staying here and not taking you away from what's really happening — that you want me to understand something, and that you can find the words to say it.

PATIENT: It feels odd. Weird. I feel like you're bored. [Story about her work.] I'm gone again. (S) I think you're being critical of what I'm saying. (S) I feel really gauzy.

In this segment, I've moved back and forth between interventions addressing a symbolic understanding of defenses when I believed she was able to
mentalize (not dissociate), to contingent communication or psychic equivalent
interventions (Fonagy et al., 2002; Bateman & Fonagy, 2004) or therapist-
centered interventions (Steiner, 1994) when I believed she was in a dissociative state. At these times, she was unable to stay in sufficient awareness or
contact with me to permit symbolic interventions requiring differentiation.

During dissociation, a patient may not be able to differentiate between internal experience and external reality; the therapist may even have "become"
the abuser or the passive enabler or observer. At these times of heightened
emotional arousal and a corresponding shutdown of cognitive functioning, interventions of contingent communication, psychic equivalence, and/or thera-
pist-centered interventions can provide a soothing and restorative link to
reestablish therapeutic equilibrium.

When a patient with a Disorder of the Self shows signs of PTSD by moving into strong dissociative defenses, an effective way to maintain "mind-to-
mind" (Bateman & Fonagy, 2004, pp. 91–94) contact, or to provide a bridge
back to contact, is through the therapist's continuing empathic presence, an
awareness of the importance of mentalizing the patient's projective identification, and a simple verbal reflection of understanding what might have happened in the moment to elicit the dissociative state. For example, "when I
said that, it confused and hurt you" reflects the therapist's understanding of
what happened, establishes that the patient's experience *can be understood* (or,
at the very least, that the therapist *wants* to understand), put into words, and
not escalated to greater conflict. During times of strong affective arousal or
dissociation, the therapist can reestablish contact with the patient best by not
calling attention to the projective aspect of her experience. That has to come
later, when the patient is able to be in a more differentiated mental state.

Moving into action, trying to offer a reassurance such as "it's safe here"
(which many PTSD patients heard from the abuser), or any other overt attempt to reassure or comfort, can undermine the patient's trust in the therapist's ability to tolerate the affect and experiences underlying the PTSD as
they are initially experienced in treatment. Overt attempts to comfort or reassure patients who are reexperiencing trauma will very likely be experienced as
communication that the *therapist* cannot endure being with the patient at such
times, and thus the patient will conclude that, once again, someone who is
supposed to provide "protection" (in this case, through understanding and
mentalization) will be unable or unwilling to tolerate the patient's "real" affective experience.

References

Aragno, A. (1992). *Symbolization: Proposing a Developmental Paradigm for a New Psychoanalytic Theory of Mind*. Madison, CT: International Universities Press.

Balint, M. (1968). *The Basic Fault, Therapeutic Aspects of Regression*. London: Tavistock.

Bass, A. (1997). The problem of concreteness. *Psychoanalytic Quarterly*, 66, 642–682.

Bateman, A., & Fonagy, P. (2004). *Psychotherapy for Borderline Personality Disorder: Mentalization–Based Treatment*. Oxford: Oxford University Press.

Bion, W. R. (1962/1988). A theory of thinking (pp. 178–186). In E. Spillius (Ed.), *Melanie Klein Today: Vol. I*. London: Routledge.

Bowlby, J. (1969). *Attachment and Loss: Vol. 1. Attachment*. New York: Basic Books.

Bowlby, J. (1973). *Attachment and Loss: Vol. 2. Separation: Anxiety and Anger*. New York: Basic Books.

Bowlby, J. (1980). *Attachment and Loss: Vol. 3. Loss: Sadness and Depression*. New York: Basic Books.

Breuer, J., & Freud, S. (1895). Studies on hysteria. *Standard Edition*, 2, 3–305.

Britton, R. (1992). Keeping things in mind. In R. Anderson (Ed.), *Clinical Lectures on Klein and Bion*. New York: Routledge.

Caper, R. (1999). *A Mind of One's Own*. New York: Routledge.

Chused, J. F. (1996). The therapeutic action of psychoanalysis: Abstinence and informative experiences. *Journal of the American Psychoanalytic Association*, 44, 1047–1071.

Ellman, S. J. (1991). *Freud's Technique Papers: A Contemporary Perspective*. Northvale, NJ: Jason Aronson.

Fairbairn, W. R. (1952/1954). A revised psychopathology of the psychoses and psychoneuroses. *Psychoanalytic Studies of the Personality: An Object Relations Theory of the Personality*. New York: Basic Books. (London: Tavistock.)

Ferenczi, S., & Rank, O. (1925). *The Development of Psychoanalysis*. (Caroline Newton, trans.) New York: Nervous and Mental Disease Publishing Co.

Fonagy, P., Gergely, G., Jurist, E. L., & Target, M. (2002). *Affect Regulation, Mentalization, and the Development of the Self*. New York: Other Press.

Freud, S. (1905). Fragment of an analysis of a case of hysteria. *Standard Edition*, 7, 7–122.

Freud, S. (1914). Further recommendations in the technique of psychoanalysis — recollection, repetition, and working through (pp. 366–376). In *Collected Papers, Vol. 2*. New York: Basic Books.

Freud, S. (1915). Further recommendations in the technique of psychoanalysis — observations on transference love (pp. 366–370). In *Collected Papers, Vol. 3*. New York: Basic Books.

Freud, S. (1916/1917). Introductory lectures on psychoanalysis. *Standard Edition*, 15/16.

Friedman, L. (1994). *Ferrum, Ignis and Medicina: Return to the Crucible*. Plenary Address, Annual Meeting of the American Psychoanalytic Association, Philadelphia.

Gabbard, G. O., & Lester, E. P. (1995). *Boundaries and Boundary Violations in Psychoanalysis*. New York: Basic Books.

Mahler, M., Pine, F., & Bergman, A. (1975). *The Psychological Birth of the Human Infant*. New York: Basic Books.

Masterson, J. F. (1981). *The Narcissistic and Borderline Disorders: An Integrated Developmental Approach*. New York: Brunner/Mazel.

Masterson, J. F. (1983). *Countertransference and Psychotherapeutic Technique*. New York: Brunner/Mazel.

Masterson, J. F. (1985). *The Real Self: A Developmental, Self, and Object Relations Approach*. New York: Brunner/Mazel.

Masterson, J. F., & Lieberman, A. R. (2004). *A Therapist's Guide to the Personality Disorders: The Masterson Approach*. Phoenix: Zeig, Tucker, & Theisen.

Mitchell, S., & Black, M. (1996). *Freud and Beyond: A History of Modern Psychoanalytic Thought*. New York: Basic Books.

Mitrani, J. L. (2001). Taking the transference: Some technical implications in three papers by Bion. *International Journal of Psychoanalysis, 82*, 1085.

Schafer, R. (2003). *Insight and Interpretation: The Essential Tools of Psychoanalysis*. New York: Karnac.

Schore, A. (2003a). On the early origins of hopelessness and hope: Clinical contributions from developmental psychoanalysis. *Psychologist/Psychoanalyst, 23/3*, 41–42.

Schore, A. (2003b). Trauma and neuroscience: Bringing the body more deeply into psychoanalysis. *Psychologist/Psychoanalyst, 23*, 42–43.

Schore, A. (2003c). *Affect Regulation and Repair of the Self*. New York: Norton.

Siegel, D. J. (1999). *The Developing Mind: Toward a Neurobiology of Interpersonal Experience*. New York: Guilford.

Spitz, R. (1965). *The First Year of Life*. New York: International Universities Press.

Steiner, J. (1994). The problems of psychoanalytic technique: Patient-centered and analyst-centered interpretations. *Psychic Retreats: Pathological Organizations in Psychotic, Neurotic and Borderline Patients*. London: Routledge.

Strachey, J. (1934/1969). The nature of therapeutic action of psychoanalysis. *International Journal of Psychoanalysis, 50*, 275.

Terr, L. C. (1991). Childhood traumas: An outline and overview. *American Journal of Psychiatry, 148*, 1, 10–20.

6

Attachment Theory and the Masterson Approach: Psychotherapeutic Reproceduring of the Real Self

DONALD D. ROBERTS, PH.D.

DEVELOPMENT AND DIAGNOSIS OF THE PERSONALITY DISORDERS

Attachment research and theory have garnered enormous attention over the past several years. What, if anything, do they have to do with the Masterson Approach? In my view, it augments, nuances, and refines our developmental, therapeutic model, despite the fact that much of that theory has been implicit in this approach all along. Two questions occur: First, how does attachment theory add to our understanding of the personality disorders? And, second, what are the implications of attachment theory for psychotherapy?

I will begin by presenting several tenets of a developmental model that amalgamates attachment theory and the Masterson Approach.

THE REAL SELF

The concept of a real self is central to the Masterson Approach. However, it does not assume that this real self will evolve optimally over the course of development. Rather, the vicissitudes of the developmental process result in a wide range of outcomes on the continuum of self-evolution.

When Things Go Right

What are the conditions that support the emergence and development of the real self?

Implicit Relational Memory

First, let us consider "implicit procedural memory," a prominent attachment theory concept. Distinct from explicit, semantic, or autobiographical memory that requires the symbolic representation of facts, events, or ideas in language, implicit procedural memory or knowledge involves representations of how to proceed, of how to do things. Thus, explicit memory is concerned with remembering "what." Implicit memory has to do with remembering "how."

"Implicit *relational* memory" (Lyons-Ruth, 1998), in particular, is about how to be one's self with others, how to relate, how to attach, how to express affection, how to get attention, how and when to joke with others, and so on. Shaped in the infant's mind from "summations" or generalizations of repeated experiences, primarily with the mother, it is "in your bones" knowledge, right-brain knowing. It is a preverbal, preconceptual, prereflective, and preconscious internal schema of how to attach, to connect, with others. And because it is not conscious, it is not volitional; it is activated reflexively, "knee jerk-like," without conscious awareness.

So I am proposing that, in the case of the healthy child, the real self is implicitly procedured to activate; this child's implicit relational knowledge involves procedures, ways of being and relating, that support real-self experience and expression.

How does this come about?

The self is born in, and its development is supported and scaffolded by a relationship that provides a secure attachment experience *and* a healthy process of separation, that is, two parallel but interrelated lines of development involving two capacities: (1) to be emotionally close (emphasized by attachment theory), and (2) to be autonomous or separate (emphasized by object relations theory). Each is the underbelly of the other. And both represent crucial developmental tasks for optimal unfolding of the real self; a healthy attachment is a prerequisite for healthy separation, because a pathological, insecure attachment experience does not provide the "secure base" necessary for separation. Thus, the flourishing of the real self is supported by the achievement of a secure attachment experience and, later, by healthy separation.

What, briefly, is attachment? According to attachment theory, the self is hard-wired to seek relationships, evolutionarily wired to attach — both for survival and for affect regulation. So the infant's drive to establish connection, a relationship with another, is of motivational primacy. But what conditions are requisite to the development of a healthy, secure attachment?

Attunement

First, a secure attachment requires an emotionally available mother who provides "good enough" attunement to the infant's needs and mental states, to the real self. Following the child's lead, the mother, through her attunement, provides what Sander (1965, 1991) refers to as a "recognition process" by which the infant comes to feel known, to know himself or herself as being known by another. This is, it seems, analogous to Mahler's (1968) concepts of a "mirroring frame of reference," "mutual cueing," or an "echo phenomenon." Similarly, Siegel (2001) references "feeling felt," while Fonagy (2001) describes one's being "aware of a mind with my mind in mind." That is, the infant's experience is reflected in the mother's attuned resonance. "When you attune to me, see me, *get* me, you help me clarify my experience of myself." This recognition process, then, supports clarification and consolidation of the real self.

Early on, attunement occurs in the context of a "right-brain to right-brain" process of mutual, reciprocal knowing. There is a shared exchange of what Stern (1985) refers to as "vitality affect" or what Siegel (2001) terms "primary emotion," as the mother's attunement evokes affective aliveness and exuberance in the child, to which the mother responds with a corresponding affective experience. It is the mother's following the affective leading of the infant.

But attunement not only means attuning to the fluctuations of affect states, but is also responsive to the infant's need to be alone, quiet, in the presence of the mother (Winnicott, 1988). This is so because the infant discovers himself or herself in *both* the mutual, reciprocal interaction with the mother *and* in quiet, alone time with her — in both attachment and separation.

Rupture–Repair Cycle

An experience of accurate attunement alone, however, is insufficient for the evolution of a healthy, autonomous self. Rather, repeated disruptions of the attuned relationship created by the inevitable misattunements that occur in the interaction between a mother and a child, *followed by timely repair*, are essential to optimal development (Beebe & Lachman, 1994; Tronick, 1989). In this way, an internal model of repair is developed that communicates to the child, "When I go away, or when you are 'bad,' or when I am mad at you, I'll come back, I won't leave you. Everything will be O.K." This child, then, is confident of the mother's emotional availability and is relaxed, with exploratory behavior. In Bowlby's (1988) terms, the child experiences the mother as a "secure base" from which to explore, to separate and individuate (Mahler, 1968), and as a "safe haven" and source of dependable comfort to which he or she can return under conditions of stress. And this becomes internalized as a template for later experiences of the self and of others.

Behaviorally, because of the secure base, the securely attached child, is able to play spontaneously, to explore with a minimum of anxiety, and to turn to his or her mother when in need of soothing. In short, there are capacities for *both* attachment and separation. Not surprisingly, a marker for the securely attached adult is the demonstration of capacities for both intimacy and autonomy.

Internal Working Models of Relationships

In the course of this early developmental process, an *internal working model of relationships* (Bowlby, 1988), an attachment term, or an *object relations unit* (Masterson, 1976, 1981), an object relations concept, forms. The child internalizes a schema of who he or she is, of who others are, and of how to establish and maintain a relationship. Based on accrued interactions with the primary caregiver, these internal working models then become embedded in implicit procedural memory. And these models have been found to be remarkably constant over time. Of course, they are not absolutely immutable, because they can be altered by significant relational experiences throughout life. The concept of "earned secure" attachments (Phelps, Belsky, & Crnic, 1998) is used to describe those insecure attachment styles that are transformed into secure attachment strategies through later relationships that afford sufficient attunement and disruption–repair experiences. This is precisely why psychotherapy can work.

In the case of a secure attachment, this internal working model of relationships comprises a representation of the other that is emotionally available, and that acknowledges, affirms, approves of, attunes to, and applauds the expression of the real self. Correspondingly, the self-representation of the child feels loved, valued, and safe. Moreover, this internal relational paradigm contains a model of rupture and repair that results in the expectation that misattunements, separations, and other forms of interpersonal disruption will be repaired promptly, at best, or, at least, experienced as tolerable.

In the healthily developing infant, the real self is implicitly procedured to activate. That is, this child's implicit relational knowledge comprises procedures supportive of real-self experience and expression.

When Things Go Wrong

However, things can, and do, go wrong. The developmental trajectory and outcome are quite different for the person with a personality disorder.

Insecure Attachment

Self disorders are fundamentally attachment disorders, implicitly procedured, that disallow a healthy separation process; both the attachment and the separation capacities are impaired. So these disorders of the self reflect an *insecure attachment* system (Ainsworth et al., 1978).

Attunement

In these cases, when there is insufficient attunement to the child's real self, when the parent's agenda takes precedence over real-self needs, the child discerns, implicitly, the conditions of attachment required by the parents — clinging dependence and helplessness, mirroring the parents, performing for the parents, becoming invisible, being a problem, and so on — the implicit procedures needed to maintain an affective connection. Thus, the insecure attachment is highly conditional on suppression of the real self; the real self is procedured *not* to activate, *not* to be expressed, not *even* to be experienced. In this regard, one patient remarked, "My mom always wanted her spotlight on me, but she shined it over there, so I had to keep jumping over there to be seen. I had to keep leaving my self and become who she wanted me to be in order to feel seen by her."

Rupture–Repair Cycle

In addition, there is a failure in the internalization of an effective model of rupture and repair. In the case of the incipient personality disorder, the repair of relational disjunctures has been either inconsistent or nonexistent, *or* the repair experiences have been contingent on the activation of a false self, and so a model of "rupture–despair," rather than of rupture–repair, develops.

Abandonment Depression

Because of the conditional attachment experience and the lack of an internal rupture–repair model, the individual with a personality disorder must cope with an underlying *abandonment depression*. This corresponds to Allan Schore's (1997) depiction of early-forming internal representations of "a dysregulated-self-in-interaction-with-a-misattuning-other."

A seemingly catastrophic complex of affects, the abandonment depression is inevitably activated by separation urges and events, or by expressions of the real self. Consequently, a core dynamic develops, "the Disorders of the Self

Triad," in which self-activation stimulates depression, which, in turn, results in false-self defensive procedures. That is, self-activation leads to abandonment depression, which leads to defense (Masterson, 1976, 1981, 2000).

This abandonment depression, or "absence despair," then becomes the "underhum" of the child's experience, so the dominant theme enacted in life involves avoidance of the full experience of that dreaded dysphoric state. In other words, for the person with a personality disorder, the real self is implicitly procedured primarily to avoid activation and the consequent experience of the abandonment depression.

False Defensive Self
Because this person is psychoneurobiologically wired to expect abandonment depression, or "absence depression," if the real self is activated, a compensatory implicit relational procedure system evolves; a "defense system" emerges instead of a "self system." In other words, a *false defensive self* (Masterson, 1981, 1985, 2000), a composite of implicit relational procedures designed to maintain an attachment to the object at any cost, and thereby to avoid the experience of the abandonment depression, emerges. The infant is evolutionarily wired to go where there is connection and safety, and thus survive. Of course, these attachment-driven, nonvolitional defensive procedures are maladaptive in that they imprison the person in a self-protective posture that precludes the possibility of real-self development.

Split Working Models
Because of the insecure attachment, there is also a failure to integrate disparate internal representations of the self and the other. These patients operate not with one, but with two distinct and split internal working models of relationships — two polarized internal object relations units, two split procedural modes. According to Masterson (1976, 1981, 1993, 2000), one of these is based on the patient's false self-attachment experiences, the rewarding object relations unit or the grandiose self-omnipotent object unit or the master–slave unit. The other is rooted in the patient's experiences of nonattachment, the withdrawing object relations unit or the empty self-aggressive object unit or the self-in-exile sadistic object unit.

Reflective Function and Other Ego Capacities
Finally, Fonagy (2001a, 2001b) and Fonagy and his associates (1991, 1996) have written extensively about the role of *reflective function* (mentalization) in the development and functioning of more severe forms of psychopathology. Siegel (1999, 2001) refers to this "mindsight" as "the ability to perceive our own minds and the minds of others." This capacity enables an awareness that

others have minds, with their own feelings, thoughts, attitudes, desires, hopes, plans, intentions, and so on. This, then, enables reflection on the derivation and meaning of a behavior, rather than on the behavior only. The capacity for reflective function develops through the implicit and explicit mirroring provided by the attuned relationship with the mother, and through the differentiation process of rupture and repair, and tends to correlate with the security of attachment. Predictably, deficits in reflective function are associated with impaired self-reflection, empathy, and reality perception. And there is evidence that children and adolescents with conduct disorders, antisocial adults, and people with personality disorders, particularly, demonstrate just such deficiencies.

PSYCHOTHERAPY OF THE PERSONALITY DISORDERS

Goals of Psychotherapy

What are the goals of psychotherapy of the personality disorders? And how does attachment theory contribute to our formulation of these goals?

Reproceduring

To begin, the Masterson Approach considers the restructuring of the internal object relations and reactivation of the real self the ultimate goal of psychotherapy. A variant of this perspective, informed by attachment theory, is that reproceduring of the real self, developing a new repertoire of procedures, of new behavioral propensities, that restructures and supports activation of the real self, is the core goal. These procedures include fundamental capacities of the real self, such as spontaneity and aliveness of affect, realistic self-entitlement, self-activation, self-assertion, self-support, commitment, and the like (Masterson, 1988).

In this regard, we have a pretty good understanding of *what* happens in successful psychotherapy. That is, false-self functioning gives way to the activation of the real self. But attachment theory refines our understanding of *how* it happens. *Restructuring* and *reproceduring* are the *what* and the *how* of effective psychotherapy.

The implicit relational procedures of the person with a personality disorder effectively suppress real-self activation, and, instead, support the activation of a substitute false self. Thus, it is necessary for the patient to discover and implement new procedures, new and authentic ways of being with one's self and with others — in order to reactivate the real self.

In addition, Klein (Masterson & Klein, 1989) has postulated a subset of prerequisite goals: containment, learning, and adaptation.

Containment

Initially, the patient with a personality disorder must come to recognize, and to contain, the acting out of maladaptive, non-self-supportive, defenses From an attachment perspective, this means to abstain from the enactment of the archaic relational procedures of the false self, what Masterson (1976, 1981, 1993, 2000) refers to as "transference acting out." It is through the interruption and control of these implicitly procedured ways of being with one's self, and with others, that the patient can begin to experience the Disorders of the Self Triad in action and can start to realize that there are more adaptive, real-self ways of living and being. Thus, this containment of the false self is, in effect, a prelude to the reproceduring of the real self.

Learning

The containment of defenses leads to an understanding of the operation and meaning of the triad of the Disorders of the Self in the patient's life. In other words, it must become apparent to the patient that the abandonment depression is evoked when old, anachronistic false-self procedures are relinquished and replaced with authentic expressions of the real self. And that defenses are likely to follow.

Adaptation

The patient then must use his or her understanding of the operation of the triad to improve adaptation, to choose more self-supportive means of managing the painful affects of the abandonment depression when it is evoked by efforts to activate, to experience, or to express the real self. This is achieved (1) by letting go of obsolete internal working models that fail to support the real self; (2) by grieving the memories of relational loss, absence, neglect, or abuse that then emerge; and (3) by consciously choosing new reality-based relational procedures uncontaminated by early implicit procedural knowledge, procedures that do support the activation of the real self. Such adaptive efforts, in effect, involve the practicing, over and over, in and out of session, of the new, real-self procedures.

For instance, Brian, a young, assertive, and successful attorney, was, somewhat surprisingly, exceptionally passive and conflict-avoidant in his marriage of 15 years. But through the process of psychotherapy, he began to understand how the Disorders of the Self Triad was operative in his relationship with his wife. That is, any efforts at self-assertion or self-support in his marriage stimulated fears of abandonment, so he passively acquiesced to his perceptions of his wife's desires and expectations, effectively suppressing the activation of his real self. With this awareness, he began to represent himself by "practicing," incrementally, self-expressive, self-supportive behaviors. And, in time, this self-supportive relational style came to characterize his marriage relationship.

As containment, learning, and adaptation are achieved, a reproceduring of the real self also occurs. As the real self is attuned to, vitalized, and scaffolded, and as formerly implicit false-self procedures are relinquished, relational procedures supportive of the real self are discovered and practiced.

What are the treatment variables that further the achievement of these goals? They are both (1) relational factors (attachment theory) and (2) technical and structural factors (object relations theory) that contribute to the change process.

Relational Factors in Psychotherapy

From an attachment theory perspective, Lyons-Ruth (1998) has suggested that "something more" than technical intervention is needed to effect change in psychotherapy. In other words, what she is proposing is that psychotherapy technique alone is insufficient to promote a reparative change process; a certain quality of relational experience is also required. The relationship itself is the contextual foundation for optimally effective psychotherapy. This is, of course, reminiscent of Rogers' (1957) "necessary and sufficient conditions" for effective psychotherapy, that is, empathy, congruence, and unconditional positive regard, so-called nonspecific reparative factors operative in the process of psychotherapy.

From an attachment theory perspective, what, then, are these relational factors that may be necessary to the psychotherapy change process?

Attitude

First, it seems that an implicit attitude on the part of the therapist that communicates compassion, respect, and regard for the patient is necessary. It seems that there is a tendency for some clinicians to take a cynical attitude toward people with personality disorders — these so-called "difficult patients," particularly as consciousness and volition are attributed to their frequently arrogant, manipulative, or otherwise provocative behaviors.

However, an attitude informed by an awareness of the fundamental role of implicit relational knowledge can be an effective corrective with regard to such a perception. In reality, the person with a Disorder of the Self lives with a formidable handicap. The false defensive-self operations and the insecure attachment strategy were formed preverbally and prerationally and remain largely unconscious and nonvolitional. As such, these are rigidly maintained behavioral propensities that, although originally driven by adaptive needs, are now self-defeating and resistant to examination or self-reflection.

The patient with a personality disorder is imprisoned by a severely skewed, rigidly perpetuated, and largely nonconscious repertoire of procedures for initiating and sustaining relationships. With few perceived possibilities, these patients are destined to reenact the chaos, confusion, frustration, disappointment, emotional impoverishment, and pain of the past. In other words, the implicit relational fund of knowledge of the person with a personality disorder lacks options, other possibilities — he or she knows of nothing else. Such patients are not so much "difficult patients" as they are patients with severe difficulties. And they will continue to be unaware of other procedural possibilities until a relationship supportive of the real self and authentic attachment is provided consistently and over time. Enter the real relationship.

From the perspective of the impaired real self, the effort to survive emotionally by establishing interpersonal connections in the only way known to be possible is almost heroic. One does not ordinarily associate the word "heroic" with "Borderline" and "Narcissistic," but these patients are worthy of respect and compassion, given their underdeveloped capacities and their limited implicit knowledge of procedural possibilities. Such an attitude on the part of the therapist can be expected to communicate a recognition of the existence of the patient's impaired real self and an empathic understanding of its procedurally determined plight, and to provide implicit support for the activation of the real self. That is, the real self, historically and intrapsychically discouraged from experience and expression, is invited to emerge.

Another facet of this attitude is that of awe or wonderment. A program for early intervention with at-risk infants and toddlers is called "Watch, wait, and wonder" (Cohen, Muir, Parker, Brown, Lojkases, Muir, and Barwick (1999). The primary intervention asked requires the mother to get down on the floor with her child, and simply to "watch, wait, and wonder" about this little person, who he or she is, and what he or she might be experiencing. It appears logical that this same sort of reverent wonderment is also needed in the therapy relationship. And this can be expected to refine the therapist's attunement to the real self of the patient.

Of course, according to attachment theory, this attitude is not communicated verbally, explicitly. Rather, it is an implicit attitude that is transmitted primarily nonverbally, prosodically, affectively, from the therapist's right brain to the patient's right brain.

Attunement

A second relational factor is the therapist's attunement to the patient. Just as the infant requires affective attunement to facilitate attachment, to develop the capacity for affect regulation, and to consolidate a coherent self, the psychotherapy patient will benefit from a consistent experience of "affect synchrony" in the relationship with the psychotherapist. As the therapist tracks and attunes to the affective fluctuations of the real self and to the deep need to be seen, recognized, known, acknowledged, and corrected in a trusting and trusted relationship, a mutual, reciprocal communications process is activated implicitly between the two of them.

That is, just as the infant and the mother reciprocally influence each other's experience, the therapist and the patient are co-creating a relational experience. And the therapist must, as much as possible, be aware of his or her own subjective resonance with the patient in order to attune more accurately to the patient's internal world of experience.

Several consequences of such attunement to the patient can be expected.

First, affect attunement can be anticipated to scaffold the underdeveloped real self. Because these patients operate out of a compensatory false self, owing to insufficient attunement to the nascent real self early in life, a primary goal is the provision of conditions that support and scaffold that dormant real self.

Attachment theory is helpful in this regard in that it makes such a compelling case for the power of the attunement process in the development of the self. Just as the infant discovers his or her self in the "recognition process" of dyadic affect transactions with the mother, the patient may find his or her self "recognized" in these analogous right-brain to right-brain interactions with the therapist. The patient begins to feel known, to realize that someone has "a mind with my mind in mind." As with the periodic experience of something like: "I think I see that you see me, that you really get me, can this really be?," so with the repeated experience of such attunement by the therapist, the patient begins to experience and clarify the real self.

However, and this is extremely important, it is imperative to distinguish attunement to the real self of the patient from attunement to the false defensive self (to be discussed further later).

Second, in addition to supporting the real self, the therapist's accurate attunement to the affective experience of the patient has been demonstrated to enhance affect regulation. When people "feel felt" and known, they are soothed and calmed, and those with personality disorders frequently demonstrate an underdeveloped capacity for effective regulation of affect. Typically, they seek to regulate affect through false self-attachment systems — clinging, compliance, mirroring an idealized other, seeking mirroring from others, or regulation of distance in relationships — through defenses. Thus, activation of the real self is disallowed.

The therapist's attunement to the patient, then, both enhances affect regulation (which, incidentally, fosters attachment to the therapist) and lays the relational foundation for clarification and the reproceduring of the real self.

Therapeutic Space

Typically, attunement is considered an active verbal process in which someone feels deeply the affective experience of someone else. But there is also a form of quiet, active attunement that is sensitive to the other's need for space, for separation, and that, therefore, regulates the level of activity in the interaction accordingly. This is probably comparable to the infant's need to be "alone in the presence of an other."

Remember, owing to an early deficit in attunement to the real self, the person with a personality disorder has developed a false defensive self designed to feel attached and to avoid feeling abandoned, but at a cost to the development of the real self. So, these patients are clearly in need of a relational experience that will allow them to be real.

Masterson (1993) has posed the challenge succinctly:

> How does the therapist go about the task of creating the conditions that help the patient . . . begin to rebuild and reactivate a real sense of self? It is important to keep in mind that a therapist cannot direct, suggest, seduce, threaten, attack, or torture a patient to self-activate. If it happens, it will be because the patient does it. The therapist can only create the conditions that make it possible (p. 67).

One of those conditions is the provision of space for the patient to be with himself or herself.

Summers (2001) has put it this way: "Creation of a new self-structure requires a relationship that provides ample room for the emergence of new ways of being and relating" (p. 639). Thus, there is a need in the therapy relationship for "open spaces," for times to be alone in the presence of the other, to be able to focus on the self, on real-self experience, and to explore alternative, more authentic procedures for being with one's self and with others — while the therapist "watches, waits, and wonders."

In these moments, the attuned therapist offers "emotional presence," while, at the same time, allowing the patient to be alone in his or her company. The therapist, then, needs only to wait and watch for that "spontaneous gesture," an interest, a desire, a wish, a longing, or a feeling, perhaps never before expressed, perhaps never before allowed to be experienced in another's presence. These are manifestations of the underdeveloped real self, to be expressed in the moment, or at a later time. This experience of self-focus in the attuned presence of the therapist, in turn, contributes to the emergence of a relational procedure that shores up and begins to reprocedure the real self. The therapist's implied message is, "It's all right for you to take your time to focus on your self. I will wait with you."

After many years of psychotherapy with a number of therapists, a woman patient mused with her current therapist about how surprising was the increasing clarity of her experience of herself over the course of several months of treatment. In her words, "I think it has to do with the fact that you don't talk much, and that I don't feel any pressure to talk, that you allow me to be quiet and to think and feel within myself. I've never experienced that before." And she proceeded to elaborate on early memories of her mother's intrusiveness.

Rupture–Repair Cycle

As is true of the infant–mother relationship, attunement and space alone are insufficient to support and reprocedure the real self. Just as the infant's real self also requires repetitive rupture–repair experiences, this is also true for the psychotherapy of patients with attachment deficits.

One component of the implicit relational knowing characteristic of all personality pathology is an underdeveloped internal model of relational repair and a corresponding implicit expectation that the connection will not be restored following its rupture. Thus, the need for the gradual internalization of such a model of disruption and repair is critical to the emergence and consolidation of the real self.

Now, it is likely that relational ruptures are created at two levels in the course of psychotherapy. First, there are the *intentional* misattunements that occur when interventions focused on defenses create a disruption of the patient's false-self relationship to the therapist, of the patient's transference acting out of early inactive procedures. For example, bringing to the patient's attention a mirroring, or a distance-regulating, or a clinging, or a detached attachment style promotes an experience of separation that is disruptive of any illusion of attunement to the false defensive self. However, the possibility of repair is afforded by just such moments in the encounter, if the therapist is willing to acknowledge the rupture empathically and to attune to the patient's real-self experience.

Thus, the therapist might say to a patient with a Narcissistic disorder: "I sense that my question about your experience disappointed you because I was not understanding you perfectly, so you distanced from me, and then inferred that I am incompetent. But I really am interested in learning more about how that experience was difficult for you."

Second, in addition to the calculated misattunements to the false self, there are also the therapist's inevitable *unintended* misattunements to the patient's real self that result in pain, fear, frustration, or disappointment — tastes of the abandonment depression. And these, too, require the therapist to ad-dress them directly, to clarify misperceptions or misunderstandings, to acknowl-edge their reality, and, when appropriate, to apologize for the failure in em-pathy or understanding.

Of course, relational disruption stimulates an experience of the abandon-ment depression for the patient with a self disorder. So these occurrences not only afford repeated experiences of relational repair to be internalized as part of a secure attachment, but they also offer the therapist the opportunity in the transference, over and over, for explicit and implicit "being with" the patient in his or her abandonment depression. The patient's affect regulation, en-hanced by the therapist's presence, and by the experience of relational repair, enables the patient to encounter the abandonment depression and separation anxiety in the context of a relationship, in the context of attachment. This "safe haven" not only renders the painful affective experience tolerable, and, therefore, amenable to exploration, but over time it also alters the internal working model of relationship itself, augmenting it with a model of disruption and repair, and gradually restructuring the real self.

For example, a 45-year-old woman patient with a Narcissistic disorder, after several years of therapy, revealed to her therapist that she had been astounded to discover that she and the therapist could have misunderstandings and conflicts, and that these could actually be clarified and resolved. She had no recollection of such experiences in her family of origin, and, in fact, until her experience in therapy, had never entertained the possibility that differ-ences might not be destructive and unsolvable.

A Real Relationship
Because implicit relational procedures are developed in a relationship, they must also be reprocedured in the relationship. Patients occasionally suggest that the relationship is not "real," but that the therapist working from this theoretical model is offering a new attachment experience, a real, albeit par-tial, relationship. Of course, the frame and therapeutic neutrality do impose limits on the relationship with the patient — the relationship is not symmet-rical — but the presence of the therapist is real.

As Masterson (1985) has written,

> The therapist must be a real object or person, not in the sense of
> sharing his personal life but rather by manifesting an emotionally
> warm interest in the patient's problems, sympathizing with his real
> life defeats, and congratulating him on his triumphs, and being em-
> phatic about the fact that coping and adaptation are vital to emo-
> tional survival (p. 55).

The relationship is real, because the real self of the therapist is relating to the patient's real self.

Schore (2003) has suggested that self-revelation by the therapist is constant, occurring at a right-brain to right-brain level of communication. If this is true, therapists work in the nude, emotionally and psychologically — they are exposed continuously.

Thus, the therapist's engagement of his or her real self in the relationship with the patient is essential for the provision of a new and healthier attachment experience to be internalized as a fresh "way of being with the other," a newly reprocedured internal whole object relations unit.

But, of course, it is not only the real self of the therapist that is engaged in the relationship; the real self of the patient is invited to the encounter, as well. In fact, the entire therapy enterprise, as formulated from the Masterson perspective, is designed to evoke the experience and expression of the patient's real self, both in the treatment session and in everyday life.

To elaborate, the real self can only be reactivated in mutual, reciprocal, coexperienced relational moments of vitality affect, or in Stern's (1998) terms, in "moments of meeting." These are those fleeting, affectively alive, real-self to real-self encounters that occasionally punctuate the therapy process. These "now moments" may occur serendipitously — when there is a flash of spontaneity, affect, or self-assertion — when there is real self expression. Or they may take place when the patient chooses to let go of old relational procedures; that is, when the abandonment depression is awakened by containment of defense.

Also, interventions focused on defenses can, and often do, elicit affective responses to the therapist. For example, the Borderline patient can be expected to experience frustration, or rejection, or anger if the therapist confronts a defense that anticipates a caretaking response. But there is always an implicit, and sometimes explicit, invitation for the patient to share, and to explore, these feelings evoked toward the therapist, as well as those associated with the abandonment depression proper. At those moments of open exploration of transferential feelings, the patient is responding to the therapist with the real self, as well.

These slender spaces, micromoments of shared vitality affect, signal the entrance of the real self into the relationship, because it is in these fleeting instants that the old relational procedures are sufficiently disrupted to allow for a moment of meeting, real self to real self.

Such a moment may be no more than a nearly imperceptible startle, or a pause, or an instant of eye contact, but it is precisely at such times that the real relationship is experienced most intensely and that new relational procedures are practiced. And each of these moments becomes one tiny dot in the emergent visibility of the previously imperceptible self.

Further, these moments, attended to by the therapist, eventually can be brought to the attention of the patient as well, and a time of co-reflection can ensue. "You don't seem to be as afraid to tell me that I frustrate you, as you have been in the past. Did you notice what you just said to me? Isn't that interesting? You never used to tell me of your disappointment in me." "I know. It's because ..."

The therapist, then, is offering a qualitatively unique relationship to the patient. The attuned encounter with the therapist invites the experience and expression of the patient's real self, perhaps for the first time with persistence and consistency. Through the real relationship with the therapist, a new object relations unit, or internal working model, one that is supportive of the budding real self, is grown. This real-self to real-self connection fosters new procedures, new ways of being and relating, that support the activation of the real self. It is an altogether new attachment experience, what attachment theorists refer to as "earned secure attachments" (Cohen et al., 1999).

This new internal working model of relationships, this new, healthier object relations unit, dilutes the potency of the earlier pathological attachments. In Masterson's (1985) words, "The patient internalizes the therapist as a new, positive object representation along with his positive, supportive attitude toward the patient's individuation and self-representation of being adequate, based on self-assertive efforts at adaptation" (p. 61).

Or, in attachment theory terms, Sable (2000) suggests: "The working model of the therapeutic relationship eventually exerts dominance over hurtful experiences and models of the past, countering the patient's image of himself as unlovable and unworthy of secure affectional ties" (p. 333).

And because this relational practice with the therapist is experienced as both a surprising and a satisfying taste, it also fuels the hunger for more real self-relating outside of the therapy relationship. The patient, then, is likely to seek to establish and enjoy more meaningful relationships in everyday life, to practice the real-self relational procedures experienced in the relationship with the therapist. Such extra-therapy self-activation is one evidence of the efficacy of treatment.

This chapter so far has not addressed technique, *what* the therapist *does*. Rather, it has focused on *who* the therapist *is*, on how the therapist is in relationship to the patient.

To summarize: The psychotherapy of the personality disorders involves a right-brain to right-brain relationship that implicitly, prosodically, and nonconsciously reprocedures and restructures the patient's internal working model of relationships, or object relations units, in the vitality moments of the therapy process. It is within this relationship that the real, core self is born into awareness — through accurate attunement and attention to the spontaneous gestures of the patient, to flashes of the abandonment depression, and through a kind and careful invitation to examine together the meaning of those moments. Then, by the practice of experiencing and reflecting on these vitality moments in the therapy hour, archaic implicit relational procedures and their related false-self behavioral constellations come to be seen as less necessary, and something new emerges out of something old. And as these old procedured defenses are found to be dispensable, they atrophy through lack of use, and the newly found relational procedures are strengthened through practice.

STRUCTURAL AND TECHNICAL FACTORS

Some attachment theory approaches to psychotherapy rely almost exclusively on the mutual, reciprocal relational dynamics between the patient and the therapist for therapeutic efficacy. In such approaches, the essence of psychotherapy theoretically is the provision of a new attachment relationship that, in and of itself, is able to revise the internal working model of relationships through implicit interactions with the affectively engaged therapist. Thus, the right-brain to right-brain relationship *is* the agent of reparation.

Lyons-Ruth's (1998) notion of "something more," however, implies the operation of "something else." That is, the "something more" of sensitive, accurate, and consistent attunement to the patient and of repeated experiences of the "rupture–repair" process, if offered in the absence of vigilant attention to structural factors and intervention strategies, is likely to limit the efficacy of treatment. Implicit right-brain to right-brain transactions and transformations alone are not sufficient. The therapy process involves both implicit and explicit experiences — we have two cerebral hemispheres!

Dr. Masterson (1985), while suggesting the need for the therapist to be real, warmly interested, and empathic with the patient, added that the therapist also must be "emphatic about the fact that coping and adaptation are vital to emotional survival" (p. 55). This is to suggest that, beyond the relational qualities discussed, there are structural and technical elements of the psychotherapy venture that are necessary to foster the reproceduring of the patient's real self.

For example, consider the supervisee who related a case of a young woman with a Borderline personality disorder who suffered extraordinary separation sensitivity. Exquisitely aware of this woman's fears and unhappiness, in general, the therapist, a sensitive and compassionate woman, consistently had been mirroring her patient's feelings of helplessness and hopelessness. However, to the therapist's consternation, the patient seemed to become increasingly more helpless, more hopeless, and, over time, agoraphobic. Feeling deeply for the patient's plight, the therapist began going to her home for therapy sessions, driving her to various destinations (providing "systematic *in vivo* desensitization" experiences), arranging extra sessions, engaging in lengthy telephone conversations initiated by the patient, and tolerating escalating verbal abuse from her. And shortly before this consultation, the patient had become enraged at the therapist for undergoing emergency surgery, and so "abandoning" her.

Conceptually, and in fact, this well-meaning therapist had been countertransference acting out by resonating with, and attuning to, the patient's projections of her false defensive self. By failing to address the real self, enfeebled and impaired as it was, the therapist not only had attuned to the *feelings* of helplessness, but also had supported both the patient's *belief* that she was helpless and her *enactment* of implicit false-self procedures. In other words, the patient had been transference acting out, and the therapist had colluded with the related projections.

What went wrong? Attunement to the most obvious affective presentation of the patient runs the risk of the therapist's colluding with the patient's false-self projections. That is, if the crucial distinction between false-defensive-self procedures and the activation of the real self is ignored, the therapist may unwittingly attune to the affective acting out of the patient's false self and fail to address the behaviors that interfere with the emergence of the real self. Thus, attunement alone may unintentionally support transference acting out on the part of the patient and encourage countertransference acting out by the therapist. From an attachment theory perspective, archaic implicit relational procedures, originally adaptive given the internal conditions of attachment, unwittingly may be supported and reinforced. From this perspective, then, we always need to be aware of the critical distinction between the real self and the false self. We need to see beyond the false defensive self into the potential real self. And this empathic way that we see what is real invites the real self to "show up."

Further, according to the Masterson model, it is important for the patient to attain an explicit, conscious, verbal understanding of his or her fundamental psychodynamics. That is, by tracking the operation of the triad, the therapist brings to the patient's attention the use of defense for protection from the full impact of the abandonment depression and separation anxiety occasioned by the activation of the real self. Masterson (1976, p. 101) conceptualizes this as providing the observing ego with an awareness of the link between self-activation, dysphoria, and defense. This, of course, requires the engagement of the left brain and a transformation of implicit procedural memory into explicit, semantic knowledge. Then, it is hoped that the patient will come to understand how the compensatory attachment system has functioned to protect him or her from the experience of the abandonment depression.

For example, the patient, sobbing, says, "All these years, and I never realized that I shielded myself from my father's control by detaching myself from him. And that's what I've done with everybody. It's no wonder that I've never had even one close relationship in my whole life." This explicit awareness resulted in subsequent explicit efforts to be more open with others, in spite of the patient's fears. In this way, the process invites the left brain, as well as the right, to participate in the reproceduring process.

So, although relational factors are undoubtedly the "something more" in the psychotherapy formula, and are certainly "necessary," they are not "sufficient." What else is needed?

Stance of Psychotherapy

The stance of psychotherapy communicates the assumption that the patient *does* have the capacity, albeit underdeveloped, for self-activation, self-assertion, self-initiative, and self-soothing. It reflects both the therapist's belief in the real self and expectations that are altogether incompatible with the patient's false-self procedures.

Therapeutic Neutrality

Therapeutic neutrality has nothing to do with a cold, detached, indifferent, dispassionate attitude on the part of the therapist — a common misconception. Rather, it is conceived specifically in relationship to the projections of the patient's false self that so profoundly color interactions in therapy. By avoiding collusion with the patient's transference acting out, therapeutic neutrality enables the therapist to attune to the real, previously invisible self of the patient, and to provide practice of the rupture–repair experience.

Thus, whereas the therapist must be neutral relative to the patient's false-self projections, he or she must never be neutral relative to a belief in the real self and its latent capacities. Consistent with the stance of psychotherapy, self-activation must be expected.

Frame of Psychotherapy

The frame is a set of policies and procedures for the practice of therapy that encourages activation of the real self and that limits acting out of the false self. As such, the frame concretizes therapeutic neutrality and the stance of therapy. It is a concrete means for the therapist to communicate to the patient's real self an expectation of self-activation and self-responsibility.

For a new internal working model to be shaped, the old procedures must be relinquished, and new self-supportive procedures implemented. The stance, neutrality, and frame, furnish the reality expectations, structure, and limits that discourage irresponsible, helpless, entitled, or distancing relating. At the same time, they also provide a vehicle that supports new ways of being that involve real-self experience and expression. Thus, reproceduring of the real self begins in the empathic, attuned relationship — but with limits and expectations.

Diagnosis-Specific Interventions

But in terms of explicit communication, how does one penetrate or bypass the false self in order to gain access to the real self? Masterson (1981, 1993, 2000) has proposed differential developmental determinants for the Borderline, Narcissistic, and Schizoid personality disorders, as well as diagnosis-specific interventions of choice. He has contended further that the particular intrapsychic morphology and defensive false selves of these disorders is what informs the clinician as to what is the most efficacious intervention strategy for each. Borrowing from the lexicon of attachment theory, accurate attunement to the real self requires a focus and form of communication that is specific to each of the personality disorders.

The purpose of the interventions is to speak to the patient's real self and its basic needs. But the portal to the real self varies across the different disorders, based on their different needs. For instance, the central implicit relational procedure, the false defensive self, of the "separation sensitive" Borderline patient with a personality disorder requires the avoidance of self-activation and the enactment of incompetence, interpersonal compliance and clinging, and passivity, in general. Consequently, the sensitive offering of confrontations of maladaptive defenses attunes most accurately to the fundamental need of the real self to assume responsibility for his or her life. It communicates, "I believe in your ability to do it for yourself, to think for yourself."

Of course, these interventions initially won't feel like attunement, because they create ruptures of the false-self connections. In time, however, the resonance with the needs of the real self will become apparent to the patient, and there will be the clear sense that the therapist is right.

The conditions of attachment for the Narcissistic personality disorder render these people extraordinarily dependent on others for a sense of personal value and well-being. Consequently, owing to this exquisite "esteem-sensitivity," they tend to be most responsive to interpretations of Narcissistic vulnerability that communicate an appreciation of both the fragility of self-esteem and the self-protective function of the defenses against that fragility.

In contrast, the Schizoid patient is intensely "safety sensitive" because of the twin fears of being controlled and of being hopelessly isolated. Consequently, interpretations of the "Schizoid dilemma," and, eventually, of "Schizoid compromises," speak empathically to the Schizoid patient's real self and the felt need for interpersonal safety.

Thus, verbal interventions, when integrated by the patient, enable a con-

scious awareness of the operation of the false defensive self that suppresses, or limits, the activation of the real self. In this way, the implicit is rendered explicit; the left brain gains access to the right brain, bilateral brain function is enhanced, and the internal model is discovered.

In this regard, it is not just that interventions interrupt the patient's defenses, allowing affects to emerge. That *is* mutative. But it is also that this occurs in the context of a relationship that becomes internalized.

To summarize, with respect to psychotherapy, one of the gifts of attachment theory is an appreciation of the nuances of the implicit, right-brain relationship between the patient and the therapist. For instance, theirs is a refined understanding of the power and imprisonment of the implicit relational procedures laid down early in life. Accordingly, an attitude toward the patient of compassion, respect, and wonder is engendered in the therapist. This, in turn, is communicated prosodically, nonverbally, to the patient. The attachment orientation also emphasizes the importance of noncontingent space for an exclusive focus on, and exploration of, the experience of the real self — in the comforting context of a safe relationship. There is an emphasis, too, on the necessity for repeated experiences of the sensitive and timely repair of ruptures in the relationship. Finally, an appreciation of the real relationship between the therapist and the patient enrichs our understanding of the therapeutic significance of the quality of relationship offered in the psychotherapy experience.

From the theoretical perspective of the Masterson Approach, however, relational factors alone are insufficient. In addition, the entire psychotherapy process must be designed and structured in such a way as to support the emergence and reproceduring of the patient's real self. This includes a stance on the part of the therapist that expects self-support, self-assertion, and self-soothing from the patient — self-activation, in general. Additionally, there must be therapeutic neutrality, the therapist's unwillingness to collaborate with the patient's false-self projections. That is, the therapist must speak always to the real self, and thus communicate a belief in its existence and capacities. Further, the psychotherapy endeavor must be structured in such a way, through the use of the frame, as to provide a benchmark for real-self adaptive functioning and to discourage the reenactment of archaic relational procedures that have undermined the development and activation of the real self. And, finally, verbal interventions addressing the fundamental needs of the patient's real self must communicate explicitly an understanding of the presence of the ruinous constraints of the false self *and* of the underlying longing to experience, and to express, the self that is real.

Another way of thinking about this is that therapists, through explicit interventions, are "showing *what*" it means to activate the real self. But of equal importance is the likelihood that the therapist, through implicit communications in the real relationship, is also "showing *how*," demonstrating how to be real. Through the stance, the frame, tracking the triad, and verbal interventions, false-self adaptation and real-self activation become defined. But it is through the relationship that real-self presence and activation are demonstrated. It seems that object relations therapists have been inclined to emphasize "showing *what*," whereas attachment-oriented therapists have tended to stress "showing *how*," demonstrating how to be real.

In essence, this approach to the psychotherapy of the personality disorders is intended to offer both the relational and the technical and structural factors necessary to reprocedure the impaired real self for experience and expression. As a therapist, one's being speaks. How we communicate is as important as what we communicate. But while we must be who we are, we must also say and do what must be said and done. Therapy involves both the left brain and the right brain, both the head and the heart, both technique and mystery.

References

Ainsworth, M., Blehar, M., Waters, E., & Wall, S. (1978). *Patterns of Attachment: A Psychological Study of the Strange Situation.* Hillsdale, NJ: Erlbaum.

Beebe, B., & Lachman, F. M. (1994). Representations and internalization in infancy: Three principles of salience. *Psychoanalytic Psychology, 11,* 127–165.

Bowlby, J. (1988). *A Secure Base: Parent–Child Attachment and Healthy Human Development.* New York: Basic Books.

Cassidy, J., & Shaver, P. (Eds.). *Handbook of Attachment: Theory, Research, and Clinical Applications.* New York: Guilford.

Cohen, N., Muir, E., Parker, C., Brown, M., et al. (1999). Watch, wait, and wonder: Testing the effectiveness of a new approach to mother–infant psychotherapy. *Infant Mental Health Journal, 20*(4), 429–451.

Fonagy, P. (2001a). The roots of violence in the failure of mentalization: A psychoanalytic perspective. Presented at the Seattle Psychoanalytic Society and Institute Conference on Disorganized Attachment, Youth and Violence — Etiology, Detection, Prevention and Treatment.

Fonagy, P. (2001b). *Attachment Theory and Psychoanalysis.* New York: Other Press.

Fonagy, P., Steele, M., Steele, H., Moran, G. S., & Higgitt, A. C. (1991). The capacity for understanding mental states: The reflective self in parent and child and its significance for security of attachment. *Infant Mental Health Journal, 12*(3), 201–218.

Fonagy, P., & Target, M. (1996). Playing with reality: I. Theory of mind and the normal development of psychic reality. *International Journal of Psycho-Analysis, 77,* 217–233.

Goodman, G. (2002). *The Internal World and Attachment.* Hillsdale, NJ: Analytic Press.

Holmes, J. (1996). *Attachment, Intimacy, Autonomy: Using Attachment Theory in Adult Psychotherapy.* Northvale, NJ: Jason Aronson.

Holmes, J. (2001). *The Search for the Secure Base: Attachment Theory and Psychoanalysis.* Philadelphia: Taylor & Francis.

Karen, R. (1994). *Becoming Attached.* New York: Warner.

Lyons-Ruth, K. (1991). Rapprochement or approchement: Mahler's theory reconsidered from the vantage point of recent research in early attachment relationships. *Psycho-analytic Psychology, 8,* 1–23.

Lyons-Ruth, K. (1998). Implicit relational knowing: Its role in development and psychoanalytic treatment. *Infant Mental Health Journal, 19*(3), 282–289.

Mahler, M. (1968). *On Human Symbiosis and the Vicissitudes of Individuation.* New York: International Universities Press.

Masterson, J. F. (1976). *Psychotherapy of the Borderline Adult: A Developmental Approach.* New York: Brunner/Mazel.

Masterson, J. F. (1981). *The Narcissistic and Borderline Disorders: An Integrated Developmental Approach.* New York: Brunner/Mazel.

Masterson, J. F. (1985). *The Real Self: A Developmental, Self, and Object Relations Approach.* New York: Brunner/Mazel.

Masterson, J. F. (1988). *The Search for the Real Self.* New York: Free Press.

Masterson, J. F. (1993). *The Emerging Self: A Developmental, Self, and Object Relations Approach to the Treatment of the Closet Narcissistic Disorder of the Self.* New York: Brunner/Mazel.

Masterson, J. F. (2000). *The Personality Disorders.* Phoenix: Zeig, Tucker.

Masterson, J. F., & Klein, R. (Eds.) (1989). *Psychotherapy of the Disorders of the Self.* New York: Brunner/Mazel.

Phelps, J. L., Belsky, J., & Crnic, K. (1998). Earned security, daily stress, and parenting: A comparison of five alternative models. *Development and Psychopathology, 10,* 21–38.

Rogers, C. (1957). The necessary and sufficient conditions of therapeutic personality change. *Journal of Consulting Psychology, 21,* 95–103.

Sable, P. (2000). *Attachment and Adult Psychotherapy.* Northvale, NJ: Jason Aronson.

Sander, L. W. (1965). Interactions of recognition and the developmental processes of the second eighteen months of life. Presented at Tufts University Medical School, Boston.

Sander, L. W. (1991). Recognition process: Specificity and organization in early human development. Presented at University of Massachusetts conference, The Psychic Life of the Infant.

Schore, A. (1994). *Affect Regulation and the Origin of the Self.* Hillsdale, NJ: Erlbaum.

Schore, A. (1997). Interdisciplinary research as a source of clinical models. In M. Moskowitz, C. Monk, C. Kaye, & S. Ellman (Eds.), *The Neurological and Developmental Basis for Psychotherapeutic Intervention.* New York: Jason Aronson.

Schore, A. (2003). The right hemisphere is dominant in clinical work: Implications of recent neuroscience for clinicians. Presentation at the University of Washington.

Siegel, D. (1999). *The Developing Mind: Toward a Neurobiology of Interpersonal Experience*. New York: Guilford.

Siegel, D. (2001). Toward an interpersonal neurobiology of the developing mind: Attachment relationships, "mindsight," and neural integration. *Infant Mental Health Journal*, 22(1–2), 67–94.

Stern, D. (1985). *The Interpersonal World of the Infant*. New York: Basic Books.

Stern, D. (1998). The process of therapeutic change involving implicit knowledge: Some implications of developmental observations for adult psychotherapy. *Infant Mental Health Journal*, 19(3), 300–308.

Summers, F. (2001). What I do with what you give me: Therapeutic action as the creation of meaning. *Psychoanalytic Psychology*, 18(4), 635–655.

Tronick, E. Z. (1989). Emotions and emotional communication in infants. *American Psychologist*, 44(2), 112–119.

Winnicott, D. (1988). *The Maturational Processes and the Facilitating Environment*. New York: International Universities Press.

7

Couples Therapy:
Movement From Dependence on the
False Self to a Real Relationship

KEN SEIDER, PH.D.

THE REAL SELF

The real self has come increasingly to the fore in the work with Disorders of the Self. Therefore, it is important to be able to distinguish a false-self organization from the real self. In 1960, Winnicott wrote a paper. "Ego Distortions in Terms of True and False Self," in which he addressed the issue of the true and false self and emphasized the dangers of conducting an analysis on the basis of the false self. False-self organization, he stated, is often associated with a high intellect and as a substitute of cognitive for true thinking — that is, left-brain thinking for an integrated left/right-brain thinking.

Dr. Masterson's concept of the real self is integrated into a more precise developmental schema. It is tied precisely to differentiated false-self organizations, and outlines the functions and capacities of the self that are developed in the individual on the way to libidinal self and object constancy. Very briefly, the capacities of the real self are spontaneity, aliveness of affect, self-entitlement, self-activation, assertion and support, acknowledgment of self-activation and maintenance of self-esteem, the capacity to soothe painful affects, a continuity of self, an ability to commit and be committed, and a capacity for creativity, as well as intimacy and autonomy, which are very closely linked. One cannot be intimate if one is not separate. Clearly, these capacities contribute to a person's being able to form a healthy relationship with an appropriate partner, whereas deficits will cause difficulties and handicaps in the formation of the partnership.

Clinically, the individual with a healthy real self feels a sense of continuity, stability, and mutuality in the experience of the self with, and without, others, both maturely attached and comfortably self-regulating. This chapter will stress the notion that attachment research and the advances in neurobiology, principally the work of Allan Schore, add to our understanding of the development of the real self and its pathology. Furthermore, these advances have profound clinical significance in the treatment of Disorders of the Self in psychoanalytic couples therapy.

ATTACHMENT

Bowlby, a British psychiatrist and psychoanalyst, and the originator of attachment research, alienated himself from both the Freudians and the Kleinians, and was a lone voice in the wilderness. He relied primarily on the work of ethnologists, applying it to human beings, and speculated that attachment was a biologically based experience. He was misunderstood and quickly dismissed by his colleagues in London, although his efforts are proving to be one of the great contributions to the understanding of development, and also to psychoanalysis. Bowlby noticed that when infants were separated from their parents for long periods of time, their behavior changed, and then when they were reunited with the parents, they seemed to be attached in a different way.

Ainsworth, a psychologist using Bowlby's work, developed a way of objectively testing for the security of attachment, which she called the "strange situation." In the strange situation, the mother and the infant are in a room. When a stranger enters the room, the mother and infant remain. The mother then leaves the room, comes back to the room, and leaves the room again, and the infant's reactions are observed. An attachment rating system was developed on the basis of these observations.

The secure attached infant shows signs of missing the parent on the first separation and cries during the second separation. The child will greet the parent actively, will crawl to the parent at once, and usually seeks to be held, but after a brief contact, settles down and quickly returns to play.

The avoidant attached infant looks like a pseudo-mature child. The infant does not cry on separation, but continues to play with toys throughout the procedure; actively ignores and avoids the parent on reunion; moves away from the parent, turning away or leaning away when picked up; and no expressions of anger or distress are present. It is as though the child is not affected by the comings and goings of the parent. Notable, if you were to attach these two infants to monitors and analyze their blood for coritsol levels, you would find that, on a physiological level, their responses were the same, although their behaviors were dramatically different.

The third category is the resistent–ambivalent. This infant is preoccupied with the parent throughout the procedure, seeming to be actively angry, and alternating seeking and resisting the parent, pushing and pulling. When the parent returns, the infant fails to settle down. He or she cannot resume exploration or play and continues to focus on the parent and to cry. Whereas the secure child is very distressed at the separation, he or she is easily comforted and able to reorganize and to resume play. The resistant–ambivalent cannot be comforted, and there is very little holding.

Mary Main, Ph.D., a student of Ainsworth, has continued the attachment research, bringing it to the representational level. She devised an instrument called the "adult attachment inventory" whereby an adult's responses in a structured interview can provide a rating of attachment. These rating styles are secure/autonomous, dismissing, and preoccupied. Another large category is that of disorganized individuals, but it will not be included here because they are much more troubled and disturbed than the patients that I will present in couples therapy.

The secure-attachment adult exhibits a coherent and collaborative attitude while the speaker describes attachment-related experiences and their affects; whether these affects are favorable or unfavorable, the subject values attachment and is able to maintain objectivity regarding any particular experience or relationship.

The adult who demonstrates a dismissive pattern in the interview normalizes and gives a positive description of his or her parents (i.e., excellent, very normal mother), but these categorizations are essentially unsupported, or are contradicted by specific incidents. Negative experiences are said to have little or no effect. The transcripts of these individuals are short, and also show a lack of memory — so they are denying any negativity and are pseudo-positive in their orientation to their past and their history. The preoccupied pattern is equivalent to that of the resistant/ambivalent infant, is preoccupied with experiences. They seem to be angry, confused; they are passive, fearful; they feel overwhelmed; their sentences become entangled grammatically or are couched in psychological jargon. Their transcripts, contrary to those of the dismissive, are very long, and often include many irrelevant facts.

The importance of the adult attachment rating is that from it one can predict, with a high degree of accuracy and reliability, that the attachment style of the adult will also be that of their children, even those who have not yet been conceived. Researchers have demonstrated convincingly that this is not a genetic transmission, but a psychological phenomenon that is transmitted multigenerationally. Thus, the ability to intervene with couples who had insecure attachments and to help them to establish more secure ones benefits not only the couples themselves, but also their offspring and family for generations to come.

What are the ingredients of a secure attachment? Peter Fonagy (2000), a psychoanalyst and infant attachment researcher in London, has presented the view that it is the capacity of the mother to mentalize the infant that makes the difference between secure and insecure attachment in the mother, and also in the child. This mentalized affectivity is composed of three elements: The mother is able to identify affect in herself and in the infant, to modulate affect in herself and in the infant, and to express affect in herself and to facilitate it in the infant. It is this capacity for mentalization that those children who are insecurely attached lack, and that the mothers also lack.

In working with couples, I try to increase each couple's capacity, both individually and as a unit, to be able to engage in mentalization (to use Fonagy's phrase), or to engage in symbolic thinking (to use the Kleinan notion), or to assume the position of the third person (to use Ronald Britton's notion), or to be on the way to self and object constancy (to use Masterson and Mahler's phrase), and to base the foundation of the personality on the real self, as opposed to the false-self organization of the personality disorders.

NEUROBIOLOGY OF THE SELF: ALLAN SCHORE

Allan Schore, in his three books on affect regulation (1994, 2003a, 2003b), has integrated, updated, and synthesized a wealth of neurobiologic research with psychoanalytic observations and concepts, and has really advanced our understanding of how the infant's environment affects the neurobiologic development of the brain. There is an interaction between caregiver and infant that will facilitate certain developments, but not others. He has shown that neurons that fire together live together, and that those that don't fire together don't survive. Much of infant caregiver communication takes place during the infant's first three years of life, and Schore has demonstrated convincingly how this is primarily right-hemisphere communication — the mother's right hemisphere to the infant's right hemisphere. Right-hemisphere functioning is primarily outside of conscious awareness. So much of what is occurring in the first three years of life is not directly accessible to explicit memory or verbal description.

Dr. Schore states that at 10 to 12 months of age, the infant's prefrontal orbital cortex undergoes a significant maturational change, which correlates with Mahler's practicing period. These changes, along with the mother's mentalizing, have a direct impact on the growth of the right orbital prefrontal cortex, where the capacity for internalized object relational units exists; that is, representations of others and the self in interaction with a linking affect.

Dr. Schore has convincingly marshalled neurobiologic evidence demonstrating how the environment stimulates the development of certain potentialities while eliminating others. He has placed affect regulation at the center in his model of the development of the self and its regulation. In his recent books, he has outlined neurobiologic models for dissociation and projective identification that are compelling and illuminating. At this point in time, it is becoming clearer that the dysregulation of affect is of central importance in the treatment of Disorders of the Self.

Dr. Masterson, for more than 30 years, has placed affect at the center of his model, and his abandonment depression is receiving further confirmation in neurobiology. The experience that he has called the "abandonment depression" most likely is located in the right hemisphere of the brain and is largely outside of the patient's awareness. Despite the fact that it is a powerful motivator of behavior. The autobiographical schematas that shape the false self are preconscious or unconscious and are not easily influenced by the higher cortical activity of the left brain (that is, language and conscious will).

Schore has outlined how psychoanalytic psychotherapy intervenes in the right hemisphere at a level similar to that where the mother intervened, and that a good therapeutic relationship can develop compensatory structures at the level of neurons that will make up for early developmental deficits.

Based on my work with couples, it is my contention that in a primary relationship — be it marriage or a committed partnership — deep unconscious attachments are activated; that the dysfunctional attachments, the insecure attachments that exist in each individual, are eventually activated; and that it is a biologically based attachment system that is being dealt with in couples therapy.

By activating intense affective states in psychoanalytic therapy, couples will rely on those attachment configurations, as well as on affect regulation that is deeply embedded in the unconscious/right hemisphere of the brain. Although they will behave in a maladaptive fashion, the activation of these units in the couple provides entrance into the couples system amd thereby the therapist can transform an insecure attachment into a secure one. This is what the attachment researchers call "earned secure attachment." If the therapist is able to "mentalize" (that is, to quote Fonagy) the couple to speak the language of the organization of the Disorder of the Self, as well as to model a real attachment, he or she is presumed to have the capacity for self and object constancy, the capacity to "mentalize," and to be an integrated, real, spontaneous, alive, creative individual. The treatment then provides for experiences that allow for the emergence of real-self secure attachments, as well as new capacities of the self and other in affect regulation, and to become less and less reliant on false-self adaptation.

NARCISSISTIC DISORDERS OF THE SELF

In the developmental self and object relations approach, the Narcissistic Disorder of the Self is characterized by a split internal world. The two units can be described as the grandiose omnipotent defensive fused part unit where the object is omnipotent and the self is grandiose and the affect is being unique, special, great, admired, adored, perfect, and/or entitled, and the underlying empty aggressive fused part unit where the object is harsh, attacking, and devaluing, and the self is inadequate, fragmented, unworthy, and unentitled and the linking affect is the abandonment depression.

The Narcissistic Disorder of the Self relies on the defenses of splitting, avoidance, denial, acting out, clinging, projection, and projective identification. Unlike the Borderline patient, the Narcissistic patient appears relatively stable in the middle and upper levels of the disorder and is able to keep the positive unit activated. The exception is in intimate relationships. Often the patient with a Narcissistic Disorder of the Self will present as very successful, whether in the academic, political, or business environment, but in his or her personal relationships has a history of doing very poorly.

In all three couples whom I will discuss, both partners suffer from a Narcissistic Disorder of the Self. There are three subtypes in our diagnostic system: First, there is the exhibitionist or movie star type, the person who wants to be admired and mirrored and to be praised by others and is constantly "on stage." Next is what we call the closet Disorder of the Self, where the focus is more on idealizing the object in order to bask in its glow. The Narcissism is hidden. The person derives satisfaction from attaching himself or herself to a powerful omnipotent object — whether it is a person, a guru, or a theoretical orientation that is the "right" one, and is revealed in some special way. These patients are fusing with something that is powerful, perfect, and narcissistically satisfying, but they do it in a closeted way. The third type is the devaluing Narcissistic individual who relies extensively on devaluation and uses the devaluing of objects to maintain his or her superiority. These are very unpleasant people who are especially difficult to treat.

Narcissistic couples tend to substitute control for agreement. They mirror idealization for love and affection and aggressive evacuation and attack for emotional expression, utilizing mirroring and compliance for reflection and agreement. The interventions used in the treatment of Narcissistic disorders in couples therapy are primarily mirroring interpretations. At times, confrontation is needed in order to contain the transference acting out in the sessions.

Briefly stated, the mirroring interpretations are empathetic with the Narcissistic vulnerability, the location of this principal affect in the self, and the description of the defensive maneuver to soothe the painful affects in the self, or to protect oneself from their full impact.

I have been thinking about how attachment and the attachment research might apply to Disorders of the Self for a number of years. I have also been interested in the work of the late W. R. Bion, a psychoanalyst in the Kleinian group in London (he also practiced and set up a group in Los Angeles in the 1970s), and who is considered by many to be one of the great Kleinians. Bion created an instrument, the grid, which he suggested that psychoanalysts might use, not in sessions, but after sessions, either to review the contents of the session or to consider ideas that might advance the scientific understanding of psychoanalysis. The grid has pros and cons, and it is a highly condensed theoretical system, but, essentially, it allows one to review one's thoughts or theories, to move up or down, to verify or disconfirm certain notions. I have used the grid in the development of my ideas of how attachment research can be used in our understanding of Disorders of the Self.

There are basically two subtypes of adult attachment ratings that might be applied to any of the Disorders of the Self: the avoidant/dismissing and the ambivalent/preoccupied. However, I believe that the patients that I'm discussing don't fit into the category of disorganized attachment, but that the latter are more troubled.

The following clinical cases involve couples in which each partner suffers a Narcissistic Disorder of the Self, and one of the above two types of attachment styles.

The two subtypes are differentiated on the basis of their defensive affect-regulation style, which roughly approximate the avoidant/dimissive, which I call the avoidant, and the ambivalent/preoccupied, which I call the anxious. The avoidant type typically uses avoidance mechanisms to deal with intimacy. The anxious subtype moves toward the other seeking contact or interaction, until he or she feels calm, soothed, and fused with. I do not claim that this is how the attachment evolves over time, but I am using these attachment styles elicited by the strange situation as a clinical model to organize my thinking about couples.

Each of the three couples at the outset had dysregulated affect, was transference acting out, and the partners were primarily related through Narcissistic false-self facades. As the work progressed, they were more able to be introspective and self-reflecting, mentalizing the other. Affects became deeper and more authentic as each partner moved to more secure states of mind.

COUPLES WHO HAVE MOVED
TO A REAL RELATIONSHIP

Clinically, the individual with a healthy real self feels a sense of continuity, stability, and mutuality in the experience of the self with and without others, both maturely attached and comfortably self-regulating. So, too, with couples whose relationship has moved to a foundation based on a real-self working alliance. These couples are able to be intimate and separate, able to discuss real problems in the relationship, and able to grow and mature in keeping with the changing landscapes of their lives. The partners are able to be a genuine source of support and love for each other when they encounter life's hardships, as well as to celebrate and share in the joys.

Three case examples will illustrate the treatment.

Case 1: Mr. and Ms. A

Mr. and Ms. A were referred by Ms. A's individual therapist. Ms. A was depressed and expressed dissatisfaction in her marriage. The couple had had a prior course of couples therapy, but with limited benefit.

In the initial evaluative sessions, Ms. A reported that she was the youngest of four children, that her family was chaotic, and that when she was 13, her father committed suicide. She was the person who took the call from the police. Following her father's death, Ms. A had an extended period of acting out. At the start of treatment, she had been sober for 10 years.

Mr. A, who grew up in Los Angeles, was the youngest of three and was the golden child. His father physically and verbally abused his mother, as well as the children. He was the only child to leave the family orbit and to live a somewhat normal life. Mr. A had no history of substance abuse and abstained from alcohol to support his wife.

I diagnosed Mr. A as an exhibiting Narcissist and Ms. A as a closet one. Their interlocking unconscious vulnerability was that the expression of need and love would result in humiliation, shame, and frightening loss. Aggressive attempts to control and direct the other were substituted for real relating.

I think of the A's as an anxious/anxious Narcissistic couple.

Sessions After Evaluation

I asked the couple if they had any comments or questions. Mr. A started by saying that I conducted myself like a game show host, with the added proviso that I was one of the biggest asses he had ever met.

I inquired of Mr. A what it was that gave him that impression. He was unable to give any concrete examples or substantive comments. I responded by confronting and limit-setting, stating that I felt that nothing I did or said warranted his comments, that it was unlikely that I was going to change much over the course of seeing them, and that if he didn't like me to the point of being unable to use the sessions, he should see someone else.

This settled things down for several sessions. Mr. A then began to miss sessions because, he said, of "important meetings." I brought things to a head by telling them that if they weren't able to attend weekly meetings, I would not see them. If they didn't feel that they could attend 50 meetings a year for perhaps several years, then it wouldn't be worth it to continue. Ms. A stated that if her husband couldn't, or wouldn't, participate, she would file for divorce.

The main characteristic of all the sessions up to this point had been one of escalating conflict between the A's, although Mr. A was the louder of the two. But Ms. A was no shrinking violet. She would curse at her husband in sessions, flip him off, and sarcastically put him down, showing her quick wit and facility with language. She was harsh and castrating. Mr. A referred to her as the queen of friction, the Leona Helmsley of the West Coast.

In the background of this attacking and angry couple were two preschool children who were being subjected to the same type of family environment in which the A's had grown up. It was through the perspective of the children that I was able to shift the couple from gross acting out to self-reflection. I wondered with the A's what they saw as models of loving relationships when growing up, and what their children were seeing now.

This ushered in the second phase.

The Second Phase: Transition

Ms. A, through the use of mirroring interpretations, came to realize that her angry outbursts were reactive to her feeling hurt, and that below the anger were immense feelings of sadness, depression, despair, and hopelessness. Concurrent with an increasing ability to tolerate her feelings of the abandonment depression and her impaired real self, her reality perception increased, so that she was able to see the destructive impact of the marital conflict on the children. This idea was repeatedly met with denial and aggressive attacks by Mr. A, who would belittle and blame his wife, giving tit for tat, essentially saying, "You do too." Eventually, Ms. A reached the end of her rope.

In a calm, considered voice, she informed Mr. A that she wanted a divorce. She kept to this position for several months. Initially, Mr. A attempted to provoke her to abandon her position. Then he fell back into an "as if" compliance, trying to behave. When this failed, Mr. A finally broke into sobs, and wrote Ms. A an authentic and heartfelt letter, which he read to her in one of the sessions. Up until this point, Mr. A had been sporadically attend-

ing individual psychotherapy, out of compliance. At this juncture, he committed, and began to be seen twice weekly, moving his individual sessions
from externalizing complaints to a focus on himself. It was at this time that
the A's were able to begin to genuinely listen to, and reflect on, what each
was saying. The tenor of sessions changed. There were occasional angry outbursts, but also more time spent exploring how they hurt each other.

The Shift to Working

As their focusing shifted to self-exploration and self-expression, sessions
were typified by an elaboration of each person's subjective experience of situations. Although tension could increase to the level of a quarrel, these conflicts would arise in the middle of the session, and be resolved well before it
ended. Whereas in the previous phase, the aftermath of a fight in a therapy
session could last for several days, the A's would now arrive in a good mood,
and leave in one.

An example of one of these conversations was when Ms. A spoke of how
she was talking to her husband about her anxiety concerning the world situation. She constructively stated that her interest was in engaging him in a
more emotionally connected way. Her reason for bringing up the example was
not to complain, but to use it as a point of entry for both of them to explore
how they connected and didn't connect emotionally. At first, Mr. A responded by bringing up an example of how Ms. A had also done the same
thing to him in the past week. Although they fought for five minutes, eventually Mr. A was able to recognize the legitimacy of Ms. A's complaint, apologize to her, and admit that he thought it was a good example, and that he,
too, wanted a deeper emotional connection. Before moving on to the example, they both spoke about Mr. A's tendency reflexively to shift the focus off
himself when he felt criticized, Ms. A also acknowledged doing so. It is this
type of more regulated affect that I think approximates emotional security for
a couple.

Case 2: Mr. and Ms. B

The B's were referred by their individual therapists. They were both depressed, and on the verge of divorce, and both were consulting attorneys.
There was a sense of desperation when the couple called, as well as on the
part of the referring therapists; it was as though the couple and family were
about to collapse. There was little hope that couples therapy would help. They
were both highly educated, successful professionals who came from severely disturbed families. They had three children (two girls and a boy), and were very
motivated to keep the family together for the children's sake.

I diagnosed both Mr. and Ms. B as suffering Narcissistic Disorders of the Self, closet type. Their interlocking vulnerability was that the expression of need, love, affection, and acknowledgment would result in frightening silence, disintegration, and intolerable painful shame. Affective deadening and becoming the perfect functional couple with no conflict was substituted for a real relationship.

I characterized this couple as the avoidant/avoidant type.

By the end of the third evaluation session, there had been a dramatic resolution to the crisis. They had been "miraculously helped," and attributed it to me. Although flattered, and secretly hoping finally to be appreciated, I knew that I hadn't intentionally contributed to the change. I hadn't made any therapeutic interventions, and was just completing my evaluation.

Sessions After Evaluation

The sessions after the evaluation were calm and uneventful, bordering on the boring. I became curious and asked the couple what they thought had made such a change. They both said it was me, but couldn't elaborate, stating that I just calmed things down. Sessions went on in a mundane fashion for three or four months. I primarily used mirroring interpretations, which moved things forward, but with little affect. There then began a series of interruptions of our meetings: holidays, business meetings, sick kids, forgotten appointments. Ms. B then reported a dream in which I was in bed with her, where her husband often was, reading a paper, and on the other side was her father. I interpreted to the couple that somehow I had gone into their bedroom and had calmed things down. However, I suspected that there were deeper issues of which they were afraid, and so distanced themselves from each other, and so their issues remained protected from painful feelings.

Transition

At the beginning of the next session, Ms. B reported a dream in which she was calmly walking through a city with a male friend and her husband. She suggested that they turn right, but her husband turned left, and a giant ocean wave appeared out of nowhere and killed him, and she woke up. (Note fusion and one mindedness.) Through mirroring interpretations, I was able to bring out into the open how afraid both were to uncover issues. They told me that over their 15 years of marriage, they had only three eruptions as large as the one about which they first consulted me, between eruptions were many years of distant and nonemotional living with each other. At this point, the couple talked about really trying to become closer and to work some of their difficulties through. This stimulated in them deep feelings of inadequacy, fears of expression, desire and emotion, vulnerability to severe attacks and feelings of being or going insane.

Working

Mr. and Ms. B began to bring up events during the week when things didn't go well. Their usual mode was to keep quiet about these conflicts and to "deaden" themselves so as not to become angry. When discussing challenging events, conflicts would erupt suddenly and intensely in sessions, and they would lose the observing ego or any perspective. During this period, my interventions were directed mostly toward analyzing defenses that caused dysregulated affect, either cutting off or flooding. As the partners were able to stay with their affect in a regulated way, they said of the dysregulated states: "It's as though we lose ourselves, it's like we are caught up in a dream-like drama that doesn't represent who we are as people. It's played out automatically, we aren't who we really are when we get caught up in it." Throughout the treatment, there never was a need for confrontation.

Case 3: Mr. and Ms. C

This, Mr. and Ms. C's second marriage, had been characterized by quarreling since it began, and they had been in various couples therapies. The last had ended when Ms. C terminated because she felt that "the therapist was unable to protect her and limit her husband's behavior." The therapy prior to that had been ended when Mr. C became fed up with the therapist's constant focus on his "anger, which wasn't the problem." The C's both came from families in which the parents were grossly Narcissistic. Mr. C's parents were loud, attacking, impenetrable, and never acknowledged his needs. Even when he shouted, he wasn't heard. Ms. C's parents were quiet and removed, almost Schizoid in their relationship with Ms. C, and the only contact she could claim was through Narcissistic mirroring of her mother.

I diagnosed Mr. C as suffering a Narcissistic Disorder of the Self, exhibiting type, and Ms. C as a closet type. Their interlocking vulnerability was that love, acknowledgment, and appreciation of who they really were would never be possible. For real relating, they substituted a relationship in which one would direct the other through life, ever vigilant and critically navigating, and the other would submit completely and perfectly accommodate to every demand.

I would characterize this couple as anxious/avoidant.

Sessions After Evaluations

I immediately got into a tangle with Mr. C, as he had clear ideas about how I should run the sessions and how outrageous his wife's failures to attend to his needs were. He was hypersensitive to slights, vigilantly scanning the environment for imperfections, and constantly zeroing in on Ms. C's shortcomings and failures. His manner of communicating was best characterized as angry and offensive. He used his aggression to control his wife, and attempted to do so with me. Very quickly, I was locked into a primarily confrontative stance with him. When I followed confrontations up with mirroring interpretations, he would back off, calm down, and allow Ms. C to reflect on some of his complaints. Ms. C stated that in large part, Mr. C's complaints were justified. She was distant emotionally, very suspicious of him and everyone else in her life, and restricted in her physical responsiveness to Mr. C's displays of affection. She had locked him out of her relationships with her son and daughter, and knew this had hurt him.

Each of the C's established a very different relationship to me. Ms. C was very pleasant and appreciative of my efforts to help her; she made me feel that I was doing a good job. Mr. C was the opposite, making me feel angry and unappreciated, and as if anything good that I did was unnoticed. Although there were elements of real relating in their relationships with me, these paradigms were primarily part-self configurations of a false-self type of relating. Ms. C was primarily mirroring me as she had her mother. Mr. C was projecting the empty aggressive unit onto me, reversing figure and ground, placing me emotionally in the shoes he had filled in his relationship with his parents.

Transition

Several months into the treatment, a dramatic shift occurred when I was able to help Mr. C stay in contact with his underlying abandonment depression, rather than his defending and acting out with angry outbursts. Mr. C began to sob in a session, expressing his despair that he would never be able to get through to his wife, or ever have the simple satisfaction of companionship and love. He cried, "I'm tired of working so hard, and I can't do it anymore." Because our time was up, I had to interrupt the couple while Mr. C was in the midst of expressing himself.

At the following session, the C's reported that Mr. C had had something of an emotional breakdown. They had sat in their car in the parking lot for almost an hour before Mr. C could control himself. They were both frightened that Mr. C would have a real breakdown. As I listened, I heard "breakthrough," not "breakdown," of the underlying affect that had been fueling Mr. C's false-self organization. I interpreted this to the C's, as well as their fears of relating. Ms. C was authentically responding to Mr. C; she reported a pain in her chest, and wept while saying it was sad that they each wanted the same thing, but it was so difficult.

Working

As the C's shifted more into working, the sessions took on a collaborative tone. There were fewer arguments and more discussions of their problems.

They began to experiment with their physical relationship; Mr. C was included appropriately in parenting. Ms. C became more generous.

Flash points now were used as points of entry to exploring their relationship. For example, one period of work revolved around Ms. C's mistrust of her husband. This pulled her back to her relationship with her mother, in which connection depended on perfect mirroring; separate needs were neglected and attacked. She knew intellectually that her characterization of her husband was wrong, but, emotionally, it was a compelling feeling. Although this "unfair" characterization of Mr. C triggered an angry outburst initially, he was able to contain himself repeatedly, and to express adaptively how Ms. C was distorting him.

In one session, Ms. C described a disturbing dream she had had the previous week. In the dream, she was walking along a road and came upon a large plastic bag. She grabbed the bag and began to drag it with her. The bag began to rip, and inside she found a dead little girl. Just then, a police siren went off, and she woke up horrified. As she started to explain the meaning that the dream had for her, she began to cry. She realized that her own representation in the dream was her internalization of her cold and disconnected mother, that it was she who now was killing the alive-child part in her, that waking up emotionally frightened her and disturbed her profoundly. She said that she had this empty hurt feeling in her chest. Mr. C spontaneously extended his hand to comfort her. His only contribution during the session was his encouragement of his wife, and his saying that his wife's mother was the coldest and most removed person he had ever met, and that he felt as though she had never really expressed love to anyone. This was marked as much by Ms. C's genuine focus on her impaired real self as it was by Mr. C's ability to have his wife's needs at the center of the hour.

The following letter from a couple I treated illustrates the changes that can occur.

Dear Dr. Seider,

My husband and I send you warm greetings . . . and apologize for not sending a note last year. We tried, but the end of the year was difficult for us, and we had trouble finding the words to explain it. Besides the turmoil of the aftermath of September 11, we also experienced the loss of my grandfather and the loss of a baby within a short period of time. We wanted to write and say that despite the struggles of my job loss, the loss of people we knew on September 11, and the loss of a family member and a baby, we felt that the work we had done in therapy served us well, and we were able to weather the difficult times with the support of each other. I felt grateful for my husband's strong and steady love and for our ability to navigate the hardships together. We wanted you to know this last year, but it was still too hard to put it down on paper.

This past year has been better. We went away alone together in February, our first nonfamily vacation in a few years. We learned to snowboard together in March. We also picked tennis up again, and play together on weekends. He's been working hard. I have managed to get fairly consistent consulting work. Most exciting of all, we are expecting a little boy. It has been a really healthy and fairly easy pregnancy, if such a thing can be said about pregnancy at all!!! Tonight, we finished painting a baby's room and we are getting it set up and ready. We will wait to name him until we meet him to decide for certain. We have also had the opportunity in 2002 to further appreciate the work we did with you. We send you our best.

References

Bergman, A., & Harpaz-Rotem, I. (2004). Revisiting rapproachment in the light of contemporary developmental theories. *Journal of the American Psychoanalytic Association*, 52(2), 555–570.

Bion, W. R. (1962). *Learning from Experience*. London: Karnac.

Bion, W. R. (1987). *Clinical Seminars and Other Works*. London: Karnac.

Blum, H. (2004). Separation–individuation theory and attachment theory. *Journal of the American Psychoanalytic Association*, 52(2), 535–553.

Britton, R. (1998). *Belief and Imagination*. London: Routledge.

Fonagy, P. (2000). Attachment and borderline personality disorder. *Journal of the American Psychoanalytic Association*, 48(4), 1129–1146.

Fonagy, P., Gergely, G., Jurist, E., & Target, M. (2002). *Affect Regulation, Mentalization, and the Development of the Self*. New York: Other Press.

Main, M. (2000). The organized categories of infant, child, and adult attachment: Flexible vs. inflexible attention under attachment related stress. *Journal of the American Psychoanalytic Association*, 48(4), 1055–1096.

Masterson, J. F. (1976). *Psychotherapy of the Borderline Adult*. New York: Brunner/ Mazel.

Masterson, J. F. (1981). *Narcissistic and Borderline Disorders: An Integrated Developmental Approach*. New York: Brunner/Mazel.

Masterson, J. F. (1985). *The Real Self: A Developmental, Self and Object Relations Approach*. New York: Brunner/Mazel.

Schore, A. (1994). *Affect Regulation and the Origin of the Self*. Hillsdale, NJ: Erlbaum.

Schore, A. (2003a). *Affect Regulation and the Repair of the Self*. New York: Norton.

Schore, A. (2003b). *Affect Regulation and Disorders of the Self*. New York: Norton.

Seider, K. (1995). Couples therapy of patients with disorders of the self. In J. Masterson & R. Klein (Eds.), *Disorders of the Self: New Therapeutic Horizons: The Masterson Approach*. New York: Brunner/Mazel.

Winnicott, D. W. (1965). *The Maturational Processes and the Facilitation Environment*. London: Hogarth.

8

Psychotherapy of the Disorder of the Self with Trauma

STEVEN K. REED, PH.D.

The treatment of Disorders of the Self (DOS) with trauma (specifically, sexual and physical abuse) is a complex, and yet relatively underaddressed, issue in the clinical literature. Extensive writings have addressed the treatment of personality disorders, or DOS (Masterson, 1981, 1985, 1988, 1995; Kohut, 1971; Kernberg, 1975; Gunderson, 1984), as well as in the field of traumatology (van der Kolk, McFarlane & Weisath, 1996; Courtois, 1988; Herman, 1992). However, comparatively little has been written about treating DOS with trauma (Orcutt, 1995, 2004) in a systematic and integrative fashion.

This is surprising when you consider that current documented findings show a prevalence rate for DOS seen by psychoanalysts in private practice of approximately 46% (Friedman, Bucci, Christian, et al., 1998). (With regard to the prevalence of trauma cases in the general population, one large representative study showed that 61% of men and 51% of women experience a traumatic event at some point in their lives, which included a lifetime prevalence of posttraumatic stress disorder (PTSD) or 7.8%. Rape was shown to be the most likely form of trauma leading to PTSD for both women and men; 65% of men and 46% of women report a rape as the trauma most likely to produce PTSD (Kessler, Sonnega, Bromet, et al., 1995). Resnick and colleagues (1993) found an overall lifetime prevalence of PTSD of 12.3% in adult female populations.

Also, in a study of a clinical inpatient population of 358 Borderline patients, Zanarini and colleagues (Zanarini et al., 1997) found that 91% of

Borderline patients reported childhood abuse, and 92% reported some type of childhood neglect before the age of 18. Furthermore, several other studies found that 30% to 50% of Borderline patients meet the criteria for PTSD (Hidalgo & Davidson, 2000; McGlashan et al., 2000). And, undoubtedly, a significant percentage of patients seen in outpatient practice have Disorders of the Self with the compounding factor of trauma.

In understanding the etiology of Disorders of the Self, Masterson has written extensively on the topic of DOS emerging out of a disordered attachment with the primary caregiver. What he essentially says is that the caregiver, limited in the ability to provide a secure attachment for the child, impairs the developmental blossoming of the real self of the child. This abandonment of the child's real self produces an abandonment depression. As the child protects against this abandonment depression, he or she constructs defenses that turn into the false defensive self (Masterson, 1981, 1985, 1988, 2004). The Masterson Approach has been strongly validated by research in interpersonal neurobiology (Main & Morgan, 1996; Schore, 2003a, 2003b; Seigel, 1999).

INTERPERSONAL NEUROBIOLOGY

Interpersonal neurobiology looks at the connection between our attachment experiences and the development and function of the brain. It draws from a wide range of different fields of research (such as attachment theory and developmental neuroscience) (Seigel, 1999). Specifically, it has validated the profound impact that disordered attachments have on the "self" of the child. This research also highlights the importance of a secure attachment for the infant in the first years of life. This attachment begins to lay down the foundational capacity of the emerging self, such as attachment patterns, sense of basic trust, safety, and affective regulation. A healthy or secure attachment between a mother and child finds a mother who is available and welcoming to the child in seeking proximity at reconnecting or reunion; thus, providing a parental balance between supporting the child's need for closeness and the need to explore the world. This, in turn, creates an expectation in the child that the mother is a safe haven in times of distress and/or times of reunion. Over time, this safe haven becomes internalized in the child. In fact, at as early as 10 to 12 months of age, this internalization of an intrinsic working model can be measured. Furthermore, in the latter part of the second year, these mental representations of the mother become increasingly complex and symbolic. They can actually be assessed in memory by the child to help regulate distressed affects. This internalized working model of attachment with the mother appears to be processed and stored in implicit procedural memory sys-tems of the right hemisphere (Schore, 2003a).

In contrast to the securely attached child, the insecurely attached child has a mother who is inaccessible for reunion, and who provides inappropriate attunement and/or rejecting responses to the child's affective expression and overtures for connection. In secure attachments, the mother helps the devel-oping infant to regulate affects by optimizing the positive and soothing the negative. This soothing of negative affects, which often comes from a misat-tunement by the mother, requires her to repair the disruptions. This repeated pattern of "interactive repair" (Schore, 2003a) and its optimizing positive affects are ways in which the mother downloads "herself" into the child's in-ternal working modern of attachment. In other words, the attachment is the dyadic interactive regulation of affect (Sroufe, 1996; Schore, 2003a). This downloading of attachment is primarily a right-brain to right-brain interaction that is particularly transmitted through mutual visual gazing, verbalization, and voice tone. As the child internalizes a safe haven within himself or herself, this provides for the growing capacity for self-regulation and the ability to cope with stress (Schore, 2003a). For securely attached children, these internalized capacities allow their emerging selves to blossom in an attached and individu-ated way, whereas for insecurely attached children, it puts them at risk for limited self-regulatory capacities, and for developing a pathological sense of self that, over time, expresses itself clinically as a Disorder of the Self.

NEUROBIOLOGY OF TRAUMA

One definition of trauma perceives it as a life-threatening event that over-whelms the person's coping skills (van der Kolk, McFarlane, & Weisath, 1996). Often, traumatic memories of sexual or physical abuse are encoded in a different way than are normal memories. In fact, research by Elliott and Briere (1995) suggests that sexual abuse has the highest degree of total amnesia (figures range from 19% to 38%) as compared with any other type of trauma. This amnesia for emotional and cognitive material appeared to be age- and dose-related. The younger the person and the more prolonged the sexual trau-ma, the more likely it is that significant amnesia occurred. The reasons why sexual abuse is considered the most likely trauma to be dissociated are not yet entirely clear.

Normal memories, which are first experienced implicitly on a nonverbal perceptual level in the right hemisphere, are then processed explicitly by the left hemisphere into long-term memory and speech. This explicit processing begins to take place at about 2 to 3 years of age, when these implicit memories can be translated into explicit verbal autobiographical memories. This signifies that they are given a context of time, space, and meaning, allowing the child to become aware of being a "self" in the world (Seigel, 1999).

Traumatic memories are also implicitly encoded on the nonverbal perceptual level. However, unlike normal memories, because of highly dysregulated affective experiences (i.e., traumatic experiences), it overstimulates the amygdala (which gives a sense of emotional meaning and significance), and then short-circuits the hippocampus, which organizes and evaluates the pieces of information). It is this breakdown in hippocampal processing that keeps the traumatic experience in a fragmented sensory state, like pieces of a jigsaw puzzle (i.e., auditory, visual, tactile, olfactory perceptions), never forming a coherent picture or recollection that can be processed into long-term memory and speech. This breakdown in memory processing has clinical manifestations. For example, because patients cannot have full coherent access (visual, tactile, auditory, narrative, and olfactory) to these traumatic experiences, they come up as flashbacks, which tend to terrify and torment the individual (van der Kolk, McFarlane, & Weisath, 1996). Charcot (1887) referred to flashbacks as "parasites of the mind" (as cited in van der Kolk, McFarlane, & Weisath, 1996). These parasites are particularly tormenting because they are often experienced as timeless. For example, Mr. M, a patient, noticed having a panic attack when a friend affectionately slapped him on his back while congratulating him on a job promotion. This tactile stimulus triggered a dissociated memory of physical abuse and make him feel as though he were 8 years old again. As stated, "I feel crazy as there were simultaneous realities (past and present) in my head — like I'm with a friend at work as a 44-year-old in the present, and, at the same time, I feel like an 8-year-old boy and that Dad is right behind, ready to slap me."

Another example is speechless terror. As the trauma is triggered, there are the traumatic somatoaffective experiences (i.e., hyperventilation, numbing, panic) that have no understanding, speech, or words that are accessible to the patient. This is caused by the deactivation of Broca's area, the verbal language area located in the left anterior frontal lobe, and its going off-line as the person experiences these flashbacks (van der Kolk, McFarlane, & Weisath, 1996). As one patient described this speechless terror, "It's like this terrifying foreign shadow force that suddenly seizes me and it's unpredictably dangerous and I feel frozen and my mouth forgets how to speak." For example, Ms. H, an abuse survivor who had been happily married for 10 years and had a satisfying sexual life, uncharacteristically drank several glasses of wine one night before having sex. During sex, she felt frozen with terror and could not speak, as no words would come. Apparently, the smell of alcohol was an olfactory trigger for her sexual trauma, as her abuser would drink an alcoholic beverage before violating Ms. H.

Another clinical manifestation is that of the patient who lives in perpetual terror of remembering, or is trapped in a PTSD feedback loop. The patient is connected to the terror of the trauma, but the actual traumatic memory is still dissociated. Thus, the patient is either being perpetually triggered or is hypervigilantly scanning her world to avoid being triggered. Van der Kolk refers to this as "phobia of memory" (van der Kolk, McFarlane, & Weisath, 1996).

As these examples show, persons with Disorders of the Self with trauma are often complex cases, as there are two clinical dimensions to treat: DOS (character work) and the trauma (trauma work).

CHARACTER WORK

The first essential stage of treatment is the character work. What is character work? Masterson has said that when treatment begins, the self of the patient is like a sieve. Thus, the goal of character work is to build a strong enough container (ego strength) by plugging up holes in this container of the self in order for it to be strong enough to contain or metabolize the affects of the abandonment depression and abuse. The character work is based on the triad concept of the Disorders of the Self. This concept essentially states that self-activation leads to the abandonment depression, which, in turn, leads to defense.

SELF-ACTIVATION ⇒ ABANDONMENT DEPRESSION ⇒ DEFENSE

This concept is powerfully efficacious in that it encapsulates the totality of treatment. Essentially, this triad helps to focus the therapy on activating the real self of the patient (i.e., areas of separation/individuation and attachment), while processing and regulating the core affects (abandonment depression) that have prevented the blossoming of the real self, and then to focus on defense analysis as it dismantles the false defensive self. These three components of the trial form the three primary cornerstones of character work. There are different triads for each of the Disorders of the Self. Generically speaking, these triads are:

1. The Borderline Triad
   Competence → Abandonment → Regression
2. The Narcissistic Triad
   Imperfection → Painful Vulnerability → Grandiosity
3. The Schizoid Triad
   Connection → Danger → Safe Distance

Thus, as the triad informs the therapist of what to focus on and what to listen to, as well as what the core dynamics are, it allows the therapist to attune empathically to the patient's experience (consciously and unconsciously). This helps to discern the difference between the real self and the false self of the patient. Often, however, neither the patient nor the therapist knows the difference between the patient's real and false selves. But as therapy helps the patient to dismantle the defenses of the false self and to attune more to the real self, a therapeutic alliance is made possible.

In addition, the DOS Triad has several therapeutic benefits. First, it strengthens the patient's sense of self, enabling the person to move toward higher levels of self-activation. Second, it also potentially allows, I believe, the therapist to zero in on the core dynamics and primary affects quickly and effectively. By knowing the specific triad of the patient, the therapist can identify the underlying object relation units (pathological intrapsychic attachment templates), that are the source of the core affects of the abandonment depression. Winnicott (1956) advocates knowing one's theory as well as if it is "in one's bones" in order to enable the intellect to proceed on cruise control, so we are better able to immerse ourselves deeply into the phenomenology of the patient's experience. This immersion or empathic attunement is largely an unconscious phenomenon mediated by the right hemisphere. Case in point: Research has shown that the right brain can appraise facially expressed emotional cues in less than 30 milliseconds, far below the perceptible conscious level of what is actually in our awareness (Johnson & Hugdahl, 1991).

CASE STUDY 1:
MS. B, BORDERLINE DOS WITH
SINGLE EPISODE OF TRAUMA

Presenting Problem

Ms. B's initial problem was chronic depression and difficulty with occupational success. She had an impression of sexual abuse by her father, but no memory of it. Ms. B was diagnosed as having an eating disorder, and also as being sexually promiscuous.

History

Ms. B had grown up in a family with three brothers and parents who were both workaholics, and she reported chronic abandonment depressions issues. "I felt I grew up alone, never really seen by my parents, even though I grew up in a good stable home." Her family history was unremarkable, and she had graduated from college with good grades. Ms. B had been in therapy for several years before seeing me, and felt it had been beneficial. She had confronted

her father in the past with her suspicions of sexual abuse, but this went nowhere. She had based her suspicions on her experience of his "looking at my
body — top to bottom — in a sexual way repeatedly, even after I told him to
stop." This always left Ms. B feeling violated.

Initial Impression

Ms. B was a "colorful" person when she first walked into my office. Her
outfit was highly artistic, featuring brightly colored beads and a shawl. She was
a nurse by profession, and my initial impression of her was split. One part of
her was superficial and seductively flirtatious (false defensive self), and the
other was real, connected with her pain, and motivated her to improve her
situation (real self).

Character Work

Ms. B's first words at our initial session were: "What's the most challenging part for you as a therapist?" This set the tempo for the first phase of developing a therapeutic alliance. I replied, "The most challenging part for me is
to help clients like you to focus on themselves." She replied, "I am not sure
if I know how to do that. Maybe that will be a challenge for me, as well as for
you." I agreed. The session that followed continued to consolidate/reinforce
that basic capacity for focusing on herself, and her becoming aware of all the
different defenses she used to avoid focusing and feeling her emotions. After
being able to concentrate on herself, Ms. B's next step was to identify her
triad. For example, she would become very angry and ashamed of herself when
she noticed how she sabotaged her success at work.

PATIENT: I was recommended for a promotion by my supervisor, but blew it
    by not showing up for work for the next two days. I am a loser, and I
    don't know why I keep trying.
THERAPIST: For this moment, perhaps you can extend to yourself the courtesy
    of curiosity as to what's behind the sabotage.
PATIENT: Well, I think that when my supervisor recommended me for the
    promotion, I freaked and blew it. When the spotlight is on me, I feel very
    scared and alone and just want to hide.
THERAPIST: Would it be accurate then to say that when you feel competent,
    it brings up the aloneness, and that's when you sabotage yourself?

Ms. B's Borderline triad was essentially: competence → aloneness and
anxiety → repression.

Therapy continued to move forward quickly, as Ms. B was middle- to
high-level Borderline. As such, the transference was not a primary focus,

except to deal with acting out. To focus on the therapeutic relationship too much would reinforce her clinging defenses. Her pattern was to look for the perpetual caretaker in life, only to feel rejected by the ubiquitous abandoning other. Ms. B continued to identify points of self-activation (pursuing further job promotions, setting boundaries with her parents, managing promiscuous relationships and her eating disorder), and processing the abandonment depression as it came up. As her external functioning increased, she began to descend into the working-through phase of dealing with the grieving, and letting go of the wish for reunion with her mother, primarily, and with her father, secondarily. Her episodes of pain and rage were increasing in their depth, duration, and frequency. The bottom of her abandonment depression was expressed in a dream in which she was driving with her mother in the car, and she was telling her mom, "I love you, but I also hate you. I know now that I don't need your approval, which I have never had from you." At the same time, she was driving over a bridge, and she pushed an "ejector seat button," and her mother jettisoned out of the car.

This was when the trauma began to surface. Ms. B was doing well with self-care, expect when it came to taking a bath. This was very difficult for her. She had always felt a disgust/shame for her body when bathing. In fact, she had never felt she could value or cherish her body by looking at herself in the mirror or while bathing. She would shower briefly in a begrudging and disgusted manner. As she attempted to take baths, she began to experience PTSD symptoms — degrees of dissociation, fragmentation of body images, nightmares of being raped, and anxiety attacks. I was moved by the intensity of her annihilation anxiety and dread, which she had never displayed during the character work. I felt relieved that we had done the character work and worked through to where we were now. As we entered the trauma work, she chose to lie on the couch. This was a significant decision, because her level of anxiety and her mistrust of men had not allowed that option before. However, her determination to get through the trauma work had galvanized.

Ms. B was aware of this intense dread in the pit of her stomach without any memories attached to it. To stay connected with this unknown trauma using different techniques (i.e., hypnosis, focusing [Gendlin, 1981], and relaxation skills) proved difficult at first. The trauma/character ratio was initially high, meaning that one session of trauma work usually was followed by many session of character work. For example, one session in which she had a mental image of an unattached penis penetrating her, flooded her with anxiety and shame. It took the next 12 sessions to help her to contain the terror, excruciating pain, shame, and dominant distancing defenses. These distancing defenses manifested themselves in her creating arguments/conflicts with her parents, her peers, and me. As these so-called "brush fires" were extinguished, one by one, she was willing to resume the trauma work. Progressively, this trauma/character ratio became more 1:1.

A trauma session was followed by a character session that focused on consolidating her character functioning. The trauma work progressed, with Ms. B recalling the dissociated memory of being raped, when she was 11 years old, by her maternal grandfather at one of the family's yearly holiday get-togethers. Once she had therapeutically abreacted the trauma, she was able to understand and to be free of the dread and the terror, as well as the body shame. For the first time, she was able to take a bath and value her body. As for her father, his visual sexualization was a reflection of his Narcissistic self-soothing, turning her into a sexual self object. Ms. B came to see this as a form of visual sexual abuse, but one that now highlighted her father's impairment. This elicited from her pity for him, rather than shame about herself.

This treatment for Ms. B was, from my experience, relatively straightforward, as the character work had developed a strong foundation for the trauma work. Treatment took four years and Ms. B was a fairly high-functioning and motivated patient. Thus, the treatment was primarily characterological in nature and the degree of trauma was confined to a single episode. In the case of Ms. B, the treatment was 90% character work to deal with the Disorders of the Self, and 10% was focused on processing the single traumatic episode. When there is chronic, more accumulative trauma, such as severe sexual abuse with high levels of dissociation, the treatment focus continues to be on the character work, which becomes more of a preparation for the trauma work, as it may actually account for the bulk of the work in the treatment.

TRAUMA WORK

What is trauma? For the purpose of this chapter, trauma is defined as any perceived life-threatening experience that overwhelms a person's coping skills (van der Kolk, McFarlane & Weisath, 1996). Thus, generally insecure attachments (i.e., avoidant, ambivalent) produce more abandonment affects, whereas traumatic attachments produce more annihilation affects in abuse or disorganized attachments. From a neurobiologic perspective, the traumatic attachments (i.e., abuse, severe neglect) are quite different from insecure attachments in that they produce a neurotoxic level of cortisol. High levels of the stress hormone cortisol are toxic to growing neurons. Several studies of brain damage have found evidence of smaller brain size and damage to the fibers connecting the two sides of the brain (Seigel, 1999; Bremmer, 2002; Teicher, 2002).

Trauma work is essentially a deeper level of the Masterson concept of the working-through phase. At the core of the working through is the letting go of the wish for reunion or the need for love and connection to the parent. This is particularly true when the parent is the abuser (an attachment paradox — *one's protector is the predator* — creating a disorganized attachment). The difficulty with giving up, or grieving for, the wish for reunion is related to the degree of trauma and the attenuating degrees of annihilation, anxiety, and sadism. The annihilation anxiety is exacerbated when there is a threat of physical death (i.e., being choked, beaten into unconsciousness, violently attacked). Furthermore, when dissociation is involved, it often turns traumatic memories into tormenting flashbacks or disruptions in mental consciousness (i.e., dissociative states).

Therefore, the treatment stance for trauma work is different from that for character work. In character work, the treatment stance is one of therapeutic neutrality, as it assumes that the patient is able to manage his or her affects, and gives the patient a vote of confidence. In trauma work, on the other hand, the treatment stance is more actively supportive in that it acknowledges that the trauma has overwhelming affects, and that the patient is not able to manage them on his or her own (Reed, 2004).

The next case to be discussed is that of Ms. S (Schizoid DOS with dissociated trauma), which illustrates the integration of character work with trauma work. Figure 1 (a schema that came out of Ms. S's treatment) shows the two main stages of treatment: the character work and the trauma work.

The character work, which deals with the false defensive self and uses the triad (increasing self-activation, managing abandonment affects, and modifying maladaptive defenses) develops a therapeutic alliance, allowing for the working through of the abandonment depression. Often, as with Ms. S, once enough character work has been done, dissociated trauma emerges. Trauma work, in my opinion, is safe and effective only when enough of the character work has been accomplished. When not enough character work has been established and the patient begins to do trauma work, that often leads to flooding or pseudotrauma work. In flooding, the patient is overwhelmed with the trauma and forced to act out, such as by terminating therapy (iatrogenic retraumatization). In pseudotrauma work, the false self is reinforced. The Borderline self becomes more regressed (i.e., the patient who wants to focus only on trauma, but is nonfunctional in daily life). The Narcissistic self becomes more grandiose, as the person expects a magical extraction of trauma. One patient said it this way, "I want the quickest and most successful surgery, but I don't care if the patient dies." The Schizoid self becomes appropriated by the therapist (the patient who has no choice but to submit to the therapist's perceived agenda).

Trauma work is based on integrating the traumatic memories into the whole of the patient's self, as well as on the therapist's becoming more actively supportive. At the bottom of this working through, as Ms. S let go of

Treatment V: False Self, Trauma, and Real Self

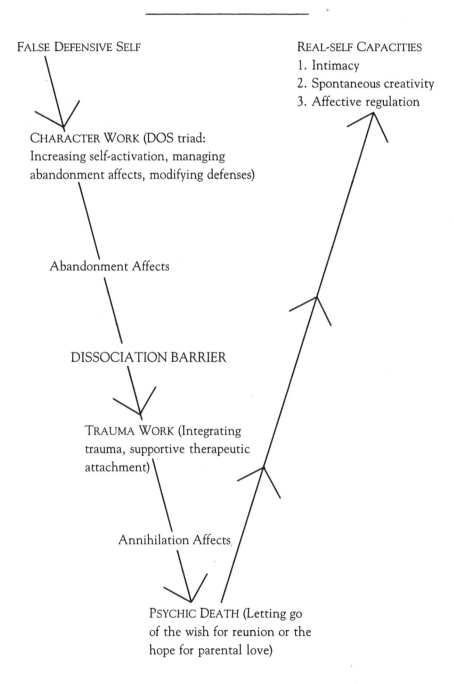

FALSE DEFENSIVE SELF

REAL-SELF CAPACITIES
1. Intimacy
2. Spontaneous creativity
3. Affective regulation

CHARACTER WORK (DOS triad:
Increasing self-activation, managing
abandonment affects, modifying defenses)

Abandonment Affects

DISSOCIATION BARRIER

TRAUMA WORK (Integrating
trauma, supportive therapeutic
attachment)

Annihilation Affects

PSYCHIC DEATH (Letting go
of the wish for reunion or the
hope for parental love)

Figure 1

the wish for reunion (Masterson, 1972), she experienced feelings of a "psychic death" (emotional and physical annihilation). After this, her real self was able to begin to self-activate without being dragged down by the trauma. The capacities of her real self began to blossom (Masterson & Lieberman, 2004).

During the trauma work, therapeutic support is necessary to help the patient to contain the level of annihilation anxiety, in order to keep therapy a safe process. This is particularly true for the more dissociative disorders, such as dissociative identity disorder (DID), where the loss of time, memory, and reality testing makes processing the trauma an unbearable experience. Therapeutic support may cause the therapist's position to shift in three notable ways.

The first is safety. The therapist needs to provide safety, particularly in the intrapsychic, intrapersonal, and environmental domains. Intrapsychic safety refers to the patient's feeling safe in connecting with his or her inner world. Thus, the therapist needs to offer ongoing reassurance regarding the patient's fears, such as going crazy, becoming a catatonic zombie, being driven over the edge, or being destroyed or lost forever in the black abyss. Interpersonal safety is the patient's feeling safe with the therapist (i.e., therapeutic boundaries are consistent, the therapist or a backup person is available for emergencies), and environmental safety, meaning that the therapist's office is felt to be a safe place.

The second area is structuring the session. Often, the therapist needs to take a more active role in pacing the trauma work. What, when, and how the traumatic memories become abreacted become a collaborative and consensual process. For example, if a patient is going to process a traumatic memory, the first part of the session is devoted to identifying what will be processed, the second part is used for processing the memory, and the third is for containment and closure. In structuring trauma work, different therapeutic techniques (i.e., focusing, hypnosis, EMDR [Shapiro, 2001], art therapy, sand tray) can be carefully selected to facilitate the process.

The third way is self-regulation and interactive regulation. The function here is to help the patient to find adaptive self-soothing skills, as well as to provide the therapeutic relationship as a primary source of affective regulation in the processing of trauma. This often requires a therapist to be more interactive with the patient. For example, I would check in with Ms. S periodically in a given session to see how she was perceiving or experiencing herself and/or me in the moment. Often, the level of dissociation would cloak her level of terror, aggression, or emotional vacancy. This level of engagement was often required to cut through her varying degrees of dissociation, depersonalization, and derealization. Trauma patients often have degrees of dissociation, which can range from PTSD to DID.

CASE STUDY 2:

MS. S, SCHIZOID DOS WITH

CHRONIC TRAUMA

Ms. S has a Schizoid Disorder of the Self with a history of severe traumatic abuse. In many ways, treatment for Ms. S differed both qualitatively and quantitatively from that for Ms. B.

Presenting Problem

Ms. S, a single, 40-year-old woman, was severely depressed. She frequently expressed suicidal intent, had anxiety attacks, was in social isolation (she lived alone with no significant relationships), and exhibited multiple somatic symptoms. She felt that she was in crisis, as she was abusing alcohol, was avoiding going to work, and was on the verge of being fired.

History

Ms. S grew up with both parents, but with her mother being an absent parent. Her father was a vague blur in Ms. S's recollection, except that she avoided him and was terrified when he got too close; she was unclear as to why. She had one older brother, who had abused her physically. She had no significant friends when she was growing up, and remembers her childhood as being isolated and barren. Ms. S had difficulty with recounting certain periods of her history. She did well in school and went on to earn a college degree, and then to become a software programmer. She had been in psychotherapy twice. The first course of treatment, which lasted for three years, was with a therapist who "wanted to work on my cognitive beliefs about my anxiety, and it was helpful for the first year, but then plateaued." The second course was for one session with a therapist "who wanted to use hypnosis right away on my anxiety and it felt too dangerous." She did not got back for a second session.

Initial Impression

My first impression of Ms. S, during the evaluation phase, was how terrified she was at being in my office and with me. She was unable to talk because of her terror (i.e., speechless terror), and I felt a strong pull to make each session, myself, and the room as safe as possible. After the evaluation phase, my usual protocol is to leave the responsibility to start the session with the patient. However, after several sessions, it became clear that she was in a state of trauma, and required more support and interaction from me to help her to manage her terror. This was one of the first of many therapeutic interactions where I had to discern how actively supported I needed to be. What is too little or too much? With her being Schizoid, the risk of my doing too little could trigger the sadistic object/self-in-exile part unit, whereas doing too much could trigger the master–slave part unit. In other words, I ran the risk of being seen as either sadistic or controlling. I attempted to interpret her Schizoid dilemma about entering therapy with a relatively unknown person. I said, "You're in a crisis. I don't know what would be more dangerous, for you to be alone and feeling out of control or for you to try to get help from somebody you don't know." She said nothing. Time was up for the current session, and we agreed to meet for a next session, as she was not sure how she felt about therapy. I wasn't sure whether or not she would come back, as I knew how difficult her Schizoid dilemma was for her. To my surprise, she not only came back, but also announced that since she left our last session, she had stopped drinking and was consistently going to work. I asked her what had made the difference, and she said that she did not know. I said, tentatively, "I am wondering if that somehow answers the question from our last session that as dangerous as it is to be in therapy, being out there all by yourself and feeling out of control is worse." She nodded, hiding a small smile of relief. Giving up the drinking and reengaging in work had less to do with me per se (unlike what my grandiosity might want to think), than with the fact that she had found a connection with the outside that would mitigate the terror and danger of cosmic aloneness (Klein, 1995). Prognostically, I knew that this was a positive sign that she would stay for the long term, and probably an indication of the depth and magnitude of the trauma she was holding.

Character Work

The initial character work focused on her Schizoid triad, which was connection → danger → safe distance.

For Ms. S, connecting with people would cause such danger and anxiety that she would use distancing defenses to retreat to safety. Therapy focused on increasing her degrees of connectivity to the outside by slowly increasing the number of social conversations with other people, forming boundaries with her parents, and pursuing outside interests (such as bird watching). As her outside connections were consolidated and her level of functioning was stabilized, she turned to the therapeutic relationships. The therapeutic relationship between us was highly charged with anxiety and danger for Ms. S. For example, after meeting for over a year, where I usually sat nine feet away from Ms. S, in one session my chair had been moved one inch closer to the spot where she usually sat, and she immediately noticed it and called that to my attention.

PATIENT: It seems your chair is closer today than usual. Can you move it back? It makes me nervous.

THERAPIST: Sure. (I move the chair back — it felt to me to be an almost imperceptible distance.)

PATIENT: It feels like I can breathe a bit easier.

THERAPIST: I find myself wondering if this interaction between us in this moment is symbolic of how dangerous connecting is, particularly if it means moving closer, and the only way to feel safer is to have me move back to my usual spot (an interpretation of the Schizoid compromise).

Ms. S's primary response to trauma was to "freeze" or "flee," rather than to "fight." The focus in the therapeutic relationship became more of her self-activating by initiating conversation with me with affect. During this phase of the character work, she would begin to describe her projections onto me — that I must not like her, that I was probably mocking her in my mind, or that I thought she was crazy (a repetitive dream she would have was of my locking her up in a psychiatric hospital). Over a period of four years, there was an unconscious shift in the transferential attachment with me, characterized by her dream of us sitting at a campfire with our backs to each other, not talking, but silently and safely sharing that space. After this dream, she asked:

PATIENT: I want to ask a personal question that feels scary and embarrassing to ask. Is it O.K. with you if I have you in my dreams?

THERAPIST: Yes. It feels like a rare privilege.

PATIENT: What do you mean?

THERAPIST: Based on my impressions of what you have told me, connecting with people has never been a safe or positive experience. So for you to want me to be a part of your inner world is taking a risk that you have never taken before.

PATIENT: People have never been safe to connect with. I am aware of the difference between my two dreams about you. The first was of you locking me up; the second was safely connecting with you.

Crossing the Dissociation Barrier

Toward the end of the fourth year, Ms. S had a flashback caused by an olfactory trigger during a session. The trigger was the smell of the new carpet that had been laid in my office two days earlier. The smell triggered a flashback of her being raped by her father on their new carpet when she was 9 years old.

Trauma Work

This flashback then began the trauma-work phase. As she began to connect with her history of chronic sexual abuse (apparently, she had been abused by her father from age 7 to 14), she became increasingly overwhelmed with annihilation anxiety. Dominant dissociative defenses increased as she lost periods of time, and experienced frozen states of terror, depersonalization, and derealization, with traumatic flashbacks of abuse.

Attachment to Therapist

This level of trauma work required her to depend more on the therapeutic relationship. Her attachment to me was shifting from avoidance to depending more on me to help her manage feelings of annihilation anxiety. Ms. S's attachment to me (as is true for most trauma-based patients) was difficult, if not overwhelming. For example, as she was relating one horrific traumatic memory (being raped by the father at 7 years of age and then having to kill her dog while her father held a gun to her head), my eyes became moist as I felt some of her trauma. She noticed, and initially became distraught. She said, "I can see that you are really with me in my trauma. It's very hard to feel your empathy because it makes my trauma more real and I can't ever remember my parents listening to me, let alone empathizing." Consequently, Ms. S was flooded by this contrast, which triggered a deeper level of her abandonment depression.

Transitioning into the trauma work, the therapeutic focus began to be on abreacting and integrating the traumatic memories. My therapeutic stance while doing the trauma work was more actively supportive, whereas it would change back to therapeutic neutrality when doing the character work. During the sessions in which I did trauma work, my therapeutic stance focused on actively supporting Ms. S's ability to process and contain the trauma by doing the following.

1. Safety. As discussed earlier, Ms. S needed reassurance that she was safe in three domains: intrapsychic, interpersonal, and environmental. The first domain, the intrapsychic, refers to Ms. S's needing reassurance concerning her specific fears of going insane, being driven over the edge, feeling suicidal and homicidal, and getting stuck in the "dark abyss with no way to come back to the world of people." The second domain, interpersonal, was about Ms. S's needing to know that the therapeutic relationship had safe boundaries. She had fears that I would be another predator pretending to be a protector, and that men sexually exploit her or betray her confidence by telling her family about her therapy. Third, the environmental refers to Ms. S's needing to know that my office was a safe place. Some of her concerns included having items in my office that could facilitate trauma work (i.e., drawing board and dolls, as well as soundproofing in the office).

2. Structuring the session. The sessions were usually one and a half hours long for planned trauma work. The first part of the session was devoted to

preparing for the trauma, the middle part (the bulk of the session) was for trauma processing, and the last part was for closure and containment. For example, one of her most traumatic memories was of the time she was raped by her father. He then forced her to kill her dog to show her what he would do to her if she ever told anyone. As he was doing this, he held a gun to her head and said, "No one loves you expect me, so don't make me kill you by telling anybody about me. Besides, no one will believe you anyway, no one! Ever!" The abreaction of this memory was broken down into different "chapters." The chapters involved:

A. Seeing herself being led into her father's bedroom as s 7-year-old and having her clothes torn off. Ms. S had me and her adult self in the room to comfort and be witnesses for the 7-year-old. After this session, a safe place to put that little girl was created in Ms. S's internal world (i.e., healing spa), as well as a vault in which to place the abuser until the next trauma session.

B. The father violently raping Ms. S's little girl. After these sessions, Ms. S felt very traumatized and unsafe because she was stuck between the past and the present realities. She would say, "I'm in between the two worlds — one world is I'm back there being annihilated by my father, and the other is the present world with you, where I'm safe." She preferred to sit on the floor during these sessions. The trauma was so intense that she vomited in my wastebasket at one point. To stay in the present reality, she needed to be assured that this was today, and that her father no longer could hurt her. Several times, she asked me to hold her hand to help her feel safe in the present as she was stuck in a flashback where she believed that her father was outside my door, waiting to rape her. I saw this as a point of self-activation for her, considering her profound distancing defenses.

For weeks to follow, she had increasing flashbacks and nightmares of other times when her dad had brutalized her. She would wake up in the middle of the night feeling like a 7-year-old girl whose father was in the room, ready to devour and annihilate her. As Ms. S lived alone, there was no one to provide reality testing or to help her snap out of her dissociative flashbacks. We decided to make her a personalized cassette tape that she could play at night when she was alone and in the dark, to help her stay in the present reality, and this proved helpful.

C. Having to kill her dog as a threat to keep her silent. Being forced to kill one of the only love objects to which she was attached involved a profound sense of loss, and eventually homicidal rage toward her father. She said, "I remember thinking at that time to myself that my dad really did hate me and he could kill me. I thought to myself that I could never tell anyone any-thing about who I am."

3. Self-regulation and interactive regulation. Discussing self-regulation or adaptive strategies was part of the trauma work. The question was: How could she manage her emotions between sessions? On the other hand, with interac-tive regulation, the question was: How could she rely on people to help man-age and regulate her emotions? By this time, she had made one friend at work to whom she began to talk. Ms. S also began to feel safe enough to call me between sessions to help manage her flashbacks.

Another aspect of interactive regulation included helping Ms. S to main-tain an optimal range for trauma processing (Figure 2). This involved regulat-ing the abreactive process, as she would cycle between states of hyperarousal and hypoarousal. Schore (2003a) states, "Behaviorally this is like 'riding the gas and the brake at the same time,' and the simultaneous activation of hyper-excitation and hyperinhibition results in the 'freeze response.'" Whenever Ms. S became overwhelmed with terror and began to freeze up (she would become like a deer caught in the headlights, speechless with terror), I would attempt to help her to regulate her emotional intensity in different ways (i.e., reassur-ance of safety, using self-soothing strategies, restoring her cognitive awareness of past versus present, providing structure and direction). Conversely, Ms. S would become detached, numb, or dissociative. During these times, I would help her to connect to her affect by asking her how she experienced herself or me in the moment and for her to scan her body for places of tension or sensa-tion, or simply to backtrack to the last point of affect. In the optimal range for processing trauma, the focus was on her being connected to me and not along in the trauma, that the trauma was not her responsibility or her fault, and that she had the power of choosing to heal and free herself from the trauma.

PSYCHIC DEATH

Ms. S touched on the deep trauma of being abused by her father, with whom she had parked the wish for reunion because her mother was too absent and neglectful to foster any thread of attachment. The father, after raping Ms. S, would take her out for an ice cream cone and talk about his work. Ms. S com-mented, "At least my father provided something of a connection in the mid-dle of the trauma, where I never saw my mother."

It was processing the trauma and, at the same time, giving up the wish for reunion with her father that seemed to be the darkest, deepest, and most despairing point in her therapy. She said, "When I connect with this trauma,

Optimal Range for Trauma Processing

LEVEL OF TRAUMATIC AFFECTIVE AROUSAL	THERAPEUTIC FOCUS
Hyperarousal: "Panic states," "speechless terror," flooding, and intense vivid flashbacks.	1. Safety 2. Self-soothing 3. Past/present cognitive balance 4. Structure

---

Optimal Range for Processing Trauma: Connectedness, responsibility, choices

---

Hypoarousal: detached, dissociation, numbing	1. Experience of self and/or therapist 2. Body scan 3. Backtracking

Figure 2

---

it feels like I am in this black hole that suffocates me and it is crushing — like my soul has a knife through my heart — it feels like a psychic death." As Ms. S was saying this, I was once again reminded why character work is needed to prepare for the trauma work. In essence, as clinicians, when we are working with a patient with DOS and trauma, we are asking the person to experience a death of sorts.

After Ms. S had done enough trauma work (nearly four years), she began to seem to be on the "upside" of her treatment, as she was able to self-activate more without getting dragged down by her characterological or trauma issues. For example, she began to live with a roommate, something she had never done before. She also got a dog for the first time since she was a child (symbolic of reattaching to a love object), and was able to express her emotions more spontaneously and to enjoy pursuing different interests.

By understanding the preparation and interplay between the character work and trauma work, we can effectively navigate the treatment of patients such as Ms. B and Ms. S, who represent complex clinical cases. Recent research in interpersonal neurobiology and traumatology underscores the impact of disorder attachments and trauma on the self of the patient. Knowing when, and how, to integrate the character work with the trauma work is challenging. The therapeutic risks are many. On the one hand, if too little character work is done before the trauma work is undertaken, the patient may be flooded and act out. On the other hand, if too much character work is done and the trauma work is minimized, the core issues are never worked through. In addition, if the therapist does not resume therapeutic neutrality after doing the trauma work, that may reinforce regression in the patient. Although other risks exist, a balanced approach between doing the character work and the trauma work will protect the integration of traumatic memories into the characterological self of the patient. This integration then allows the emerging real self to blossom.

References

Bremmer, J. D. (2002). *Does Stress Damage the Brain?* New York: Norton.

Charcot, J. M. (1887). Lecons sur les maladies du system nerveux faites a la Salpertriere (Lessons on the illness of the nervous system held at the Salpertriere), Vol. 3. Paris: Progres Medical en A. Delahaye & E. Lerosnie.

Courtois, C. A. (1988). *Healing the Incest Wound: Adult Survivors in Therapy.* New York: Norton.

Elliott, D. M., & Briere, J. (1995). Epidemiology of memory and trauma. Presented at the annual meeting of the International Society of Traumatic Stress Studies, Chicago.

Friedman, R. C., Bucci, W., Christian, C., et al. (1998). Private psychotherapy patients of psychiatrist psychoanalysts. *American Journal of Psychiatry, 155,* 1772–1774.

Gendlin, E. T. (1981). *Focusing* (2nd ed.). New York: Bantam Books.

Gunderson, J. G. (1984). *Borderline Personality Disorder.* Washington: American Psychiatric Press.

Herman, J. L. (1992). *Trauma and Recovery.* New York: Basic Books.

Hidalgo, R. B., & Davidson, J. R. (2000). Posttraumatic stress disorder: Epidemiology and health-related considerations. *Journal of Clinical Psychiatry, 61*(7): 5–13.

Johnson, B. H., & Hugdahl, K. (1991). Hemispheric asymmetry in conditioning to facial emotional expressions. *Psychophysiology, 28,* 154–162.

Kernberg, O. (1975). *Borderline Conditions and Pathological Narcissism.* New York: Science House.

Kessler, D. C., Sonnaga, A., Bromet, E., et al. (1995). Posttraumatic stress disorder in the national comorbidity survey. *Archives of General Psychiatry, 52,* 1048–1060.

Klein, R. (1995). Intrapsychic structures (pp. 45–68). In J. F. Masterson & R. Klein (Eds.), *Disorders of the Self: New Therapeutic Horizons.* New York: Brunner/Mazel.

Kohut, H. (1971). *The Analysis of the Self.* New York: International Universities Press.

Main, M., & Morgan, H. (1996). Diorganization and disorientation in infant strange situation: Phenotypic resemblance to dissociative states (pp. 107–138). In L. K. Michelson & W. J. Roy (Eds.), *Handbook of Dissociation: Theoretical, Empirical and Clinical Perspectives.* New York: Plenum.

Masterson, J. F. (1972). *Treatment of the Borderline Adolescent: A Developmental Approach.* New York: Brunner/Mazel.

Masterson, J. F. (1981). *The Narcissistic and Borderline Disorders: An Integrated Developmental Approach.* New York: Brunner/Mazel.

Masterson, J. F. (1985). *The Real Self: A Developmental Self and Object Relations Approach.* New York: Brunner/Mazel.

Masterson, J. F. (1988). *Psychotherapy of the Disorders of the Self: The Masterson Approach.* New York: Brunner/Mazel.

Masterson, J. F., & Klein, R. (Eds.) (1995). *Disorders of the Self: New Therapeutic Horizons.* New York: Brunner/Mazel.

Masterson, J. F., & Lieberman, A. R. (Eds.) (2004). *A Therapist's Guide to the Personality Disorders: The Masterson Approach.* Phoenix: Zeig, Tucker & Theisen.

McGlashan, T. H., Grilo, C. M., Skodel, A. E., et al. (2000). The collaborative longitudinal personality disorders study: Baseline Axis I/II and II/II diagnostic co-occurrence. *Acta Psychiatr. Scand., 102,* 256–264.

Orcutt, C. (1995). Uncovering "forgotten" child abuse in the psychotherapy of a borderline disorder of the self (pp. 205–227). In J. F. Masterson & R. F. Klein (Eds.), *Disorders of the Self: New Therapeutic Horizons.* New York: Brunner/Mazel.

Orcutt, C. (2004). Trauma in borderline personality disorder (pp. 111–119). In J. F. Masterson & A. R. Lieberman (Eds.), *A Therapist's Guide to the Personality Disorders: The Masterson Approach.* Phoenix: Zeig, Tucker & Theisen.

Reed, S. K. (2004). Countertransference to patients with personality disorders and trauma (pp. 119–132). In J. F. Masterson & A. R. Lieberman (Eds.), *A Therapist's Guide to the Personality Disorders: The Masterson Approach.* Phoenix: Zeig, Tucker & Theisen.

Resnick, H., Kilpatrick, D. G., Dansky, B., et al. (1993). Prevalence of civilian trauma and posttraumatic disorders in a representative sample of women. *Journal of Clinical and Consulting Psychology, 61,* 984–991.

Schore, A. N. (2003a). *Affect Dysregulation and Disorders of the Self.* New York: Norton.

Schore, A. N. (2003b). *Affect Regulation and the Repair of the Self.* New York: Norton.

Seigel, D. J. (1999). *The Developing Mind: Toward a Neurobiology of Interpersonal Experience.* New York: Guilford.

Shapiro, F. (2001). *Eye Movement Desensitization and Reprocessing: Basic Principles, Protocols and Procedures.* New York: Guilford.

Sroufe, L. A. (1996). *Emotional Development: The Organization of Emotional Life in the Early Years.* New York: Cambridge University Press.

Teicher, M. (2002). The neurobiology of child abuse. *Scientific American,* March, 68–75.

van der Kolk, B. A., McFarlane, A. C., & Weisath, L. (Eds.) (1996). *Traumatic Stress: The Effects of Overwhelming Experience on Mind, Body, and Society.* New York: Guilford.

Winnicott, D. W. (1956). *Primary Maternal Preoccupation Through to Psycho-Analysis.* New York: Basic Books.

Zanarini, M. C., Williams, A. A., Lewis, R. E., et al. (1997). Reported pathological childhood experiences associated with the development of borderline personality disorder. *American Journal of Psychiatry,* 154, 1101–1106.

9

Masterson Supervision:
"Nice Guys Finish Last" —
Supervision of the Psychotherapy of an
Individual with a Schizoid Disorder of the Self

JAMES F. MASTERSON, M.D., AND JOSEPH P. FARLEY, M.F.T.

Ms. S is a 48-year-old single, Caucasian woman. She is a civil engineer and lives alone. She came to see me four years ago after being referred by a colleague, and described herself as "an absolute emotional cripple." She complained of a general dissatisfaction with life and various physical problems, including irritable bowel syndrome, asthma, and migraine headaches. She said that she had no close relationships, neither friendships nor romantic involvements. She said, "I want to make more friends and connect with people and be more intimate with people. I want to learn what I really like because I don't think I really know. I want to be able to do things that I enjoy and not feel selfish."

I thought that was a pretty good presenting complaint. It's not often that we have patients who encapsulate their issues in this way. Of course, she had been in therapy four times previous to this and gained some insight into her condition.

She had ended her prior therapy because she felt it wasn't getting anywhere (she and her therapist agreed to that), and for months, she was searching for the perfect therapist. She realized after several months that she would search in vain and that there wasn't one. At that point, she called me.

Ms. S had a history of physical complaints going back to high school, as well as a history of social isolation. She had made very few friends throughout her life; friendships she had were distant, and usually revolved around a shared interest in the game, "Dungeons and Dragons." She had only one sexual part-ner in her 48 years, a young man who lived across the hall from her in the college dorm. Over the past several years, as she aged, she worried increasingly that she might not ever have a sexual relationship again.

As I reported previously, she had been in psychotherapy four times before. The longest was a year and a half with her prior therapist, the one who re-ferred her to me. This therapist knew that I worked in the Masterson Ap-proach and that this was a Schizoid patient who she thought that she might benefit from this approach.

At worst, Ms. S felt incapacitated by her depression. She had suffered probably 20 years of depression, but had never been treated with medication. At some points, she couldn't get out of bed. Although she rarely missed work, she often showed up one or two hours late. During weekends, she would stay in bed much of the time. She reported that this was the case for the first few years prior to starting therapy, as well as during the first year of treatment.

There was a precipitating stress around the initiation of therapy. She had received a card from her mother, with whom she hadn't been in contact for years.

Ms. S. denied any addictions other than watching television and surfing the Internet on her computer, and for those reasons, she had given away her television set and computer — she couldn't cut herself away from them. She reported drinking two to three times a week, one or two drinks at a time.

In terms of physical or sexual abuse, her mother did used corporal punish-ment. She spanked her when she was younger and on a few occasions, when she was an adolescent, she slapped her in the face. Her father was very passive and withdrawn and didn't punish the children. She said that she has no clear memory of sexual abuse, although she did have a faint image of a time when she was probably around 10 years old when (she doesn't call it a memory) she has an image of something inserted into her vagina, and its being very painful, and believing that her mother had something to do with it. She started menses around that time, and I suppose it's possible that her mother was in-structing her how to use a tampon. It is also the case that she had a very com-plicated tonsillectomy around that time so I'm wondering if she might have been catheterized and that might have been the experience. I'm not sure.

She does meet the criteria for major depressive disorder, moderate, recur-rent. So let me talk a little bit about her family history.

(Dr. Masterson comments) The Borderline and the Narcissistic child know that there is a pathway to the relationship with the parents — they just have to find it. The Schizoid child feels there is no pathway to the parents, and often that is demonstrated in the history by the severity of the emotional ill-ness on the part of both the mother and the father.

This was the case with Ms. S. Her mother was a secretary at a local church. She describes her as sadistic, cruel, and withholding. She felt as though all contact between them had to be on her mother's terms. She would frequently second-guess Ms. S, and tell her she how she had made mistakes and how she ought to have done things. "She had to be right if there was ever any dispute — she would win and I would lose all the time." She describes her as arbitrary in her limit setting and as not having enough time for any of the children, except for her handicapped sister who was in a wheelchair. She felt that her mother had never truly loved her. She remembers, at age 5 or 6, wanting to be held by her, and actually being able to ask for that, and being told to leave the mother alone. In her free time, her mother absorbed herself in romance novels and volunteer activities in the community. Ms. S remembers in latency having the awareness that her mother was incapable of loving her and to this day it is a great source of conflict for her. On the other hand, she recognizes her mother's incapacity to love her, but on the other, she continues to hope that she will.

(*Dr. M comments*) When you're doing your evaluation and you're getting the history, particularly the family history, it's important not to think about it just in terms of the details of the history of the personality, but also to start to think about what it means for the intrapsychic structure. That we will find an object representation in her head that has to do with being rejected and over-controlled seems pretty clear from the description of her relationship with her mother. And also, you ought to begin to think about how you're going to react to this, because it will be the kind of thing that can evoke a counter-transference.

I was thinking as she described this, and as I was writing it up, that it reminded me of Fairbairn's paper on the Schizoid personality which says that these patients come to believe that their mother's don't love them in their own rights as persons. So the paradox here is that she wanted her mother's love, felt that she didn't get it, and hated herself for wanting it. Again, it makes me think of Fairbairn's antilibidinal ego that hates the object-seeking libidinal ego.

So, let's go back to the family history. Because of conversations she had with her sisters, she believes that her grandfather molested her mother.

Ms. S's father was a physicist. He worked long hours and was rarely around, although my patient remembers fondly their vacations at their beach house where she and her father would take long walks or occasionally go fishing. Those are the few moments of contact with her parents she remembers positively. Her father, who was Obsessive-Compulsive, required everyone in the family to disinfect the phone after they used it, and wipe it down. She was the second of three children, and has a disabled sister two years older. The paternal grandparents are the other significant caretakers. They lived within walking distance of her home. I think they really saved her, in a way. She remembers that their cupboards had food that she liked to eat. She would often go there after school to get something to eat and to hang out. I thought that this nourishment seemed to be the metaphor for what they provided for her and what her parents couldn't provide.

From the history, I assumed that her mother was either Narcissistic or Schizoid with posttraumatic stress disorder (PTSD) and that her father was Schizoid with Obsessive-Compulsive Disorder.

As for her earliest memories, there were no memories from age 0 to 3. From 3 to 5, she remembers having difficulty with starting kindergarten, anticipating that she wouldn't know anybody there and being anxious about it. She also recalls a very vivid memory of walking home from school, and when she arrived at home, nobody was there. Her family had been discussing a move to the East Coast and she remembers imagining that they had decided to move without telling her. She was terrified, believing that she would have to make do on her own. Her mother arrived one or two hours later. Ms. S was quite relieved but the mother was furious because she hadn't remembered that she was supposed to meet them at the grandparent's house after school.

In latency and adolescence, she participated in a lot of activities: girl scouts, swimming, and fencing. It appeared that her mother got her involved in activities, not so much to support her, but to get her out of the way so that she could have more free time. This, at least, was my patient's impression. She had very few friends in high school. She joined the chess club and had a few distant relationships there, mostly with boys.

She went away to college and lived in the dorm for the first year. She returned home because she just wasn't able to do it. "It was too far away from home. And it was too intense living with so many people that close in the dorm. I became claustrophobic. The tiny dorm rooms were too much."

Ms. S graduated with average grades. She then took a year off and traveled across the country like a drifter. She would take a job for a few months, and then move on. She came back to the Bay Area and secured a job in an engineering firm. To date, Ms. S has worked as an engineer at four different firms and appears to be fairly frugal. She was laid off during the first year of therapy with me, and it took her about six months to find a job. She didn't seem too anxious about it, because she had saved quite a bit of money.

Her mental status exam was unremarkable, except that her speech and affect were flat. There was very little affect in the first year of treatment.

She came in with a diagnosis from the previous therapist. This was helpful, although sometimes I find it misleading, since some therapists have only a cursory understanding of the model and diagnostic issues. In this case, I found the formulation right on. I also found her presentation to be consistent with a diagnosis of Schizoid Disorder of the Self. Her social isolation and the impossibility of an intimate relationship were striking. I hadn't ruled out the possibility that she was a distancing Borderline, however, although her mother did withdraw libidinal availability when she self-activated. For example, after learning how to ride her bike, she showed her accomplishment to her mother. Her mother's response was to make her ride her bike to piano lessons, so that she wouldn't have to take her. So there was abandonment for self-activation. There didn't seem to be a rewarding object relations unit in place. There is no clear genetic history of that, and certainly it didn't seem to be a theme in her life. There is no evidence of clinging, although that is sometimes difficult to see with a distancing Borderline.

Likewise, I ruled out Narcissistic Disorder of the Self. There didn't appear to be a defensive fused part unit, and I saw no clear evidence of a self-representation of being unique, special, admired, or adored. There is no evidence of a sense of entitlement or fantasies of unlimited success, power, brilliance, or beauty. My countertransference reactions tended to be less a desire to take care of her or to mirror her, than they were to take control of her, or to feel that she had control of me. My early interventions were a bit sloppy and looked more like interpretations of Narcissistic vulnerability than Schizoid interpretations. Her response to those interventions was not to deepen her experience; rather, she seemed to feel intruded on and appropriated.

Ms. S exhibits the split object relations unit of the Schizoid Disorder of the Self. The attachment unit consists of a cruel, sadistic, and withholding object that enslaves the self and demands compliance and obedience. The object always has to win, and the self must lose or give in. The self is represented as ineffectual, weak, helpless, and passive, without a voice and infirm. The self-in-exile unit consisted of a distant, uncaring, unavailable, critical, and self-absorbed object along with the self-representation that is insignificant, wounded, hideous, alone, and self-contained. In her own words, "a garish, bug-eyed monster locked up in a dark barrel." When Ms. S self-activates in sessions by focusing on herself or exploring genetic material with affect, she triggers the attachment unit and fears being taken over, controlled, shamed, or made wrong. She protects herself by being self-contained and talking about the news of the week. When she is successful and self-activates, or if she feels competent, she triggers the self-in-exile unit. This is similar to when, as a child, she learned to ride a bicycle and was put into exile by her mother. She's been able to verbalize her fear of my throwing her out of therapy if she gets better — that she won't deserve to be here.

(*Dr. M comments*) The title of the presentation, "Nice Guys Finish Last," is, of course, a metaphor. We're not trying to say that you shouldn't be

thoughtful and interested, but that if, and when, in response to countertransference, you veer into trying to please the patient in order to relieve your anxiety, then you're getting into trouble.

That's a little prelude to the countertransference issues of this case. It's
one of the things that is so wonderful, and, at the same time, so horrifying
about individual supervision with Dr. Masterson. He's really able to make you
identify your countertransference and to work on it.

(Dr. M comments) I don't like the way you say that. I'm just saying that,
as a whole person, it's got two sides. I would be lying if I said it was always
wonderful.

(Dr. M comments) What kind of a reaction would you expect from this patient right off the bat? What would the patient's principal concern be right off
the bat? And would it be projected on to you? She's going to take control of
her fear of being controlled. We see where that comes from historically, right?
And we could figure that out from the history. So as soon as we start the
therapy, what should be in your head is, "I should look out for her fear of
being controlled by me."

So I referred her for medication.

(Dr. M comments) Control no. 1.

I stepped into it and she resisted. I said, "You need to do this." I told her
that she had a major depressive disorder and that I thought there was a great
deal of . . .

(Dr. M comments) She struggled with feelings that she didn't deserve medication. She's saying, "I don't want to be controlled by you." And, of course,
you're going not by your emotional perception of her, but by your intellect.
And she really should have the medication.

The other piece of this was that her fantasy of going to the doctor was
that the doctor would put her through a host of tests and give her various
medications, and that she would be without a voice or any control of her
treatment. The authority would step in and say, "This is what is going to
happen." So that's why she struggled.

(Dr. M comments) I don't think she was talking about that. She was talking about what she felt was going on with you.

Yes, I think you're right. She eventually made an appointment, but I
think that she felt coerced by me. Over the course of the next 18 months, she
was on a variety of medications: Prozac, Anafranil, Zyprexa, Wellbutrin . . .

(Dr. M comments) Never mind all those.

The list goes on and on. She eventually stopped the medications. She
said, "They helped a little bit with the depression, but it was like tricking
myself. I felt better at the moment, but it didn't help the sadness, it didn't
take away the sadness." She also gained 30 pounds on the medication.

For the first year of the treatment, my interventions were fairly unfocused. In one session she reported: "You had asked me when we first met who I connected with as a child. I had stuffed animals, a teddy bear named Barney. I remember losing him and becoming very distraught. My parents replaced him, and somehow it was okay. When I was 10 years old, I made a cardboard building for a class project. I didn't want scotch tape, I wanted masking tape, but my parents didn't have any. I was so angry that I destroyed the little building. I destroyed it rather than make do with scotch tape. With Barney, I wonder if maybe I got angry and threw him away. Maybe I threw him away."

I said, "It seems that you fear your anger will destroy those things and people you love or need." (I was receiving supervision from a Kleinian at the time.) I interpreted her bowel problems as her body's rejecting nourishment and need of any kind. It was an attempt to be self-sufficient and not to require even physical sustenance. She replied that she always needed to be perfect and be loved, and that she likewise required that her love objects be perfect, that she have the perfect therapist. This wasn't the perfection that a Narcissist seeks, but perfection in a way that is not attainable, so it keeps the love object at a safe distance.

(Dr. M comments) So we're back at ground zero. What has always been fascinating to me is that patients will keep after you, and after you, until you get it right. In this way, they educate you about what you have to do.

She ended one session by saying she wanted more feedback from me, and then, in the following session, she said she was very angry. I asked her if she might be angry at me, and she said that she didn't think so. She then reported a dream of a composite character from childhood who was selfish and wouldn't share her toys with the young Ms. S. I interpreted that perhaps the dream reflected her feelings toward me — that I was withholding my toys or valuable thoughts from her. She responded, "Perhaps," and then went on to ignore what I had said.

(Dr. M comments) So he's fishing around, he's pushing holes and buttons to see if he finds one that fits.

In one session, she talked about feeling lonely one evening, and eating a very large piece of cheesecake. She felt sick later. She then talked about engaging in a conversation with a coworker about antique dolls. She became aware that the coworker's interest in the subject was waning and she wanted to cut the conversation short. But Ms. S kept it up. She felt that she was holding the coworker hostage in a dull conversation.

(Dr. M comments) Again, I think that she is talking about the transference acting out.

I responded to her with the following: "It seems you have an appetite for contact with another person — you had it the other night — but mistook it for appetite for food. You tried to satiate it with food, by stuffing yourself in order to fill the emptiness inside. In a similar, but perhaps reverse, way, you stuffed your coworker. You filled her up with something she didn't want, but I believe that underneath it was your own appetite — you had your own need for some kind of connection."

I though these interpretations were wonderful. But upon reflection, she didn't seem to be moving.

(Dr. M comments) I think the whole thing here is about her relationship with you, but in your intervention, there is none of this one-to-one quality. So even at this time, you must have felt a need to back off from her projection onto you. You're going to get more psychiatric-like, more complex, more intellectual, and so forth.

So there's another trap I stepped into. I can see that it was easier to talk at a distance than about what's going on between us.

Dr. Short said that treatment is not about explanation; it's about experience. Well, I started to explain some things to her — continued to do that. I was also a bit confrontational. She was avoiding taking care of herself in basic ways. For example, she didn't replace her broken eyeglasses for several months, and didn't schedule doctors' appointments to follow up on her asthma problems. She said that when she did support herself, she felt unworthy and feared being taken control of, and that there was a backlash of unpleasant feelings when she did so. I told her that she needed these feelings if she wanted to work through them, and that avoiding supporting herself would get her nowhere.

(Dr. M comments) That's giving her lots of direction.

Yes, it was. I also mixed up my interventions. Some of my interpretations were Narcissistic interpretations. She talked about the futility of life, being hopeless that things would never get better for her, and she started to talk about suicide as an option.

(Dr. M comments) Why is she doing this? She's giving up. She's tried all these metaphorical efforts to convey to you, probably, her fear and anger at being controlled by whatever it is you did, and as she did it more and more, and you were not able to pick up on it, she began to feel more depressed and hopeless. She says to herself, "I'm running out of ploys here. What should I do now?"

So she would talk about that, and then she would start to talk about some details of the week, and then I would make a Narcissistic interpretation that basically it seems that as she focuses on herself here, she starts to feel despair and hopelessness about her situation's ever getting any better, and to soothe herself, she turns her attention to the details and activities this week. She would often come late to sessions — 5 minutes, 15 minutes. One time, she came to a session 20 minutes late. I would typically ask her what she thought the meaning of her lateness was. She would respond with some practical reasons, such as bad traffic, a task at work that she needed to finish before leaving, or having to sit on the toilet at work before she left. (It's really hard to sort out because she does have a severe irritable bowel syndrome).

(*Dr. M comments*) Did her lateness start at this time or was it ongoing?

I think there was some of it in the beginning, but I think it got worse around the time that we started supervision.

(*Dr. M comments*) It's a form of Schizoid withdrawal, as a protection.

Anyway, I would try to link what happened in the last session with her coming late and suggest that perhaps there were some feelings that were very painful for her, and she would say I was making too much of this lateness and was trying to read something into it. At this point, I would either drop the issue or take her view of it as having no meaning. The approach didn't lead anywhere obviously, and seemed to have no impact on her lateness.

(*Dr. M comments*) When any patient is late, this is a direct strike at the treatment, so mind you, you have to deal with it until the patient arrives on time, no matter how long it takes. It's transference acting out in the office.

I eventually did this, but in the meantime, she did report some dreams during that period of time. I would ask her about her associations. If she had none, I would comment on or interpret her dreams. She recalled a dream in which she was looking at a toy model of an armored car. There was a question in the dream of ownership. To whom did the car belong? The car then expanded in size, and she noticed that the sides had come off, so that one could see inside. There was a brief discussion of the dream, in which she did say it might indicate some feelings of a need to go into battle. I said, "At times, you've indicated that therapy feels like a battle to you and you anticipate being attacked by me as you explore yourself here. Perhaps the armor on the car represents your feeling a need to protect yourself here. At times, you've taken your sides off. Let me peek inside as you explore yourself here, but you end up feeling extremely exposed. Maybe the question of ownership of the car speaks to the question of ownership of the therapy. You've often spoken of therapy as something your mother would tell you to do and you fought against it for this very reason. So there is the question of whom you are doing this for. Do you do it in response to the demands of another, or do you do it for yourself?

(*Dr. M comments*) There is more of a Narcissistic quality of the interpretation here. When you're doing it, the words are very important. With the Schizoid patient, the two important words are *fear* and *safe*. You are frightened that I will control you, and the way you make yourself safe is to come late, is to avoid, or whatever he or she does. So it is important that you contrast the fear with being safe.

At one point, when she was feeling utterly desperate and I also was feeling desperate, I said, "You might want to think about keeping track of your dreams." I gave her a directive. So part of her reporting dreams to me was, I believe, in response to that.

She reported one dream in which she was in a castle engaged in a battle for her life, and there were spirits in the castle who helped her fight off the enemies outside. At one point, in exploring the dream, she realized that the greater fear was not of being killed by the outsiders, but rather of not being able to escape the castle itself. She came to be aware in the dream of the fact that those spirits who helped her fight off the invaders were actually enslaving her in the castle. I interpreted, "So it seems to be in your life that the very things that keep you safe from others — your self-sufficiency and sleeping through the weekends — end up, in fact, isolating you and enslaving you. She seemed to gain some insight from those interpretations, but, again, there was no affect.

(Dr. M comments) Again, she was talking about the treatment. She fears being caught up in it and is afraid of being enslaved.

That I completely missed.

(Dr. M comments) One other general point, in my view, is that the less you say, the better. Your interpretations and your comments should be short, but pointed in the right direction. Some of my fanciest interpretations with patients, which I was so proud of, didn't affect the patients at all. So that's what happens when you get into a rambling interpretation. It loses focus and it puts up a defense for the patient — he or she can't focus on it and integrate it.

What happened in her life was that she lost her job in a round of layoffs in her company, and she attributes this to the downsizing, but also to the fact that she often was late. At this time, I began supervision with Dr. Masterson and it became clearer and clearer as to what I needed to do. I needed to make Schizoid interpretations, not Narcissistic interpretations, and I needed to hold the frame around the time. What I would like to do is to really focus around the frame of the time, and how that led her into genetic material and affect.

She would come late to sessions, and at the first session at which we did supervision, she came late, and I started to interpret her lateness. I first asked her if she had any thoughts about being late. "It's just too hard for me to get out of the house on time. I've been staying up late and it's hard to get up in the morning," she said. I said, "I think that coming to therapy represents a step toward helping yourself, and also a step toward opening up with me. And, as you open up here, I think you start to become frightened of being controlled by me, and so, to feel safer, you seize control of the session by coming late and regulating the session's length." "No, I don't think so," she said. "I do that everywhere in my life, it's not just here."

My intention was to pursue it in the next session.

(*Dr. M comments*) So, if you miss an opportunity in a session, don't worry. It will come up again.

I waited, and it did come up again. We had the same discussion, and she said, "I keep telling you I'm late at everything, you just don't seem to get it." So I said, "I wonder if perhaps in other areas of your life as well, if you start to apply yourself, you begin to feel anxious about losing control as perhaps here, and arriving late is one of the ways you can feel more in control." She replied, "I just don't know what way to go here. There are other things, by the way, I'd like to talk about. I don't want to spend the session just talking about being late. I just can't get myself organized in my life." Then she goes on to talk about the details of her life. I said, "I think, as I bring up this issue with you about being late, you become afraid that I will try to impose my view about it onto you, and so to keep in control, you cut that exploration off and focus on the details of your life."

(*Dr. M comments*) You did use fear, but you should have followed it with "in order to feel safe, you cut the exploration off — it would have been just right." My hunch is that you partly got to her here.

There was a long silence here, and then she said, "I'm angry that I have to do this. I used to be more organized, this is just too hard." Then she started to cry. "I just don't know what I'm doing here. I don't know where to go. I don't feel there is a clear road or a path to take and I feel that you are telling an invalid to get up and walk. It feels as though you get some kind of sadistic pleasure from blindfolding me and throwing me out in the woods and saying to me, 'Find your way home.' It's like pricking me with needles when I'm already in pain."

(*Dr. M comments*) You got her!

Yes. And I knew it. I said, "I was thinking about what you were saying right now, and I wonder if, in some way, what I have been saying to you is that the road lies in exploring yourself. I've been pointing out the road. It's not that you don't know the road, or that you haven't heard this from me, but that the problem is that when you start to explore yourself with me, you start to fear that I will torture you, that I will use you for my own sadistic purpose. So, to keep safe, you decide to take another road — talking about the details of your life. On this road, you feel you have more control and can navigate it safely, but, unfortunately, it doesn't take you anywhere."

(*Dr. M comments*) That's what we call interpreting the Schizoid compromise. You interpret the fear and safety and then point out the reality price that the patient pays. The Schizoid compromises derive from the notion that Schizoid patients have a kind of tract that they follow. They move toward the object, and this triggers their defensive unit, and they feel afraid of being abandoned, or enslaved, etc. Then they pull away by withdrawal, and get so far that they trigger their sadistic object and are alienated, like somebody who goes into outer space. Their capsule disappears and they are left to turn over and over in complete isolation. And so, the work goes back and forth, back and forth, back and forth. Look at her response:

She says, "That road is just too hard. I always had to do it my mother's way. She was always in control." And then she pauses for about two minutes and says, "I suppose you might be right."

(Dr. M comments) See . . . your last interpretation was interpretating the projection, and it got through.

Yes, it seemed to get in. She was late for the next session though. (Dr. M says, "Shucks.") She comes in and her first line is, "I don't want to hear any crap about why I'm late. It feels like you've been making accusations and demands." I said, "I wonder why you heard my attempt in the last session to help you explore yourself as accusations and demands?" She said, "You assumed I was trying to avoid the sessions and that it was different from other areas of my life in which I'm late."

(Dr. M comments) You see, that interpretation really hit home. Now you're getting a different kind of resistance to it, and the tendency would be to back off. You might think, "I must have done something wrong."

And that was indeed my tendency. That is where I got a lot of support from Dr. M to stay in there and not to back away. I responded to her, "Actually, I think it may be similar here. I think that as you apply yourself to therapy or to the process of finding work [she had been avoiding trying to find a job], you start to fear that you will need to give in to the other, whether it's me or a prospective employer. This fear of giving in is so distasteful that you try to gain control of the situation by controlling the time and arriving late. Unfortunately, it doesn't get you anywhere in therapy and undermines your reasons for being here in the first place." She responds to me, but her voice is so quiet that I can't hear what she is saying. After I tell her that I can't hear her, she continues to speak but again so softly that I can't hear. I say to her, "I think the process of exploring this with me here frightens you. I think you worry that I will try to dominate and control you. So again, to seize control, you talk in a voice that is so soft and quiet that I can't hear. This way, you have blocked me out and kept me at a safe distance." She starts to cry.

(Dr. M comments) Now, when you can get a Schizoid patient to cry in the office, you really have something.

She says, "I feel so depressed and discouraged. I feel myself fighting you like I fight everyone else in my life. I just can't give in. That means death to me. I can't get myself to look for work — I just feel lethargic, I stay home, maybe it's a safe place for me. I'm afraid that if I get a job, I will start the problems all over again. I'll have a boss telling me what to do." And she goes on to explore her fears of recreating the same situation she was in before. This process continued for several sessions over a two-month period, and she continued to come late and I continued to bring it up with her and to explore it with her, and she would continue to get angry at me — and I interpreted to her that she seemed to use her anger with me to keep at a safe distance, and to keep herself feeling safe and in control. She began to explore this, and how it was much safer for her to be angry than open or close. "I'm feeling so overwhelmed and angry, I just can't get it together. Maybe you're right. I think I feel like I'm giving in if I come here and arrive on time. This is something my mother would want me to do."

(*Dr. M comments*) See, there is a beautiful description of the projection.

"My only power is to say No. It might be connected to having to go to bed. As a kid, I remember wanting love and attention from my parents. It seemed that they always ignored me."

(*Dr. M comments*) There she goes. Did you pick up on that? She's gone from the here and now back to history, which is the beginning of the work with affect.

"They would go out for the evening and I would want them to be home. When they did get home, I had this hope of getting a little morsel of time with them, and they would tell me to go to bed immediately. Going to bed meant losing. I wouldn't get what I wanted. They dismissed me. That's why it is so hard to go to bed now. I stay up all night sometimes. If I go to bed, I'll lose. But in the end. I lose if I don't."

She started arriving at sessions on time, and in the last 18 months, she has only been late on two or three occasions. The explorations of her lateness led to a good deal of genetic material.

(*Dr. M comments*) What has happened is that she has stopped projecting and acting out that object on the therapist. She has contained the projection that allows the feelings and the memories — against which it was a defense — to emerge. It is also important for the patient to notice that you did not say a word about this kind of content. It is vital for it to come spontaneously as a consequence of your interpretations, so that the patient will own it. That is the way the patient owns it most, and gets the most benefit from working through on it.

What was striking to me is how the model really predicts this. When she contained her acting out, in fact, at the very first session to which she arrived on time, it was the most affect that she had ever shown. And it was here I saw the most genetic material. She says, "I felt so controlled by my mother when I was younger, my only way of having control was to be negative. Being late was my only control. It's been such a problem for me for so long. At times, I've noticed a desire to be here early at the sessions, but I fight it.

Maybe coming here and talking feels like surrendering. It's not that you'll tell me what to do, but it's not like you're passive either."

In supervision with Dr. M, he pointed out that I had been too active. My interpretations were too elaborate and complicated. He got me to back off, and to simplify my interpretations. Then the next problem was for me to step up again, when I needed to.

She continued, "If I come here on time, I'm admitting that they were right, that you are right, and that I'm capable of getting here on time. I'll be saying that there aren't any problems in my life. I must be okay. I don't need anyone's help. What's all the whining about? I can't show them or you that I'm capable. If I do that, more will be required of me. I'll lose control of my life, or I'll be tossed aside. God damn it, I hate this."

There was another issue that came up in the sessions, as I was reading the process notes (the process notes are so helpful for this reason), was my discovering that I was only doing the first part of some of my Schizoid interpretations. I would only get the first half down on paper, and she would interrupt me. She would cut me off, so I never got the last half of it. So, as I began to get some awareness of that, I started to interpret that in the same manner as well. "I wonder, perhaps, as you start to share with me and I start to speak, whether it brings up more feelings of being unsafe and fears of being controlled by me. To keep safe, you interrupt me and you seize control of the conversation, so you won't feel the need to submit to my comments." She responded, "That is the way it was with my mother. I would have to submit to her lectures without responding. In those moments, I wanted to explode, but felt I had to become the silent, penitent child as she droned on." Sitting with her in the room, I at times felt like that silent child, waiting to explode as she droned on. Through projective identification, she was communicating her experience to me.

(Dr. M comments) We clearly have an example of an implicit procedural memory being reenacted in this segment. And it also illustrates how, for years, these patients were considered untreatable. Here you have seen a good example of the transference acting out of a projection, and what they used to do was to use some kind of interpretation about an oedipal conflict. You can see why they wouldn't get anywhere with it, and then they would blame it on the patient, saying, "These patients aren't treatable." They hadn't learned what the key to accessing the patient's defense was.

I would do the same type of interpretations around her list of physical complaints; there was a way of going through the list that she was using to erect a wall between us. So I would interpret that it seemed that this was her way of keeping safe from the fear of being controlled, to erect a wall of complaints.

I'd like to talk a little about the therapeutic alliance and a process that I think illustrates her shifting from transference acting out to transference and therapeutic alliance. She said, "If I feel good, others will feel bad, and someone will have to pay. That's the way it always is; one wins and the other loses. I felt bad last time because I was talking about things and not about myself. You pointed it out and I felt criticized by you. I felt you were saying that you were right and I was wrong. What you said sounded so critical. Then I wondered how it would be possible for you to point out that I was playing it safe and for me not to feel criticized, without my losing. And I don't think there is a way. I think I will feel that regardless of what you say. The other thought I had was that everything I do, I do to avoid myself. Is there anything I can do that isn't some attempt at safety? I was thinking last time that maybe the particular words that you use with me are the same words that my mother used when she was trying to control me. She may have mouthed the proper and correct words, but it was the feeling behind it that trapped me. Maybe you are saying the same words with okay feelings behind them, but somehow I'm sensitized to them and they sound to me like the same old trap." I think this is the beginning of transference and therapeutic alliance. She is beginning to acknowledge the reality of who I, that I'm here to offer help to her, not just to trap her, but she has the feeling, and the fear, that it may not be so.

There was a session that really struck me as an example of the talionic impulse that I wanted to read: She had made significant progress in her life since she started therapy. She found a higher paying job; she was able to speak up in support of herself at work; and she developed a relationship with a coworker, and he's been talking about marriage these last months; she has greater access to her feeling states and has attempted to negotiate a closer relationship with her siblings and her father. Dr. Masterson writes that the person with a Disorder of the Self lacks the capacities of the real self, one of which is to acknowledge self-activation. She has great difficulty with this. Even though she has had these successes, she tends to hide them from me. I have to infer her successes, and it seems that I only get hints from time to time, from what slips out accidentally.

She recently elaborated on her difficulty in acknowledging her accomplishments with some genetic material. "It felt intolerable for me to give into her. If I did what she asked of me, I was giving in and she won. Getting better to me means that she wins. If I live a normal life, it means that she wasn't so bad. 'Look at her daughter, she's not so bad, she must have a good mother.' It seems that the only way for me to speak is to say No, that's where I feel I have some power. No, I won't get better. By being in so much pain, I imagine that somehow I am punishing her. This all doesn't make sense to me. I don't see her; I haven't seen her in years, so why do I think I am punishing her. Why do I think I can get back at her by failing? Even if she were to die tomorrow, I think I would still have this feeling. I loathe the idea of being successful. It vindicates her. That's why I hate the car. [For the last four years, she's been driving a car that breaks down every week and she just bought herself a new car.] The car says to the world that I'm successful. It's not only that I don't feel I deserve it, but I think it tells everyone that she was an okay mother. Maybe I want her to notice how much pain I'm in. If I can be pathetic enough, maybe she'll have to pay attention finally. It's crazy though — it's never worked, and I know it never will."

Dr. Masterson writes: "Unable to express his hurtful rage because of her need for, and fear of, her parents, she attempts to master it by internalizing it, using the mechanism of identification with the aggressor. She discharges the rage by attacking herself, fantasizing revenge on the parents and fulfillment of her talionic impulses by destroying their possession herself. There is also a compensatory accompanying fantasy that if she dramatizes her sorrowful states sufficiently, the parents will provide the wished-for response." I think my patient's thoughts express what Dr. Masterson has called the talionic impulse.

(*Dr. M comments*) What about countertransference?"

I had none. The Mr. Nice Guy was my biggest countertransference reaction here. I was trying to be helpful, and in being helpful, I would offer these wonderful, elaborate interpretations that I thought she would just accept and appreciate. That didn't happen. I also felt that once I really honed in on it, I was going to bring her to the point of a lot of pain, and that just wasn't a nice thing to do. And I was raised in a family of nice people, and we don't do those kinds of things. So, during the time that I was receiving supervision, I started riding horses. I had this experience of going horseback riding on the beach. I was on this Arabian mare, named Misty. The owner told me that this horse wouldn't go into the water, but I was welcome to try it if I wished.

Touching Water

It is my first ride to the beach
My horse, Misty, plods along
The six-mile trail unremarkably.
At the first hint of an ocean breeze,
However, she stops dead in her tracks.
I'm told she was at the ocean once before
But stayed clear of the water

Coaxing and pushing her along,
We make it to the sand
But she makes it clear to me that

She isn't going near the water.
Firm, unrelenting pressure
From my landward leg
Keeps her a few feet from the thin
Sheet of salty liquid gliding toward us

We gallop down the sandy beach
Slowing down to weave in
And out among the large jagged rocks.
Finally, a dead end.
We turn around in the cove
And head back,
The ocean now on our left

Firm pressure both legs.
With her momentum, a canter.
I guide her into the water
Just barely one hoof in.
She slows and resists.
She retreats backward.
She rears up,
Perhaps to shake me off
I kick with both heels,
Closing the rear exit
She darts ahead.
I pull firm on the reins.
The forward exit is closed also.
She crabs her body right,
And with the firm pressure
Of my right leg
I squeeze her toward the water
And close the side exit

There is only one way to go

With trepidation, she inches
Toward the water
One hoof, two, three, and then all four
Standing in a few inches of water
That feels to her
More than enough to drown in
If I let up, she will flee

Her entire body now shakes with fear
Twitching muscles, unsteady frame.
The current of fear passes through
Me as well

I hold her still.
I breathe.

She breathes
I move her deeper
She retreats
Against my primitive impulse
I close the exits again
Over and over again
She goes deeper
Her shins, her knees
Eventually water laps at her side
And a wave breaks on my thigh
Boots and horse soaked

The shaking, almost completely gone
Misty, calmer now
On the edge of enjoyment
Exhilaration, Euphoria, Confidence
She breathes
I breathe

What is it about us
That avoids the water at all costs?
Staying dry from tears
Avoiding fears
That threaten to destroy us
Missing out
On pleasures both simple and profound
And knowing the shape
Of our own true self

— Joseph Farley, October 2001

(Dr. M comments) I was doing to you what you were doing to Misty.
Yes, indeed.

10

Therapeutic Neutrality
Under Challenge

JERRY S. KATZ, L.C.S.W.

In the last two decades, therapeutic neutrality has come under challenge in the psychoanalytic literature as a basis for how psychoanalytically oriented therapists approach their work. As various developments inside and outside of the field have led to alternative perspectives on the nature of the psychoanalytic interaction, doubt about whether neutrality on the part of the therapist is either possible or desirable has been increasingly voiced.

The main challenge to therapeutic neutrality derives from what has come to be called relational psychoanalysis. This term is used to denote a wide (although not sharply defined) range of theoretical schools that view human relatedness or attachment, as opposed to instincts and drives, as the central impetus in human development and motivation. Object relations theorists, such as Winnicott, Guntrip, and Kohut, are considered as falling within the overall relational umbrella and, based on the above definition, the developmental, self, and object relations approach of Masterson could also be described as a relational one.

However, the main thrust of the relational school comes from theorists of the intersubjective (see Stolorow, Brandchaft, & Atwood, 1987), the social-constructivist/perspectivist (see Hoffman, 1991), and especially the interpersonal (see Mitchell, 1988, 2000; Aron, 1996) schools. Some of them integrate into their theories the object relations model of intrapsychic structures that reflect the individual's historical and current senses of self within the interpersonal world, and agree that individuals bring to any relationship the projection of early object ties. All of them reject the concept of developmental arrest; they see human behavior as too contextual and too malleable to be "fixed" in this way. Mitchell (1988) argues that the developmental-arrest model lends itself to viewing the patient through the metaphor of the baby, which leads both the analyst and patient to view the latter as a passive victim of early childhood events.

These theories reflect the postmodern critique of positivism, and the doubting of all certainties. They also echo ideas from feminism, constructivism, and cultural relativism. Relational theorists reject the idea that the therapist is an authority who studies the patient's mind from outside the relationship, comes up with objective findings about it, and reveals these facts to the patient from a neutral position.

They maintain that in the psychoanalytic relationship, as in any other human interaction, the therapist and patient continuously influence each other in aware and unaware ways. "Countertransference," therefore, is seen as omnipresent, and is neither a discrete nor an abnormal event. An inextricable participant in an intersubjective field, the therapist cannot separate out his or her ideas about the patient from his or her embeddedness in this field and its powerful multidirectional pulls and tugs. To these theorists, then, objectivity and therapeutic neutrality are impossible. Nor do they see this as a problematic state of affairs. Since:

> The analyst's personality affects not only the therapeutic alliance or the so-called real relationship, but also the nature of the transference itself ... the impact of the analyst needs to be examined systematically as an intrinsic part of the transference, which is thought to be based on the mutual contributions of both participants to the interaction (Aron, 1996. p. 50).

The systematic examination of the impact of the therapist involves discussion not only of what the patient thinks the therapist thinks and feels, but also of the actual subjectivity of the therapist. As Mitchell (1998) puts it,

> The kind of inquiring stance the analyst strives to establish and invites the analysand to join [asks such questions as]: How did we get into this? Why do you experience differences between us as assaultive and disrespectful? Why do I often find myself assaulting (or wanting to assault) you? How can we together find a way of talking with each other which allows you your self-respect and me some possibility of being and using myself more authentically in a way that might be helpful to you? (p. 296).

§ § §

What follows is an exploration of therapeutic neutrality as it relates to the psychoanalytic psychotherapy of individuals with personality disorders. After explaining what is meant by therapeutic neutrality in the developmental, self, and object relations approach, vignettes from the treatment of a woman with a personality disorder are used to illustrate why therapeutic neutrality is necessary in work with such individuals *if* the goal of the treatment is a change in character structure. The vignettes will also illustrate how bringing a discussion of the therapist's subjectivity into the therapy may strengthen the patient's unrealistic view of self and others, as well as the patient's maladaptive behavior.

It should be mentioned first that therapeutic neutrality is not a posture that needs to be assumed with all patients, or even with some patients, throughout the course of their therapy. Bringing the therapist's subjectivity into discussion in the session might meet the needs of a patient who does not have a personality disorder, or one who does but who (for financial, scheduling, motivational, or other reasons) is not likely to benefit from therapy that focuses on character structure. And it might become appropriate with a patient who no longer has a personality disorder, having worked it through in prior therapeutic work.

The term "therapeutic neutrality" has had a wide variety of meanings throughout the history of psychoanalysis and across theoretical schools. Within the developmental, self, and object relations approach, it is viewed in light of the internalized object relations (called the intrapsychic structure), and deficits in the capacities of the self, of a person who presents with a personality disorder. In the first three years of life, such an individual had relationships with primary caregivers (particularly the mother) that often left him or her in an affective state, which Masterson (1976, p. 38) calls the abandonment depression: depression, rage, panic, guilt, passivity and helplessness, and emptiness and void. The only way to avoid the abandonment depression is to maintain a split of his or her affective states, as well as of the self and object representations that develop along with those states, into unmodulated and unintegrated "good" and "bad" ones.

As life progresses the person continues to employ defensive splitting to avoid reactivating the affects of the abandonment depression. Critical aspects of the development of the self and its capacities[1] have to be sacrificed in the

---

[1] The capacities of the self are spontaneity; self-entitlement, self-activation, assertion, and support; acknowledgment of self-activation and maintenance of self-esteem; soothing of painful affects; continuity of the self; commitment; creativity; intimacy; and autonomy.

struggle to survive psychologically, and, as a result, the ability to activate the real self has been diminished (Masterson, 2000, p. 62). The individual comes to function on the basis of a false self, which is based on fantasy and denial, instead of on the mastery of reality. This false self serves to defend against the painful affects of the abandonment depression. Whole- self and object-representations were not formed, and repression of childhood impulses of love and hate could not take place.

In the initial, testing phase of treatment, this patient is: "relating through massive projection and transference acting out, without awareness of the independent existence of the therapist" (Masterson, 1993, p. 76).

Masterson makes the critical distinction between transference and transference acting out. The former characterizes neurotic or healthier patients, and occurs when the patient acts toward the therapist on the basis of projecting past relationships. Here, the therapist is experienced as a whole object, and, therefore, as a separate center of thought and motivation containing a mixture of good and bad qualities. Transference acting out is typical of patients with personality disorders. It takes place when this patient acts toward the therapist on the basis of the projection of past relationships, but here, owing to defensive splitting, the patient experiences the therapist as containing only good or bad qualities and motivations at a given moment. Upon entering therapy, therefore, a patient with a personality disorder has a split and rigid view, both of himself or herself and of the therapist, a view that is distorted and omits significant aspects of what is and what is not present in both participants, and in their interaction.

Expecting the therapist to see the world in the same split way, and denying the possibility of distorted perceptions, this patient behaves in a manner designed to coerce the therapist to act accordingly. If the therapist accepts this implicit pressure and resonates with the patient's projections, he or she confirms the patient's belief that this is the only basis on which the patient can relate. Only when the therapist is standing outside of the projections is he or she able to point them out to the patient, and to promote their examination.

Therapeutic neutrality is the stance whereby the therapist attempts to avoid acting in accordance with the projections that reflect the patient's split-self and object representations. It includes maintaining the therapeutic frame in such practical matters as beginning and ending sessions on time, setting up missed-session arrangements, making payments, not socializing with the patient, and not working with the patient's relatives or friends. Beyond that, the therapist works to be aware of feeling "tugged" toward a particular sense of himself or herself or of the patient, to understand the tug and to separate what is the therapist from what is coming from the patient, and to use this information to avoid resonating with the projection.

Therapeutic neutrality has nothing to do with emotional flatness, unresponsiveness, detachment, or a failure to show interest in the patient or the important events in the patient's life. It is different in its nature, and in its aim, from the blank screen of classical psychoanalytic-drive theory.

In classical psychoanalytic theory, neurosis is seen as resulting from the weakened ego's failure adequately to repress dangerous infantile impulses. These impulses are derivatives of the basic instinctual drives (libido and aggression). Since impulses are considered to be a form of energy (or cathexis) within the closed biological system that is the individual, the partially repressed impulses will seek gratification through other pathways. In neurosis, these impulses break through in disguise and achieve partial gratification in the form of neurotic symptoms. The treatment of a neurosis requires the highlighting of disguised drive derivatives as they are expressed in the transference to the therapist — who replaces early figures as the object of the patient's instinctual drives. In this way, they can be brought into the patient's awareness and eventually renounced through secondary process thinking. The therapist presents a blank screen to the patient in order to facilitate projections ("You act so coldly and uncaringly to me!") of the impulses onto the therapist. If the therapist gratifies the impulses (for example, by responding to the reproach with displays of affection), they will not show up in the patient's associations or dreams, and, therefore, not be available for interpretation. The analysis thus must be conducted in a state of abstinence from gratification. In the classical model, then, the goal is to uncover and then accept infantile impulses.

In the developmental, self, and object relations approach to work with personality disorders, in order to highlight or evoke unconscious impulses, therapeutic neutrality is used, as the patient's defensive splitting has left affects of love and hate quite conscious. Nor is it employed to promote projections onto the therapist, since the patient projects powerful affects from the start of the therapy. Instead, therapeutic neutrality provides the basis for looking at the patient's acting out of conscious, but contradictory, affective and representational states so that they can be examined against a background of other possibilities and seen as inimical to the individual's long-term goals. The goal is the integration of contradictory affective states so that the development of the self can resume.

§ § §

Andrea was a 26-year-old who had entered therapy feeling "completely lost." Her dress, carriage, and hairstyle made her appear much younger than her actual age — girl-like, in fact. Her presenting complaints were of being obese (with prediabetic symptoms) and feeling unable to reduce her food intake; finding herself alone after each of her three romantic relationships had ended with the man's leaving her for another woman (during each of these, Andrea had experienced herself as "completely devoted and sure that this one would last"); finding that her administrative job gave her little satisfaction and did not utilize her (considerable) intelligence and creativity; and having difficulty with deciding how to spend her time and accomplish such tasks as cleaning her apartment, paying bills, buying clothes, and grooming herself. She claimed to have "no clue" as to why she was having these difficulties. She also maintained that she was unable to think in any productive way about these issues, and that she would become confused and get headaches when she tried.

Andrea had been in psychotherapy several times before, each time for at least two years. She said that she had liked all of her previous therapists, and that in each course of therapy, she had learned something about herself, but none had led to any significant changes in her presenting problems, or given her any sense of control over her life. She had felt particularly understood by, and comfortable with, the woman therapist, who frequently hugged her at the end of a session. It was not Andrea's decision to leave any of her therapists, but she had accepted the suggestion of each that another therapist might be of more help to her. She described herself as continually miserable and as seeing no point to her life (although she denied ever seriously contemplating suicide).

At the suggestion of her prior therapist, Andrea had begun using an antidepressant medication a year earlier, but complained that it did not help her to do anything with her life, or make her feel significantly better.

She described her mother, with whom she spoke on the telephone at least once a day, as "a good person, who is always 'there.'" Andrea said that she had always felt close to her mother, and that since childhood, her mother had confided in her with complaints about the father. The mother saw herself as a victim of the father's neglect, his poor management of his income, his lack of ambition, his quick temper, and his "lower-class family and interests." She regretted that her husband had never helped her to return to college to complete her degree. "My mother always seemed sad and lonely," said Andrea, who remembered spending many weekend nights during her childhood and adolescence accompanying her mother to movies and cultural events.

Andrea described her father as "no father to me." As the basis for this perception, she explained that he had often failed to provide her with enough money to buy clothes as nice as those of her friends, that he was self-involved and had only occasionally asked her about her future plans, and that he called her irregularly, and sometimes did not return her calls for several days. Andrea was unsettled about her relationship with her father, was frequently angry in her thoughts about him, and often refused to return his calls. At the same time, she became anxious when she hadn't heard from him in a while. She wondered if it might not be better to just sever the relationship completely. She mentioned having discussed this relationship "ad nauseum" in her previous therapies, but felt that nothing had changed in her feelings or her behavior toward him.

Andrea had no siblings. She had a number of long-term, fairly close friendships with women. She denied any history of physical or sexual abuse, and I could find no indication that these had occurred. She also denied any abuse of alcohol or illegal drugs. Andrea mentioned that, as a child and adolescent, she had occasionally scratched herself (making shallow cuts) and pulled hard on her hair (rarely pulling any out), but she had not done either of these in over 10 years. She had completed one semester of college, dropping out when she found herself preoccupied with other things while trying to study.

From the first session, I was struck by the fact that she did not explore her motivations or her feelings in any depth, and by her shock and dismay that I would expect her to do so. While she exhibited much affect, this was usually in the form of tearful expressions of her inability to control her behavior, or rage about what I did or, especially, did not do.

She began the third session of her once-a-week therapy by describing how upset she was about something that had happened earlier in the week. One evening, despite having promised herself on her way home from work that she would make a start on cleaning the kitchen, Andrea had instead spent the evening eating popcorn and watching television. She criticized herself for this, saying, "That's what I always do, and it makes me sick about myself! I can never get anything organized or done." She began to weep, saying that it just showed how out of control her life was. She then stopped and waited.

When I said nothing, she began to plead with me to tell her what to do with this material. "I don't know where to go with this! You've been listening to me for three weeks; I *know* you have ideas about what's causing this. *Please* help me here." When I questioned the ease with which she gave up her efforts to understand her behavior or the feelings behind it, Andrea whiningly and angrily denounced me for withholding this direction from her. "You're my therapist, yet you're giving me nothing to help me! My other therapists always helped me out; they suggested an area for me to think about, or made some connection that helped me learn something about myself."

Andrea had manifested both sides of her split object relations units; she had gone from seeing herself as helpless and me as a benign parent to seeing herself as deprived and victimized and me as withholding. Her history, the deficits in her self-functioning, and her pattern of responding to significant others and to me, indicated that she had a Borderline personality disorder. Most crucial in coming to this diagnosis were the many indications that her intrapsychic structure consisted of split self-representations and object representations. The Borderline intrapsychic structure consists of two sets of internalized templates of the object and the self, each split off from the other. On one side of the split is a rewarding object relations unit, consisting of a maternal part-object representation that is approving and rewarding of regressive behaviors (such as clinging and acting helpless), and a part-self-representation that is a good, passive, compliant child. The representations in this unit are linked by the affects of feeling good; being taken care of; feeling loved, fed, and understood; and feeling gratified by the wish for reunion. On the other side of the split, the withdrawing object relations unit consists of a part-object representation that withdraws or is critical in the face of efforts at separation and individuation, and a part-self representation of being bad, inadequate, and defective. The representations in this unit are linked by the intensely unpleasant affects of the abandonment depression.

This description of a typical early session with Andrea certainly indicates an interaction that is co-created by the patient and therapist. Andrea wanted something from me (direction), and I did not give it to her. I not only remained silent in the face of her pleading, but responded by questioning the value to her of asking for it. This resulted in her intense feeling of frustration, an experience clearly stimulated by my way of responding in the session.

Beyond that, I undoubtedly participated in ways of which I was not aware, and, therefore, could neither describe, weigh, or analyze. My facial expressions, posture,[2] tone of voice, and numerous other factors no doubt communicated information about me and my subjectivity, and, to some unknown extent, influenced Andrea's experience of the interaction. Likewise, aspects of Andrea's way of being in the session undoubtedly communicated aspects of her subjectivity of which I was unaware, and unconsciously affected how I felt and, consequently, acted with her. This, in turn, would have affected her experience and behavior. Moreover, I was observing my patient with tinted clinical lenses, since I had come to the session looking for certain classes of information based on my theoretical orientation. While trying to be open to all kinds of input, I could not avoid missing some information that a therapist approaching the session with different lenses might have picked up.

Nevertheless, I made several crucial observations about Andrea based on the assumption that I could, at the same time, stand outside of the interactive field. Proceeding from this assumption, I concluded that she had initially displayed a posture of helplessness in the face of the therapeutic challenge to

---

[2] Aron (1996) mentions that he sometimes uses the analytic couch with patients. It is surprising to me that an approach that relies on exploration of the impact of each participant's subjectivity on the other would forgo facial and postural information.

explore her thoughts and behavior, and that this helplessness was incongruent with her intellectual and developmental capacities. I also concluded that my acting on the basis of these observations during the session had led Andrea to experience me as her victimizer. These observations could not be absolutely objective, and yet I used them as one basis for determining that her internalized object relations were based on the use of defensive splitting, and thus could become a focus of treatment.

Given that there can be no absolute objectivity in clinical work (or in any form of observation), on what basis does the therapist decide what it *is* possible to know about a patient?

It seems to me that clinical work requires judgment calls on the part of the therapist that rest on the belief that he or she *can* step outside of the interaction with the patient — at least part of the time, and in some sector of the therapist's own mind. The following comments by Weston (2002) on this question are pertinent:

> Is objectivity possible? Of course not. Hume knew that, as did Marx, as did Freud, as did Heisenberg ... We get ourselves into trouble when we take this truism and transform it into a romantic glorification of perspectivism that none of us who acts in the world, let alone who acts with patients whose pain we hope to alleviate, could really believe ... "Genuine" and "relatively objective" do not imply that we understand every aspect of ourselves or of another, or that someone could not suggest other plausible explanations for what we or they do, think, or feel. It simply means that we have reason to believe that our understanding has some substantial validity and that what we believe about the patient has a greater probability of making sense out of the data than other hypotheses we may have entertained (pp. 916–917).

Aron (1996) supports this view by observing:

> Those psychoanalytic authors ... who have most persuasively advocated constructivist approaches have repeatedly pointed out that those approaches do not reduce the need for intellectual and professional discipline and *a certain kind of analytic objectivity* [italics mine] (p. 261).

And also when Aron quotes Racker (1968):

> The analyst's objectivity consists mainly in a certain attitude towards his own subjectivity and countertransference ... True objectivity is

based upon a form of internal division that enables the analyst to
make himself (his own counter-transference and subjectivity) the object of his continuous observation and analysis. This position also enables
him to be relatively "objective" towards the analysand (p. 132).

Relative objectivity is, then, the best a therapist can hope for. The therapist must combine his or her observations with a search for other forms of
information about the patient (comparison with DSM-IV criteria, reports of developmental history, family history, medical history, available test data, information about interactions with friends, coworkers, and romantic partners)
that may inform, corroborate, or challenge these observations. But I believe
that all clinicians assume — and must assume — that at least some of their observations while interacting with a patient are generalizable, and thus are valid
predictors of what is actually true of the patient outside of the therapy office.

Given that there is no absolute objectivity, how do relational theorists jus-
tify the therapist's presenting himself or herself as a professional who has the
skills to facilitate the patient's discovering truths about himself or herself that
previously had been hidden? They handle this by, for example, describing the
therapeutic relationship as (see Aron, 1996):

> mutual but inevitably asymmetrical, [since] while influence and regu-
> lation move in both directions, that influence is not necessarily equal,
> nor do patient and analyst have equivalent or corresponding roles,
> functions, or responsibilities (p. xi).

Mitchell (2000) states a similar view:

> the analyst is always *trying* to be responsibly analytic, trying to do the
> "right thing." . . . We ask of the analyst that he love and hate re-
> sponsibly, allowing feelings to emerge, but never without also taking
> into account their implications for the analytic process, of which he
> is the guardian (pp. 131–132).

But on what basis does the therapist decide, for example, what is a "responsible" amount of feeling to show the patient before disturbing the analytic
process, or how much of this feeling comes from the therapist's own history
and how much from the interaction with the patient? And how does the
therapist decide how much "asymmetrical influence" he or she is justified in
exerting, for example, in communicating the view that the patient is acting
self-destructively?

As with objectivity, the most a therapist can achieve is relative therapeutic neutrality. This involves understanding that during the flow of the session, the therapist is subject to numerous unconscious, as well as conscious influences. It also involves the willingness to search for confirming or disconfirming data in the patient's reaction to interventions, to acknowledge the possibility that he or she is misunderstanding the patient, and, especially, to pay attention to and explore countertransference. Only with such armor against bias can the therapist achieve — to paraphrase Winnicott — good enough therapeutic neutrality.

The relational theorists do not, however, believe that neutrality is a desirable goal. They argue that the therapist's subjectivity should be considered as central a focus of the analytic work as is the patient's. For these theorists, an interpretation must be created by the therapist out of awareness of what is going on in the patient's subjectivity, as well as how that subjectivity is having an impact on the therapist's own subjectivity. Furthermore, the interpretation must be offered as an observation of an interaction created by both parties. In other words, how the patient is affecting the therapist needs to be made explicit — at least some of the time, based on the therapist's judgment of its value to the patient — and it must then form part of the discussion. Relational theorists refer to this as a "two-person psychology," to differentiate it from a so-called one-person psychology, in which only the patient's subjectivity is the focus of discussion.

§ § §

In the developmental, self and object relations approach, the fundamental intervention for each personality disorder is based on the intrapsychic structure of that disorder. In the face of the unrealistic and self-destructive behavior, thoughts, and feelings of a Borderline patient, the fundamental intervention is confrontation. Its goal is to bring to awareness what the patient is avoiding or denying. My aim in the session with Andrea was to make her aware that she was dealing with the challenge of exploring her internal processes (that is, self-activation) by avoiding it through helplessness.

The defense of helplessness is so pervasive in Borderline patients, and is so often used to avoid all attempts at self-activation, that dealing with it early on and consistently is a necessary prelude to progress in the treatment. When I confronted her helplessness by saying, "How do you think it could help you understand how to deal with your problems to have me tell you how to think about them?" Andrea became tearful and enraged. She slammed both fists down on my chair, and shouted, "Who needs this? I *told* you I can't do this by myself! I have so many problems, and this isn't helping me at all to solve them! How long is it going to go on like this?"

The above sequence is explained by what Masterson refers to as the Disorders of the Self Triad. This predicts that for individuals with personality disorders, attempts at self-activation will lead to the painful affects of the abandonment depression, which then lead to defense against these affects. My confrontation had touched on the possibility of Andrea's activating herself by exploring her feelings. This evoked the painful affects of her abandonment depression. She immediately defended against these affects by externalizing them, directing her rage at me, and thus making *me* the problem.

I could instead have chosen to acknowledge my role in creating her experience, confirming her perception that I was not giving her what she wanted. Following Aron's example (1996, p. 237), I could also have said that whereas I did not intend to withhold something from her that I thought she needed, and, in fact, did not know how she should proceed with her material, I might have presented myself in ways of which I was unaware. I could then have invited her to tell me what it was about how I had presented myself that made her experience me as she had.

What might have been the impact on this patient of an exploration of my subjectivity, and her experience of my subjectivity? Nothing in her "good" or "bad" views of herself and me suggests that she could have taken responsibility for co-creating our interaction; she would likely have continued to see "the problem" as arising exclusively out of my refusal to meet her needs. Introducing my limited awareness of my subjectivity would have raised the possibility that I had not recognized my true motivations. This might well have reinforced Andrea's belief that I was withholding desperately needed direction, and have resulted in a strengthening of the patient's defenses against the affects of her abandonment depression. She would have felt understood by me — finally! — and also more comfortable in the therapy. But the good feeling would have come at the price of her not seeing herself in a more realistic and capable way.

The concept of mutuality implies the validity of *both* participants' experiences. Interventions aimed at exploring such mutuality — aimed at A *Meeting of Minds* (the title of Aron's book) — run the risk of validating the patient's distorted and polarized view of the world, and thus the acting out of defenses that result from that view. This would preclude progress in the treatment, since an individual cannot gain insight into his or her defensive behavior while acting it out.

One major way in which individuals with personality disorders avoid painful affect is to focus outside of themselves, on other people. In therapy, this can take many forms. For example, the patient may focus on what the therapist is doing or thinking. Discussing my subjectivity with Andrea thus would have provided her with yet another vehicle for avoiding the task of self-exploration.

Does all of this ignore the part the therapist plays in co-creating the patient's experience? Although it is true that each participant has some responsibility for the creation of the interaction, it is also true that the amount of responsibility may be very unevenly distributed; to use Aron's phrase, the responsibility is mutual but asymmetrical. This asymmetry is especially pronounced in work with individuals with personality disorders. The stance of therapeutic neutrality is designed to make it difficult for the patient — who is prone to placing responsibility for what he experiences on his or her environment — to avoid taking responsibility for his or her feelings in the therapy, and in life.

Does all of the above place the therapist in a position of greater power and authority than that of the patient? Perhaps so, although no more than in any other arrangement in which one individual voluntarily seeks out another for his or her expertise. Since virtually all therapists are sought out (either originally or by the patient's continuing to attend sessions) by their patients, all are given some power and authority to do what is necessary to shed light on the patient's problems. This does not mean that the therapist is infallible or unchallengeable. But it is hard to imagine that any therapist can avoid situations in which he or she must assert to the patient a view of him or her or of his or her behavior that is foreign, or may be denied.

When a patient engages in behavior that is, or may become, self-destructive, most therapists would feel required to point out the consequences of this behavior, perhaps repeatedly, and in the face of the patient's rationalizations. In doing this, the therapist is asserting a different and, he or she assumes, objective reality for the patient's benefit. This intervention is highly attuned to a need the patient has, but of which he or who is not aware, and may be denying.

An individual with a personality disorder frequently denies the maladaptive consequences of his or her defensive behavior. In the developmental, self, and object relations approach, all forms of acting out are viewed as self-destructive. The therapist, therefore, must come in at this point with an intervention aimed at pointing out the consequences of this denial. As Masterson (1993) puts it:

> The therapist assumes that the patient will always behave in a self-activated, mature, adaptive, responsible manner so that when the patient does not do so, the therapist can explore it with the patient ... Since the patient's problem revolves around the lack of autonomy of the self and he or she is caught up in self-destructive defenses, the therapist must, on the one hand, use great caution to avoid further trauma to that self by taking over for the patient functions that he or she must learn to perform for himself or herself in the session. On the

other hand, since the patient is metaphorically devoted to avoidance of self-activation, the therapist must be equally devoted to the adaptive virtues of self-activation; that is, that the patient who does not activate his or her self will pay a price for it that he or she will not like (pp. 68–69).

Because I viewed Andrea's outburst as a defense against the affects of her abandonment depression, this, too, required confrontation. I asked her, "Why do you become enraged with me when I point out that you're avoiding the effort to understand yourself, since you won't make progress in the things you've come here for unless you do understand yourself?" I was not surprised that this produced more exasperation, pleading, and anger on her part (although no further physical displays of rage), since Andrea's defenses were very well entrenched. A therapist working with any personality disorder must expect to repeat the basic intervention again and again, in sequences where the specific content continually changes to follow the patient's resistances wherever they lead.

In this first, or testing, phase of therapy, the patient is putting maximum pressure on the therapist to see the world in the way he or she does, and to react from his or her perspective. As illustrated in my session with Andrea, the therapist's presenting a different perspective evokes considerable anxiety. In her attempts to avoid this anxiety, Andrea dismissed my implicit assumption that self-activation on her part was both possible and valuable. It is only if the therapist continues to *demonstrate* the expectation that the patient will self-activate — by refusing to resonate with the patient's projections, for as long as necessary — that the patient will understand that the therapist really believes in, and will continue to stand for, this deeply respectful position. Only when the patient has been convinced of this, will he or she be confident that the therapy provides sufficient external structure for him or her to risk containing maladaptive behavior, and risk tolerating the dysphoric affects and memories that come with doing so.

§ § §

Andrea's therapy continued in this way for many months; she would start most sessions by mentioning something she had noticed about herself, stop, wait for me, and become angry when I confronted her giving up. I began to notice that she reacted to almost anything I said to her — clarifying and neutral comments, as well as confrontations — with anger and disagreement. It was only following the few times I made soothing comments to her (in reacting to unfortunate events that befell her over which she had no control) that she thanked me, and then asked me to continue treating her in this way. On several occasions, she stormed out of my office, although each time she would return within a few minutes, or for the next session, sheepishly apologizing for "acting inappropriately."

I often felt frustrated, ignored, and exasperated. My own feelings of inadequacy emerged when I questioned my diagnosis: whether I really knew the best ways to confront in general, and to confront her in particular, and whether I had the theory right, or the right theory. As time went on and I began to conjecture that she was perhaps hopeless and, in fact, helpless, the strongest and most frequent unpleasant feeling I had was guilt. I felt I was "torturing" this poor young woman, and even accepting her money for doing so! Was I staying the course, or just meeting her "stubbornness" with my own? I criticized myself for treating her like a theory, rather than as a human being.

On a few occasions (of which I am aware), I acted out my countertransference reactions to these feelings. I resented being made to feel "bad" when I was trying so hard to help her, and slipped a sarcastic edge into some otherwise accurate confrontations, to the effect that her motivations in particular situations were not always as benign as she liked to think. To relieve my guilt, but also to get back at her for making me feel inadequate, two or three times, I directed her in a situation in which she claimed not to know how to proceed, but did so with a tone of not-so-subtle devaluation of her for acting helpless. On each occasion when I became aware of having acted out in these ways, I immediately apologized to her and explained why my response had been inappropriate. But for the reasons described earlier regarding other aspects of my subjectivity, I did not discuss what I had been feeling, or its relationship to my acting out.

I believe I was able to keep my countertransference acting out to a sufficiently low level so that I could continue effectively to maintain a stance of therapeutic neutrality. What was most helpful to me in controlling it was my awareness that she was actively, although unconsciously, trying to make me feel like the bad object of her internalized object relations.

§ § §

Approximately a year after the start of the therapy, while Andrea continued to react to most of my interventions with anger and tears, I noticed several significant changes unfolding in her functioning outside of the sessions. Without mentioning that she was doing so, she began to lose weight; Andrea eventually shed more than 40 pounds, and has continued doing so. She improved her style of dress and changed her hairdo, looking and carrying herself in a much more adult manner; she now looked rather attractive. She had a short-term romantic relationship in which she put limits on her compliance with the man's wishes, and asserted a few of her own. Andrea returned to college, pursuing a degree in a field involving the expression of her musical creativity. She became much more decisive about how she spent her leisure time, and began budgeting and paying bills on time.

Clearly, Andrea had curtailed her acting out of helplessness in several areas of her life. Once she began self-activating in a particular sphere, she did not ask me how to proceed, but seemed rather decisive, and sometimes simply mentioned in passing what she had accomplished. She said with much affect that she felt very good about all of this, and that her life had changed very much for the better.

Despite these changes, however, she continued defensively splitting by treating me as a bad object. It became clearer that she also treated her father in this way, viewing everything he did, and did not do, as insufficient, withholding, or uncaring. She reacted to him with anger and withholding alternating with anxiety and clinging. From what I could gather through her reporting, her father seemed to try to meet her demands, but could never satisfy her. Her mother was rarely discussed; when she was, it was usually to praise her for understanding Andrea and "being there" for her.

I began to confront Andrea's generalized anger toward me. For example, I said, "I notice from your reactions that whatever I say displeases you or makes you angry. At the same time, since you say you've made so much progress here, I'm surprised that you never express agreement or satisfaction with what I say. Why is that?" She would either remain silent, seeming to ponder this, or say she hadn't thought she was being so angry or disagreeable. I noticed, however, that there was a change in how Andrea began sessions. She would stay far more often with material she brought up, go more deeply into her thoughts and feelings about it, and make connections from other situations and relationships in her life; that is, she was self-activating in the therapy.

Andrea then decided to try to make a change in her relationship with her father. She told him how she felt about him, and how she had experienced him as neglecting her. This preceded a more recent session in which she appeared in my waiting room looking somehow different; she again seemed childlike, in her dress, and in her posture in the chair.

She mentioned that she had forgotten her check. When I began to inquire about this, she declared, "I refuse to spend a lot of time on that in this session! Some important things have happened this week." Sensing that something significant had indeed occurred for her, and expecting her to get to it, I did not intervene. After complaining in a pouting manner that she didn't know what to bring up first, she went on to discuss incidents with friends and coworkers. In each of these, she had viewed the interaction differently than she had in the past, and behaved in a new, more self-assertive way. Still, I had the feeling that she was not bringing up something more important that was in the background. I decided to approach this by going back to her apparently regressed manner and failure to bring payment. I confronted these forms of transference acting out by saying, "I wonder why you've come in today putting yourself in a childlike, guilty, and 'bad' position in relation to me."

She immediately began to weep, and said softly, "In the last couple of weeks, I've started to scratch myself again. I've regressed, and I don't know why. It's very upsetting." After briefly discussing this, she changed the topic. When I confronted her doing so, Andrea again cried, this time more intensely. She said, "I've started acting differently with my father, but he still doesn't call me when I hope he will. I know it's only a couple of days since he called, so I don't know why I'm so upset. But I want to hear from him! Maybe I did something bad when I spoke to him. I feel so awful and negative about myself."

Andrea began the following session by saying that she was sure that her scratching herself (which did not draw blood) was related to her feelings about her father. She mentioned that she had called him, and that his having not returned her call on the same day had left her "overcome with sadness" for the rest of the week. She began crying, and said, "All I find myself wanting now is my father. I feel very, very vulnerable, and I know I have a lot more to cry about." And later, "I feel angry at him, but I know he doesn't deserve it. It seems to be about what *I* need. I really want a hug from him."

Andrea was beginning to experience some of the affects of her abandonment depression. My recent confrontations of her transference acting out of the withdrawing object relations unit had led her to self-activate more, not only during sessions, but also in her relationship with her father. As she split less with me and with her father, she was thrown back on her impaired real self, and on the affects this defensive splitting had avoided. Showing considerable courage, she was, for the first time, exploring and questioning her demands on others, and how these demands related to her own denied affects.

§ § §

Relational psychoanalysis, emerging from philosophical and cultural trends that question authority and power, emphasizes the examination of the mutuality between the subjectivities of both participants in the dyad as the primary basis for successful treatment. In the developmental, self, and object relations approach, on the other hand, the therapist, through his or her stance of therapeutic neutrality, advances a perspective about the patient that is quite different from, and fundamentally in conflict with, the personality-disordered patient's experience of himself or herself. Whereas the patient expects, and demands, that the therapist act on the basis of the patient's subjectivity, the therapist using this approach communicates that it is just that subjectivity that is unrealistic, and that must be examined if the patient is to move toward healing.

The most critical factor motivating the patient to begin this examination is the consistent presentation of the therapist's alternative subjectivity: the belief that the patient possesses the capacity to negotiate both internal and external worlds successfully in a healthier way, and the expectation that the patient will do so. This belief resonates with the patient's motivation to develop and express the real self.

But *discussing* this, or any other, aspect of the therapist's subjectivity with the patient — as advocated by the relational school — will not motivate the patient to question his or her experience of himself or herself; in fact, as indicated above, doing so is likely to promote defense, and thus preserve the status quo. As the work with Andrea illustrates, the individual with a personality disorder maintains his or her distorted subjectivity with great tenacity, and places intense pressure on the therapist to accept that subjectivity. In the face of this powerful attempt at control, the only way for the therapist to convey his or her alternative subjectivity convincingly is actually to *demonstrate* it by acting from a position of therapeutic neutrality. While the healing that occurs in psychoanalytic psychotherapy does indeed result from an intersubjective process, the therapist's subjectivity is expressed far more compellingly through his or her unwillingness to resonate with the patient's subjectivity than through the willingness to discuss his or her own.

References

Aron, L. (1996). *A Meeting of Minds: Mutuality in Psychoanalysis.* Hillsdale, NJ: Analytic Press.

Hoffman, I. Z. (1991). Discussion: Toward a social-constructivist view of the psychoanalytic situation. *Psychoanalytic Dialogues, 1,* 74–105.

Masterson, J. F. (1976). *Psychotherapy of the Borderline Adult.* New York: Brunner/Mazel.

Masterson, J. F. (1993). *The Emerging Self: A Developmental, Self, and Object Relations Approach to the Treatment of the Closet Narcissistic Disorder of the Self.* New York: Brunner/Mazel.

Masterson, J. F. (2000). *The Personality Disorders: A New Look At the Developmental, Self, and Object Relations Approach.* Phoenix: Zeig, Tucker.

Mitchell, S. A. (1988). *Relational Concepts in Psychoanalysis: An Integration.* Cambridge, MA: Harvard University Press.

Mitchell, S. A. (2000). *Relationality: From Attachment to Intersubjectivity.* Hillsdale, NJ: Analytic Press.

Racker, H. (1968). *Transference and Countertransference.* New York: International Universities.

Stolorow, R. B., Brandchaft, B., & Atwood, G. E. (1987). *Psychoanalytic Treatment.* Hillsdale, NJ: Analytic Press.

Westen, D. (2002). The search for objectivity in the study of subjectivity: Reply to commentary. *Psychoanalytic Dialogues, 12,* 915–920.

11

Representations of Reality:
The Analytic Quest for
the Unnarrated Self

JUDITH PEARSON, PH.D.

We had the experience but missed the meaning,
And approach to the meaning restores the experience
In a different form . . .

— *T. S. Eliot*

The experience of reality is constructed by the
activity patterns of neuronal groups clustered into
functional units capable of representing experience
in different modalities . . . Subjective reality is the way
individuals assemble particular neuronal activations
within themselves.

— *Daniel Siegel*

As part of its evolution, the umbrella of psychoanalysis has been stretched to encompass virtually all significant dimensions of human experience: conscious and unconscious (now, often, nonconscious), developmental, biological, re-membered and forgotten, current and historical, intrapsychic, interpersonal, intersubjective, cultural — the list could go on. Which is why, perhaps, each practitioner's work comes to be more or less informed by one and/or another of a diverse array of therapeutic approaches, none of which has been able to don the privileged mantle of known truth.

The questions that have lurked behind the curtain, informing each approach, each technique, and ultimately each practitioner, are those involving assumptions concerned with the nature, locus, development, and functioning of the (mind) self and its relation to both internal and external reality. The conceptions underlying these assumptions have, in turn, determined notions about the way in which the psychoanalytic endeavor best understands and facilitates self-knowledge, self-coherence, self-regulation, and self-activation — in fact, those elements that compose self-growth.

To explicate perspectives surrounding the nature of the self and its experience could be a topic as exhaustive as the whole of human history, and even a cursory examination of models of the mind demonstrates, not surprisingly, that none of them can be easily extricated from the governing scientific and philosophical zeitgeist of their time. (This, in itself, is a testimony to the constant and complex process of revision, transcription, and transformation that occurs in the face of what for some is "understanding," and for others is "creating" subjective human experience.)

What's more, there exists a real possibility that the station may be moving with the train, such that not only the theories, but also the self, may be undergoing changes over time. So, for example, as Julian Jaynes (1976) proposed, there existed "a race of men who spoke, judged, reasoned, solved problems, indeed did most of the things that we do, but who were not conscious at all," and that this race of men existed in a time as recent as the *Iliad*[1] (p. 47). Whatever the timing, it is clear that the emergence of consciousness as a central aspect of human subjectivity has left the psychological man (or woman) with the riddle posed by the relationship between his conscious subjective experience and the unconscious processes that underlie it.

The stumbling block encountered by all theorists attempting to derive general principles about un(non)conscious processes based on overt patterns of behavior has been succinctly elaborated by Mahler and her colleagues (1975) in their discussion of conclusions drawn from observations made in the laboratory of the therapeutic nursery. In presenting their work, they offer the following caveat:

---

[1] Jaynes' exploration of the development of consciousness is fun and fascinating reading, and thinking about it gives rise to the possibility of many tempting digressions, one of which might focus on the possibility firmly adhered to by Freud that the ontogenesis of the self does indeed recapitulate elements of its phylogenetic history. And, in fact, Jaynes' thesis accords well with current neurobiologic theories that stress the primacy of nonconscious processes as primary organizers of the self.

The question of the kind of inferences that can be drawn from direct observation of the preverbal period is a most controversial one. The problem is complicated by the fact that not only is the infant pre-verbal, but that the verbal means of the observer–conceptualizer lend themselves only very poorly to the translation of such material. The problems of psychoanalytic reconstruction here find their parallel in the problem of psychoanalytic construction — the construction of the picture of the inner life of the preverbal child, a task in which co-enesthetic empathy, we believe, plays a central role (pp. 13–14).

Although these authors consign their difficulties to the issue of estab-lishing psychodynamic principles based on the behavior of preverbal children, the problem of inference surrounding the essential and irreducible gap that exists between the unconscious inner world and the consciously perceived, re-membered, and/or narrated version of that world, is intrinsic to all analytic domains, ranging from what Schafer (1983) has dubbed the "master narrative" of theory, to the story of a single life told and heard in psychotherapy. Further, as shall be demonstrated, this gap exists as both isomorphic to, and in direct consequence of, the structure of the brain itself, which consists of two hemispheres, each of which is engaged in a different mode of receiving, struc-turing, and imparting information. Thus, even though these disparate struc-tures are, in their turn, subject to integrating structures and processes, the findings of psychoanalysis, as well as those of neurobiology, indicate that left-brain, explicit, secondary process linguistically symbolized representations can never be completely faithful reproductions of right-brain, implicit, primary-process, presymbolic-and affectively determined events.

This chapter — as much reverie as research — will attempt to trace some of the ways in which the conundrum of psychoanalytic (re)construction has been dealt with by theorists with a variety of perspectives in their quest to discover the "real" reality, the "real" mind, the "true" narrative, and, ultimately, the "real" analysis.

MAPPING REALITY

The epistemological problem — how we acquire knowledge of reality and how reliable and true that knowledge might be — occupies contemporary philosophy no less than it occupied Plato.
— *Paul Watzlawick*

And no less than it occupies contemporary psychoanalysis.

FREUD'S DOMAIN

I have said before
That the past experience revived in the meaning
Is not the experience of one life only
But of many generations — not forgetting
Something that is probably quite ineffable.

— *T. S. Eliot*

Freud's vision with regard to the relationship between the mind and reality was caught, like much of his theory, somewhere between the blinding light of clarity and the shadow of ambiguity. Thus, he placed himself squarely in alignment with the positivist viewpoint of his day wherein the "truth" of an observation was anchored in an objective reality. Still, as elaborated by Moore (1999):

... throughout Freud's psychoanalytic career the basic premise on which he based his clinical approach was that an objective material reality is initially directed and consciously perceived and simultaneously fully recorded in "memory traces" whose fidelity is essentially that of a contact print. One fact must not be ignored, however, if Freud's relation to the past is to be understood. It was never the past per se, but always exclusively mental representations of that past that were psychologically operative in his patients, and these key faithful representations were also necessarily unconscious (p. 18).

Freud's conceptions found their way into his work in his focus on replacing reliance on conscious explication of the patient's subjective experience with attention to the conveyors of the unconscious representational universe — symptoms, dreams, associations, and, most formidably, repetition, primarily as evidenced in the transference. The analyst's function was to provide a neutral backdrop against which the unique outlines of the patient's material could be discerned. The quest was for the hidden reaches of "historical truth," but again Moore sounds a warning note:

By "historical truth" Freud . . . meant something quite distinct and in fact almost directly opposite from the way in which the term is currently used . . . for, rather than using the term to refer to the accurately rendered objective past, Freud used it to refer to the "kernel of truth" in distorted subjectivity, the element of causal symbolic connection between some actual past event stored in the unconscious and what is currently, and erroneously, consciously thought to be the past or present material truth (p. 25).

What becomes quite clear is that Freud's embeddedness in the positivist tradition did not prevent him from taking the radical step of emphasizing psychic, as opposed to material, reality — a step he saw as necessary, but one that was for him, and for those who followed in his footsteps, forever fraught with ambivalence; for the moment that psychoanalytic reality became reliant on the inferred data of the unconscious was the moment that it lost its claim to Freud's longed-for dream of scientific provability.

Freud's psychology has also most commonly been thought of as a one-person affair in which the impact of object relations took a back seat to the intrapsychic world of wish and drive. But here, too, there is room for debate. Thus, despite his abandonment of the seduction theory and his consequent reliance on the internal world of what Mitchell (2001) has called "fantasy,"[2] Freud never disregarded the impact of early relationships on the psyche, nor was his theory devoid of internalized object-relational content, as can be seen in his postulation of an ego born of "abandoned object-cathexes" (1924, p. 19), and a superego born of the dual identifications of the complete Oedipus complex, which, "by giving permanent expression to the influence of the parents ... perpetuates the existence of the factors to which it owes its origin" (p. 25). It is also this same agency of the superego through which, famously," the shadow of the object fell upon the ego" (1917; 1957, p. 131). One is, then, inclined to agree with Mitchell, who indicates, "Freudian drive theory always remained, necessarily, a *kind* (emphasis Mitchell's) of object relations theory, in which fantasies about others rather than the actions of others were crucial" (2000, p. ix).

Despite Freud's fabled dictum that sometimes a cigar is just a cigar (a formulation that arguably killed him), it is, in fact, questionable as to how far at any level meaningful to the human psyche the "actions of others" can be

---

[2] It is important to note that the meaning of "fantasy" as conceived of in Freud's metapsychology differs from the meaning implied in everyday usage in that Freud's construct of "wish" referred to an unconscious rather than a conscious construction. This distinction is clearly delineated by the British Middle School, which uses a linguistic convention to separate unconscious fantasy and the conscious daydreaming ordinarily associated with the word "fantasy." This distinction needs to be kept in mind when reading statements such as the one referred to by Mitchell, who indicates that Freud's work was involved with fantasies of what people do, rather than their real actions.

separated from the representational content they both structure and evoke. And, in fact, it is around just this issue that the argument of psychoanalysis swirls, circling endlessly like the dancers in the caucus race in *Alice in Wonderland* (Carroll, 1862/1960).

This notwithstanding, it must ultimately be conceded that Freud's was indeed a one-person psychology in the sense that in his world, it was not the struggles between individuals, but the struggles and compromises undergone by the agencies of the mind as they wrestled with the vicissitudes of the instincts, Eros and Thanatos, that became the ultimate determinants of conflict and character. Comments Rieff (1961):

> No doubt many of Freud's personal biases are frozen into his instinct theory . . . [nonetheless] the liberal revisers of Freud, in their efforts to avoid the pessimistic implications of his genetic reasoning, tend to let the idea of the individual be absorbed into the social, or at best permit it a vague and harried existence, [whereas] Freud himself, through his mythology of the instincts, kept some part of character safe from society, restoring to the ideal of human nature a hard core not easily warped or reshaped (p. 35).

THE DOMAIN OF RELATIONALITY

There is no such thing as an infant.

— *D. W. Winnicott*

Nowhere are Rieff's distinctions seen to be more true than in the post-Heisenbergian era with its emphasis on the inextricable connection between the observer and the observed, a connection that was carried into the psycho-analytic universe in a diversity of theories that have come under the collective rubric of "relationality." All theories included in the relational matrix place human attachment over instinctual drive,[3] and all, in one form or another,

---

[3] The work of the British middle school has been shoved into the procrustean bed of relational theory. However, Melanie Klein's adherence to the drives — carried later into the psychologies of theorists like Fairbairn — as well as the pervasive notion of internalized object relations carried forward from the British school into modern American object relations theory by Masterson and Kernberg make the object relations theorists an awkward fit for any theoretical framework that largely rejects constructs based on drives, or on the notion of a prefigured intrapsychic universe needing to be discovered by a neutral analyst.

emphasize the Sullivanian notion of the participant–observational nature of the analytic relationship. In addition, all, to varying degrees, focus on the here-and-now data of the psychoanalytic inquiry, the co-constructed nature of reality, and, for some, the central importance of the shaping force of language.

The relational school was largely the brainchild of Stephen Mitchell, who was, before his tragic death, its cofounder, along with Jay Greenberg. The theory's initial incarnation saw these authors attempting to synthesize elements of Sullivan's interpersonal theory and the object-relational perspective of contemporary analysts of the British school. Since its inception, however, an increasingly broad spectrum of analytic theory has been caught up in relationality's inclusive net. Say Mitchell and Aron (1999, pp. xi–xii): "The term grew and began to accrue to itself many other influences and developments: later advances of self psychology, particularly intersubjectivity theory; social constructivism in its various forms; certain currents within contemporary psychoanalytic hermeneutics; more recent developments in gender theorizing; the important contributions of Merton Gill on the centrality of transference–countertransference interaction; and, with the English translation in 1988 of his *Clinical Diary*, the rediscovered legacy of Sandor Ferenczi.

It is beyond the scope of this chapter to survey all the vast landscape encompassed by the relational school, however, a brief look at some of its more substantive constituents may serve to demonstrate how, in attempting to bypass the singular-psyche-as-analyzed-by-neutral-analyst-seeking-historical-truth Scylla of Freud, many postclassical analysts have steered themselves into a Charybdis of constructivist confusion.

Winnicott's (1960) formulation, "there is no such thing as an infant — only the infant–mother unit" (itself a paradox of pointed meaning and enigma), has become an iconic precept of both relationality and the intersubjective theory of Robert Stolorow. For both, the statement is as applicable to the patient–analyst relationship as it is to the infant–mother relationship, in that both perspectives agree that the participants in these dyads "create" each other. As will be seen, however, each perspective focuses on a different dimension of what it means to "create" experience. Thus, Mitchell's use of Winnicott maintains shades of his interpersonalist perspective, stressing, as it does, "the real actions" of people. His position contrasts sharply with Stolorow's intersubjective formulations, which center solely around the participants' subjective experience of such actions.[4] In examining segments of each theory, it can be seen that neither a focus on real interaction to the exclusion of the

---

[4] As shall be seen shortly, Stolorow aims for this perspective, but his position winds up being far more muddled than this statement implies.

representational content attendant on those actions nor a focus on the phenomenal intersubjective field to the exclusion of an extant reality provides a satisfactory solution to the problem of psychic reality.

Following Loewald, Mitchell (2000, pp. 20–21) elaborates on Winnicott's statement, stripping it of it's Winnicotian core of illusion. Thus, he states: "The baby's need for the nursing experience is impossible to separate from the mother's need for the nursing experience. The baby's cry produces a 'letting-down' response in the mother's breasts, to claim that the baby has, in some sense, created the readied breast is no illusion."

As was seen before, Mitchell sacrifices the key element of psychic representation to the impact of the "real" action. He then locates this action in the realm of constructivism. Working from within the constructivist perspective, it is impossible to discredit Mitchell's statements, but the question does arise as to how far one can take this stance before its psychological usefulness reaches the vanishing point. Thus, from the same philosophical vantage point, it is equally possible to say that there is no such thing as a wolf pup, based on the fact that the same letting-down response occurs in the wolf mother, or that there is no such thing as an eagle chick, based on the fact that the chick's eliciting behavior toward the parent eagle results in food regurgitation. But the reciprocal behaviors of fixed action patterns are, one would think, but a small piece of what Winnicott intended by his statement, which is aimed primarily at pointing out the inextricable connection between the representational and the real dimensions of the infant–mother dyad.

Mitchell's formulation has been used here to exemplify a particularly interpersonalist kind of failure to join these two disparate, but inseparable, dimensions of human experience.[5] In viewing the intersubjective position advanced by Robert Stolorow, we will become aware of a different, and graver, kind of failure.

THE DOMAIN OF INTERSUBJECTIVITY

> . . . we cannot be conscious of what we are not conscious of.
>
> — *Julian Jaynes*

---

[5] I am using Mitchell's statement to exemplify a point. I am, however, fully aware that the statement does not represent the totality of his position, a point he makes as well through the use of his persectivistic qualifier "in some sense." No such equivocation exists in Stolorow's work.

> To be aware of a conscious datum is to be sure
> it has passed. The nearest actual approach to immediate
> introspection is early retrospection.
>
> — E. G. *Boring*

Stolorow and Atwood (1992/2002) also iconocize Winnicott's statement, using it in the frontispiece of *Contexts of Being*, their treatise on intersubjectivity, in which the authors try to have it all ways, postulating both a reality that is solely the creation of a subjectively experienced contextually determined phenomenological field, while, at the same time, proposing their own set of universal cognitively constructed conceptions about the structure of the mind. All serious analytic discourse must deal with both of these aspects of psychoanalytic reality as they apply to both theory and practice. But instead of enhancing each other, these central tenets of intersubjectivity do no more than cancel each other out, presenting the paradox of a theory grounded in an extant reality that includes an extant psychoanalytic reality while simultaneously proclaiming that reality is unknowable except as intersubjectively co-created (Moore, 1999).

In setting forth his theory, Stolorow[6] first makes sure to distinguish his notion of intersubjectivity from the word as it is used in Daniel Stern's developmental theory, which presupposes a self having attained a developmental level of integrity and separateness sufficient to allow it to recognize the separate feelings and intentions of another (preconditions also emphasized by Fonagy in his concept of "mentalization" and by Siegel in his concept of "mindsight"). Thus, Stolorow and Atwood put forth the following disclaimer:

> We wish to emphasize here that our use of the term "intersubjective" has never presupposed the attainment of symbolic thought, of a concept of oneself as a subject, or of intersubjective relatedness in Stern's (1985) sense. Unlike the developmentalists, we use "intersubjective" to refer to *any* [emphasis theirs] psychological field formed by interacting worlds of experience at whatever developmental level these worlds may be organized.

---

[6] For the sake of brevity, and because he is the theorist most associated with intersubjectivity, Stolorow's name will, from here on, be used to reference the ideas contained in the theory. Since the central reference I have used is *Contexts of Being*, a work on which Atwood collaborated, Atwood's name can be read along with Stolorow's.

Stolorow's rejection of the developmental perspective that conceptually frames both the "inter" and the "subject" in intersubjectivity[7] is but one example of his almost fanatic refutation of all theoretical points of view that he sees as subscribing to what he has termed "the myth of the isolated mind" (Stolorow, 2000, p. 7). In addition to classical psychoanalysis, these points of view include all or part of ego psychology, object relations theory, Basch's focus on building a bridge between analytic theory and neurobiologic theories, Schafer's perspectives on narrative, and the elements of Kohut's self psychology that include assumptions related to a nuclear self.

Stolorow discredits Mitchell's relational perspective at the level of practice, criticizing Mitchell on the grounds that "insufficient attention is given to the patient's becoming a coactor in the *analyst's* [emphasis Stolorow's] drama ... so that ... in his clinical approach Mitchell's elegant relational model ultimately collapses into a variant of the myth of the individual mind" (p. 22).

Kernberg's (and, by easy extension, Masterson's) work is discredited at the level of theory, which again is seen, on the basis of its formulation of intrapsychic structure, to be mired in the myth. In Stolorow's words:

Kernberg (1976) has offered a revision of Freudian drive theory in which he pictures the basic building blocks of personality structure as units consisting of a self-image,[8] an object-image, and an affect. Units with positive affective valence are said to coalesce into the libidinal drive, while those with a negative valence form the basis for the aggressive drive. Although Kernberg acknowledges the developmental and motivational importance of affect, once integrated into enduring self-object-affect units, affect states are seen to behave as drives, stirring within the confines of an isolated mind and triggering all manner of distorting defensive activity. The lifelong embeddedness

---

[7] When encountering Stolorow's idiosyncratic use of the word "intersubjective" in which he cuts away the developmental platform upon which the word commonly rests, I could not help but think of Humpty Dumpty's assertion to Alice: "When I use a word, it means just what I choose it to mean — neither more nor less." Humpty's practice of paying a word overtime for strained usage would seem quite applicable here.

[8] Stolorow and Atwood steadfastly refuse to use the word "representation," indicating that it has meanings for both structure and content. They, therefore, settled on "image" to refer to the representational content, and "subjective world" to refer to the representational universe — as they, not Kernberg, Masterson, or others, conceive of it.

of affective experience in an ongoing intersubjective system thereby becomes lost" (p. 16).

In line with this objection, Stolorow notes that the myth of the isolated mind denies "the essential immateriality of human experience by portraying subjective life in reified, substantive terms" (p. 7).

It is instructive, if puzzling, to observe Stolorow's critique of other theorists and then be made aware of his own theoretical and clinical work. Thus, despite his quite explicit disavowal, Stolorow proceeds to detail his own highly substantive formulation about the patterning and durability of early object relational experiences, delineating a structuralization of self-experience as a consequence of "recurring patterns of intersubjective transaction within the developmental system" that "result in the establishment of invariant principles that unconsciously organize the child's subsequent experiences." He goes on to explicate: "It is these unconscious ordering principles, crystallized within the matrix of the child–caregiver system, that form the essential building blocks of personality development" (p. 24).

These formulations accord well with current neurobiologic and psychological theories, and, in fact, could be seen as a variant of the Kernbergian and Mastersonian precepts Stolorow vehemently refutes. In fact, however, the theory that Stolorow's assumptions most consistently refute is his own.

Aware themselves of the theory's inconsistencies, Stolorow and Atwood note:

Some may see a contradiction between the concept of developmentally preestablished principles that organize subsequent experiences and our repeated contention that experience is always embedded in a constitutive intersubjective context. This contradiction is more apparent than real [for] a person enters any situation with an established set of ordering principles (the subject's contribution to the intersubjective system), but it is the context that determines which among the array of these principles will be called upon to organize the experience (p. 24).

One is, indeed, hard put to operate at this level of integration; and Stolorow's case report does little to resolve the contradiction, failing to indicate any coherent way in which context can be construed as an eliciting determinant different from what other theorists might propose who do subscribe to the "myth of the isolated mind." Rather, as his word "invariant" itself indicates, these organizing principles make themselves known as operating across a wide variety of contexts, which include, as seen in the case of

"Jessica," the context of the patient's threatening and coercive family environment, as well as the presumably safe and noncoercive context of the
therapeutic situation. Further, Jessica's developmentally organized "invariant
principles," consistently and unsurprisingly reflect the operations Stolorow
discredited in Kernberg's theory, "triggering all manner of distorting defensive
activity." How these distortions can be explained by the patient's becoming
a "coactor in the analyst's drama" is a mystery that is neither resolved by the
authors nor discernible in any other way based on the information given.

As an example, Stolorow and Atwood report that for the patient, the absence of "books on the shelves, pictures on the wall, and papers on the desk
... symbolized for her the imminent threat of abandonment. . . . Hence from
the first hour the therapist saw the emotional results of Jessica's early experiences with loss, abandonment and inconsistency (p. 69).

This is a reasonable therapeutic hypothesis; however, the therapist's inferences, including the inference of the patient's having an unconscious engaged
in mental functions that symbolize, as well as the inference (so evocative of
Freud's "kernel of truth") as to the meanings inherent in the symbolization,
point to the fact that both therapist and patient are engaged in, and conceptualized as being engaged in, operations that can only be products of the contents and processes of their own (isolated) minds. It is further evident that
these contents and processes cannot be discernible in the "immaterial" phenomenal data of the experiential intersubjective world of patient and therapist.
Rather, they are inferred hypotheses applied to, but not co-created in, the
intersubjective moment.

Stolorow (Stolorow et al., 1987/2000) expresses his belief in the intersubjective foundations of analytic knowledge by his assertion that "anything that
is not *in principle* (emphasis his) accessible to empathy and introspection does
not fall within the bounds of psychoanalytic inquiry." He then confuses the
issue further by postulating a tripartite unconscious (p. 5). However, as Moore
(1999) rightly points out, "All three of intersubjectivity's unconscious structures are *by definition* (emphasis his) not subject to either empathy or introspection. They clearly cannot be known through psychoanalytic inquiry as defined
by Stolorow and colleagues" (p. 80).

Some leeway might be granted based on the fact that the mental operations relied on to build a theory of psychoanalysis must, as Moore indicates, be
different from those Stolorow proposes as at the heart of the practice of psychoanalysis. But, in reviewing his case report of Jessica, one can see that
Stolorow's analytic practice mirrors his theory in its reliance on hypothetical
constructs. Thus his report is peppered with such formulations as repetition,
archaic transference bonds, erotization, clarification, and even analytic investigation of behavior (pp. 69–72), all of which have roots in developmental and

psychoanalytic theories that are far from "immaterial," and that stand well apart from the intersubjective phenomenal context they are used to describe. Like his patients, then, Stolorow brings invariants to the analytic table that can only be seen as products of his quite separate mind.

Addressing the irreconcilable inconsistencies posed by intersubjective theory, Moore comments (1999):

> Stolorow's critical allegiance to subjective experience is strained with (his) late inclusion of a formative and not malleable personal history ... Overall, the creation of a powerfully controlling force from the past which never attains any substance in the psychological structure seems to reflect a strained attempt to maintain the limit of the self's theoretical domain to conscious and present experience of itself. Stolorow may be insisting on looking under a streetlight for what Freud has already found in the dark. It is difficult to imagine any way [in which] any psychoanalytic theory could more completely eviscerate either the unconscious or its roots in the past (pp. 86–87).

What Freud found in the dark, and what he hoped for in terms of further illumination, will be addressed in the next section, but what must be highlighted here is that the visceral and immediate processes of intersubjective understanding that Stolorow emphasizes are essential and constitutive ingredients operating at the implicit heart of any effective therapeutic encounter. However, Stolorow's (Stolorow & Atwood, 1992/2000) intersubjective theory carries the need for attunement to an analytically untenable degree, noting that "any threat to the validity of perceptual reality constitutes a deadly threat to the self and to the organization of experience itself" (p. 94). By definition, this formulation excludes any possibility for psychological growth derived from differences in point of view between mother and child or patient and analyst, even when those differences are a reflection of the analyst's (or mother's) greater maturity or more integrated perspective, which can then be offered as a corrective for the patient's (or child's) subjective distortions. This subject will be discussed further in this chapter when we explore the ways in which differences in reality perception between the parent and child and the patient and analyst are a necessary ingredient of self-development. It can, therefore, be concluded that Stolorow's prescription for practice entirely misses the notion that empathic understanding is not an intervention, but a baseline from which the therapist must work to choose which way to go.

To this point must be added the fact that for both the analyst and the patient, any conscious, verbal interpretation of the data afforded by affective "knowing" of the intersubjective universe, whether in the immediate context

SORDERS

of the therapeutic encounter or in the domain of theory, must remain in the realm of the hypothetical. For, in Daniel Stern's (1985, 2004) memorable phrases, the "present moment" of "pure lived experience" can be captured by affective processes, such as empathy and introspection, but the instant the data are consciously and verbally presented is the moment the data are changed. And the nature of this change, as well as its inevitability, is a direct consequence of the structure of the human brain.

THE DOMAIN OF NEUROBIOLOGY:
AFFECT ATTUNEMENT AND THE RIGHT HEMISPHERE

> If the preceding model is correct, there might be some residual indication, no matter how small, of the ancient divine function of the right hemisphere.
> — *Julian Jaynes*

> The core of the self is thus nonverbal and unconscious, and it lies in patterns of affect regulation.
> — *Allan Schore*

The evolutionary base of the "ancient divine function of the right brain" referred to by Jaynes was made strikingly apparent to me on one afternoon of a summer vacation. My driver and I were sitting in the van watching a water buffalo try to resolve a dilemma. At the bottom of the hill was the water. To get to it, he had to pass six lionesses basking in the golden glow of the African sun. For almost a quarter of an hour, the old bull was immobile, eyes fixed on the lionesses. Finally, he made his move, walking slowly by them, then glancing once back over his shoulder in a gesture I could only interpret as triumphant. "What," I asked my driver, "was going on in his mind? Was he terrified? Was he strategizing? Was he figuring out whether there was another way?" Eric, in the slow and patient way to which I had become accustomed, answered me as a parent might an overexcited child. "No," he said, "he was watching their expressions."

The light flashed on. "Of course! Allan Schore!" was all I could think.

What Freud found was a universe of unconscious representation. The "dark" he found it in was the void presented by the lack of any substantive biological foundations upon which to anchor his theories; a lack he discussed in the *Project for a Scientific Psychology*, as well as in a letter to Fliess, in which he begged the latter to "supply me with solid ground on which I shall be able to give up explaining things psychologically, and start finding a firm base in physiology" (Fine, 1973, p. 11). It may be that the recent findings of neurobiologic and developmental theorists have gone a long way toward answering Freud's prayer, as these findings both validate the existence of the intrapsychic representational universe and demonstrate the underlying neurobiologic mechanisms responsible for its creation and ways of functioning.

In addressing the interface between clinical models and neurobiologic research, Allan Schore informs us that "a deeper understanding of the fundamental processes that drive development, of why early experience influences the organization of psychic structure and how this structure comes to mediate emergent psychological functioning, or the origins of the human mind, is now within sight (in Moskowitz et al., 1997, p. 2)." And indeed, Schore's own work has gone a long way toward covering these bases, synthesizing the findings of neurobiology with developmental research and psychoanalytic theory and practice.

At the heart of Schore's theory is the finding that affect transmissions between a mother and child mediated by the prefrontal orbital structures of the right brain (so named because of their close association with the visual system) that occur during the first two years of the child's life establish a template that will have an enduring impact on the child's future neurologic and psychological functioning. Thus, the hard-wired capacity of the evolutionarily "ancient right brain" to read and respond to the semiotics of facial expression, kinesthetic tone and gesture, and the prosody of vocal productions demonstrated by the water buffalo is seen by Schore as constituting the unconscious substrate that lies at the core of the human psyche.

As a part of his massive body of work, Schore provides an outline of how these biological and psychological processes unfold during those critical first two years. He indicates that the process of affect transmission is seen first in the form of mutual gaze transactions between the mother and child Thus, in the interaction he describes, mother's pupils enlarge in response to her baby's glance, which elicits smiling and enlarged pupils in the baby, which elicits caregiving behavior in the mother. Further, the biochemistry induced by the mirroring of overt facial expressions leads, in its turn, to an internal physiological mirroring of affect states. In this way, the downloading of the affect states of the mature right hemisphere of the mother becomes the mechanism for psychological and neurobiologic growth in the infant. What was formerly metaphorized as an "auxiliary ego" can now be seen to exist in the form of the infant's reliance on the mother's brain as the structuring agent of his or her own immature nervous system.

The degree of affective attunement that exists between the mother and child becomes a central determinant in these processes. Attuned responses from the mother that generate states of positive arousal result in the release of

endogenous opiates in the infant (p. 21) that are responsible for shaping specific growth attributes of neural wiring, as well as for providing an experiential
substrate that promotes attachment. On the other hand, where prolonged
states of misattunement, neglect, or abuse occur, neurotoxic chemicals are re-
leased that inhibit, or are destructive to, the growth of both neurologic and
psychic structures and functions, eventuating in, among other things, enduring
internalized representational structures of insecure attachment.

Schore's description of the latter half of the first year is one of symbiotic
reliance on the mother, where object seeking on the part of the infant re-
volves around the mother's face. Attuned mirroring on the part of the mother
leads to positive arousal states on the part of the infant that lay the groundwork for secure attachment.

As the period of intersubjectivity emerges, at around 9 months of age,
such facial mirroring becomes a method for allowing the infant entry into the
mother's feeling states. Affective self–other experiences are stored as representations within the psyche of the infant in the form of "an internalized
object relation consisting of a self representation, an object representation, and
a linking affect state" (p. 29). The existence of an internalized representational
structure of a regulated self with an attuned mother results in object constancy, which then allows the infant to shift from external reliance on the mother
for affect regulation to internal reliance on the evoked representation, which
serves as a tool for self-regulation, even in the absence of the mother.

In reviewing this developmental premise, along with others to follow, it
is instructive to note how Schore's neurologically based formulations lend
credence to the psychological unfolding of separation/individuation described
by Mahler (1975) as "the psychological birth of the human infant." In her
work, Mahler, as Schore, describes an initial state of symbiosis with the
mother, during which the child's high arousal states are based on the mother's
mirroring responses, which reinforce the child's sense of merger. Like Schore,
Mahler sees these processes as being intrapsychically encoded as a fused object
representational structure of (presuming "good-enough" mothering) the self
and the mother linked by a state of high positive arousal.[9] But as Schore and
Mahler both indicate, further developmental advances on the part of the child
have a transforming impact on the mother–child interaction. Thus, Schore
notes:

---

[9] It is beyond the scope of this chapter to give a full account of Mahler's theory,
which proposes two split representational units for each of the phases of separation/
individuation, one a libidinal and one an aggressive unit. I am focusing here on the
libidinal unit as the predominant unit because it does dominate in the situation of
healthy mother–child attunement.

In optimal growth-promoting environments, the interactive mechanism for generating positive affect becomes so efficient that by the time the infant begins to toddle he is experiencing very high levels of elation and excitement. Developmental neurophysiological studies reveal a significant increase in positive emotion from 10–13.5 months. As the practicing stage proceeds from early to late infancy, however, the socioemotional environment of the caregiver–infant dyad changes dramatically, and the nature of their object relations is significantly altered (pp. 16–17).

The sequence of affective transmission between the mother and child that Schore is describing here correlates highly with Mahler's description of the psychological changes occurring during the child's advancement from the practicing to the rapprochement subphase of the period of separation/individuation, such that the rapprochement child's increasing self-capacities result in a shift in emotional transactions within the mother–child dyad that eventuates in a separation of the intrapsychic representations of the self and mother.

Although Schore does not make explicit reference to Mahler's formulation, his description of the processes that take place during later toddlerhood could easily be seen to constitute the neurobiologic and psychological mediators underlying the intrapsychic separation of self and object representations that Mahler predicates as happening during rapprochement.

Thus, Schore's description shows the mother in the child's second year shifting her function from that of "a caregiver to a socialization agent," such that whereas in the practicing subphase, her responses were primarily centered around "affection, play, and caregiving ... the mother of the 13–17 month old toddler expresses a prohibition on the average of every 9 minutes, as she must now persuade the child to inhibit unrestricted exploration, tantrums, and bladder and bowel function, i.e., activities that [the child] enjoys ... In other words, in order to socialize the child, she must now engage in affect regulation to reduce the heightened levels of positive affect associated with the pleasure of these activities" (p. 18).

The mother's new stance does not comply with the child's previously encoded representational system, which had been structured to anticipate a match between the internal states of the self and the mother. The failure of this match to occur sets off, in Schore's words, "a sudden shock-induced deflation of positive affect." This deflation corresponds to what he labels the "attachment emotion of shame," which is experienced by the child as a failure of the mother's affect-regulating function.

The lack of correspondence in the internal states of the mother and child, along with the consequent shame-generating and deflating emotional disruption, can be seen as the mechanism that drives apart the fused intrapsychic representations of the self and mother that characterize the practicing subphase, leading to the creation of the separate self and object representations that Mahler attributes to the rapprochement subphase. The validity of this assumption is supported by the findings of Schore, who indicates that "in the prototypical object relation of shame, a separation response is triggered in the presence of and by the mother, who spontaneously and unconsciously blockades the child's initial attempt to emotionally reconnect with her in a positive affect state." This attempt to "emotionally reconnect" has its conceptual analog in Mahler's notion of the rapprochement child's wish for reunion.

The shame state occasioned by the mother's failure to engage in reunion has the neurobiologic consequence of releasing corticosteroids, as opposed to endogenous opiates, which results in the child's experience of a state of tension that is beyond his or her capacity to self-regulate. The mother's response to this state is critical, and largely depends on her capacity to regulate her own affect. Where the mother's own affect state is such as to permit her to reestablish positive attuned responses to the child, interactive repair can occur. Repeated episodes of such "distress–relief" sequences ultimately result in the child's developing, in Schore's words, "an internal representation of himself as effective, of his interactions as positive and reparable, and of his caregiver as reliable" (p. 20).

Schore's delineation of the neurobiologic bases of developmental psychic processes has highly significant implications for psychoanalytic theory and practice. His explication of the mechanisms and consequences of affect transmissions between the mother and child goes a long way toward creating a theoretical platform capable of containing and integrating the conflictual perspectives we have reviewed regarding the significance of real actions, intersubjective experience, and the existence of an enduring intrapsychic object-representational universe. Thus, his formulations incorporate each of these dimensions, showing how real interactions and their intersubjectively constituted affective substrates are encoded as enduring psychic structures.[10]

In terms of clinical practice, Schore's work on affect transmission provides solid grounds for the mysterious process of projective identification, conceptualized by him as a manifestation of rapid-processing right-brain to right-brain transmissions that occur between the patient and therapist. Additionally, his

---

[10] Schore's formulations fit well with the precepts of Piaget and others, who indicate that interactions with the external world become internalized as schemata that operate in accord with Werner and Kaplan's "orthogenetic principle," which sees such schemata as developing in ways that demonstrate increasing levels of differentiation and hierarchical integration.

formulations underscore the need for therapeutic attention to the processes of affect attunement and affect regulation as a central part of clinical work, indicating that the capacity to regulate disruptive emotional states in the patient (as seen, for example, in negative therapeutic reactions) will be largely dependent on the therapist's own capacity for affective self-regulation. Schore's work thereby lends specific meaning to the analytic constructs of countertransference and therapeutic neutrality, removing from the latter its negative connotations of sterility and disengagement, and substituting the requirement that the therapist must be able to process and regulate his or her own emotional responses to the patient's affective states. Schore does, however, underscore the fact that therapists, like mothers, are prone to experiencing frequent misattunements, so that the processes of repair and reattunement are as significant in the therapeutic world as they are in the developmental one.

SCHORE'S NEUROBIOLOGY AND MASTERSON'S DOMAIN OF DEVELOPMENTAL SELF AND OBJECT RELATIONS

In explicating the mechanisms underlying the formation of object relational structures, Schore's neurobiologic model offers conclusive support for the existence of the affectively determined intrapsychic object relational structures that form the cornerstone of Masterson's developmental self and object relations theory. In addition, the developmental trajectory Schore proposes, which accords with Mahler's theory of separation/individuation, validates Masterson's developmental formulations, which are largely based on Mahler's model. In line with these developmental precepts is Schore's explication of how different developmental issues require different responses from the mother. Masterson's clinical theory recognizes this finding in its systematic focus on the need for constructing interventions specifically tailored to meet the differing needs of patients whose psychopathological issues reflect structurally divergent modes of insecure attachment.

The correspondence between Schore's findings and Masterson's theory becomes particularly salient in Schore's explication of the need of the rapprochement child to have a mother who can promote adaptive behavior in the face of the child's (and her own) emotional pull toward the "reunion" state of mother–child affective attunement. In Masterson's view, the Borderline personality disorder is a consequence of the mother's failure to withstand this pull as it occurs during the rapprochement subphase (Masterson, 1976). Thus, the mother's own needs and anxieties prompt her to forgo her (in Schore's term) "socializing" function in order to avoid a disruption of her own or her child's positive state of attunement. As a result, the child will thereafter sacrifice his or her own adaptive functioning in order to defend against the dysphoric emotions consequent to actions that serve to foster separation and/or individuation. These dynamics then become manifest in the characteristic regressive and self-destructive behaviors of patients with Borderline personality disorders.

The therapeutic interruption of these maladaptive defensive behaviors is, in Masterson's view, implemented clinically by the intervention of confrontation, which is designed, like Schore's "socializing" function of the mother, to focus attention on adaptive functioning, prioritizing it over the good feeling of the reunion state by continuously confronting the patient with the negative consequences of his or her regressive and self-destructive behaviors.[11]

In this vein, it cannot be too heavily stressed that whereas Schore's findings indicate the need of therapists to be affectively attuned to their patients, attunement does not always signify, as Stolorow has proposed, a therapeutic response that strives only to mirror and validate the patient's subjective experience. Rather, Schore's work, like Masterson's, supports the notion that the effective therapist, like the effective mother, must sometimes resist his or her need to stay on the same emotional page as the patient in favor of creating a context that is optimally conducive to the patient's psychological growth.

As a brief example, consider one of my patients, a young woman with a Borderline disorder stemming from a highly dysfunctional childhood that included physical abuse by her father and total neglect by her mother. As might be predicted, the patient had succeeded in getting herself into a series of destructive and dysfunctional relationships with men and substances. Quite early in the treatment I began to confront what I labeled her "dumb blonde routine." As I write this, it has been six months of essentially confrontive work, during which she has improved her functioning considerably, breaking off her disturbed relationship with her boyfriend and effectively curbing her drinking. Recently, she informed me: "You know, this therapy has helped me so much more than my last. My last therapist would just try to be empathetic and feel sorry for me, and it only brought me down. I think I stayed weak to be with her. I got worse, and she started calling me at home, and then I began to use drugs because she sent me to a psychiatrist, who would give me a prescription whenever I asked for one."

There is no doubt that this young woman's history contained much that

---

[11] A full explication of the dynamics and treatment of patients with Borderline disorders can be found in Masterson's (1976) seminal work, *Psychotherapy of the Borderline Adult*.

was worthy of feeling "sorry for." However, her former therapist's mirroring of the patient's subjective sense of hopelessness only led to further regression. By contrast, my confrontive responses did not signify for her a lack of attunement, but were experienced instead as supportive of her struggle to live a more adaptive life.

In this example, it can be presumed that my therapeutic impact was the result of some combination of affective tone, verbal construction, and theoretical inference. Schore's work emphasizes only part of this equation, stressing, as does Jaynes', the notion that, like the water buffalo, we have many significant dynamics that operate at levels that are unconscious and non-verbal.[12] Unlike the water buffalo, however, we are a species immersed in the vicissitudes of language.

THE DOMAIN OF LANGUAGE[13]

> Whereof one cannot speak, thereof one must be silent.
> — *Ludwig Wittgenstein*

> ... The verbal construction that we create
> not only shapes our view of the past, but indeed,
> it, a creation of the present, becomes the past.
> — *Robert Wallerstein*

We have seen the monumental significance of the right hemisphere. What use then is the left? And why, if the right hemisphere is, as Schore indicates, the neural seat of the self, has psychoanalysis always stressed that it must, to be effective, remain "the talking cure."

Daniel Stern's (1985, 2004) poignant longing to capture "the present moment" of "pure lived experience" pervades his writings, reminding me always of a story I once read of someone trying to catch the last ray of light before nightfall. For Stern, then, some part of the acquisition of language is akin to

---

[12] Schore does not neglect the significance of language, indicating that it has a major role as a tool for connection and self-regulation, but he has also indicated that it is possible that psychodynamic theories have overemphasized the verbal, as opposed to nonverbal, elements of psychoanalysis.

[13] This section regretfully excludes (in the service of brevity) theoretical perspectives, such as Lacan's, that indicate the way in which the unconscious itself is structured like a language, focusing instead on language as it is commonly referred to, involving conscious thoughts or verbal constructions.

a loss of innocence. Stern's work depicts the Janus face of language, indicating how it is at once a tool for greater intersubjective access to the other and to culture, while, at the same time, having the potential to deny and distort self-experience.

Because of the differing modes of processing undergone by the right sensation-representing hemisphere, as contrasted with the left linguistic-representing hemisphere, there is, in fact, some undeniable way in which "lived" subjective experience does indeed lose something in the translation. In his simplest example, Stern (1985) depicts a child's experience of a patch of sunlight, replete with all the complex intermingled textures of amodal perception. He then describes how this experience is affected by a verbal statement, "*Oh*, look at the *yellow* sun*light*" [emphasis his], noting how that statement anchors the experience to a particular sensory modality. In this way, language reifies selective aspects of amodal global experience such that the verbal representation becomes the official version, driving the amodal experience underground (p. 176).

This set of sequences is a normative, if in some ways regrettable, consequence of our species' linguistic capacities. (It is, perhaps, possible that the water buffalo experienced the warm African sun more fully than did I.) However, Stern amplifies his explanation of the experience-distorting capacities of language to encompass the interpersonal sphere, where they are seen to have potentially toxic effects. He indicates:

> Experience in the domains of emergent, core, and intersubjective relatedness, which continue irrespective of language, can be embraced only very partially in the domain of verbal relatedness. And to the extent that events in the domain of verbal relatedness are held to be what has really happened, experiences in these other domains suffer an alienation ... Language, then, causes a split in the experience of the self. It also moves relatedness onto the impersonal, abstract level intrinsic to language, and away from the personal immediate level intrinsic to the other domains of relatedness (p. 163).

Thus, where the verbal version of experience, handed down by parents, caregivers, or, for that matter, therapists, is at odds with the as-yet-unlanguaged self-experience of what-is-happening (as, for example, in the crazy-making situation described by Gregory Bateson as "the double bind"), language can drive apart interpersonal self-experience as lived and as verbally represented. What remains are two versions of reality, one a false-self view based on conformity to the needs of the object, and the other a true-self view that more accurately represents self-experience. In this way,

Gradually, with the cooperation between the parent and the child, the false self becomes established as a *semantic construction made of linguistic propositions about who one is and what one does and experiences,* [while] *the true self becomes a conglomerate of disavowed experiences of self which cannot be linguistically encoded* (pp. 226–227) [emphasis mine].

Stern's formulations are but a step away from the Whorf–Sapir hypothesis, which lets us know that the multiple designations that Inuits have for snow allow them a greater perception of their snowy reality that even winter-bound New Yorkers could ever dream of. Language, therefore, not only represents, but also creates, the only reality we can ever know. That this fact holds true for the internal world of feeling, as well as for the external world of perception, is exemplified by the words of a patient who sat down with a piece of paper in her hand, and said, "I never had the words for these feelings before, so I had to write the feelings down, so I could tell myself how I was feeling."

Finally, then, the very linguistic capacity that is so readily recruited in the service of distorting self-experience proves to be the only channel through which this same self-experience is able to be restored and reintegrated as a "known" aspect of the self.

THE DOMAIN OF NARRATIVE: THE UNSUNG COUNTRY

"So the land," I said, "must first exist as a
concept in the mind?
Then it must be sung?
Only then can it be said to exist?"

— *Bruce Chatwin*

In his book *The Songlines*, Chatwin (1988) recounts the creation myth of the Aborigines, which indicates that the land at first existed only in "the dreamtime." To take the land from the realm of the dreamtime and make it real, the Aborigines believe that they must walk it, all the while singing it into existence. Psychoanalysis, in its fashion, also sings what was before located only in the dreamtime, believing that what is curative for disavowed experience is the process of narrating it.

Donald Spence (1982), perhaps the grandfather of narrative theorists, draws a distinction between narrative truth and historical truth, putting aside Freud's "kernel of truth" in favor of the truth of narrative itself. Thus, he notes: "Narrative truth has a special significance in its own right, and . . . making contact with the actual past may be of far less significance than creating a coherent and consistent account of a particular set of events" (p. 28). In this view, the work of the patient and the analyst, who together co-construct the narrative, as well as the coherence and comprehensiveness of the narrative itself, are agents of therapeutic healing that are far more powerful than the "recovery" of the historical past.

Spence's view is borne out by the developmental and neurobiologic findings of Daniel Siegel (1999), who gives a detailed description of the different ways of knowing reality specific to each hemisphere, ultimately concluding that the co-constructive work of creating a narrative that occurs between a parent and child or a patient and therapist is the source of both neurologic integration, resulting in the linking of the differing representational systems of each hemisphere, and intersubjective integration, resulting in the coherence of self states and self-experience, as well as the establishment of conditions that promote secure attachment.

Siegel thus points out that the right hemisphere is engaged in "analogic fast-acting, parallel . . . holistic processes, specializing in nonverbal representations of images, sensations, and the nonverbal, polysemantic . . . meanings of words." Also in the verbal realm, the right hemisphere is seen as contributing to the understanding of metaphor, paradox, and humor (tools of good therapists, advertising agencies, and bad politicians, all of whom recognize the power of these constructions to reach the affective territory of the right brain). The right hemisphere also, and significantly, is more active in the reading of stories than in the reading of scientific literature. And, as Schore indicated, this hemisphere is (in Siegel's terms) the locus of the "internal world of the mind," housing self and object representations, as well as "mindsight" (i.e., the theory of one's own and others' mental states).

By contrast, the left hemisphere demonstrates a mode of processing that is "more slowly acting, linear, sequentially active, and concerned with temporal . . . processes," and "the (digital) verbal meanings of words," which are "a primary mode of processing for the left side." Siegel notes that the linear mode of the processing of the left brain dominates language-based modes of communication.

And, in a way, that echoes Stern's emphasis on the difficulty of creating verbal representations of the nonconscious data of the right hemisphere, Siegel informs us that it is possible to translate right-brain analogic modes of representations of reality into left-brain "digital forms within words," but adds that "the translation is never complete."

In summing up the differences in hemispheric modes of processing, Siegel (1999) draws on the work of Michael Gazzaniga, who explained that whereas the right brain "sees things as they are with little alteration," the left brain is "structured to find meaning, using reason to create cause and effect narratives," even with limited information (pp. 179–181).

Siegel's findings demonstrate other significant hemispheric differences too numerous to delineate here. Ultimately, however, he concludes that "the whole brain creates the mind" (p. 185) in that asymmetry in hemispheric functions allows for a multiplicity of representational formats, which are then integrated to achieve a sense of self-coherence across space and time. This integration of representations of self-experience Siegel labels "autonoetic consciousness" which he attributes directly to "a narrative mode of cognition" (p. 330).

He, therefore, writes that the process of creating a coherent-self narrative both depends on and constitutes the integration of the differing modes of functioning of each hemisphere, in that the narrative process must draw on both the analogic, imagistic, mentalizing representations of the right hemisphere and the interpretive, detail-oriented, linguistic capacities of the left hemisphere. He goes on to conclude:

> We can propose the following bilateral integrative process for narrative: *The left hemisphere's drive to understand cause–effect relationships is a primary motivation of the narrative process. Coherent narratives, however, require participation of both the interpreting left hemisphere and the mentalizing right hemisphere. Coherent narratives are created through interhemispheric integration* (p. 331) [emphasis Siegel's].

It is instructive to note how Spence and Siegel's focus on the significance of being able to create a coherent narrative is exemplified in the findings of Goldwyn and Main's Adult Attachment Interview (AAI), which proved to be able to predict the attachment style of a child based on the response of his or her parent to 18 questions designed to determine "an individual's state of mind regarding attachment." What is of interest here is that the scoring of the AAI was independent of content, resting instead on the degree to which the parent's responses followed Grice's "cooperative principle of rational discourse," which itself rests on the capacity of the narrator to be "succinct, yet complete; relevant to the topic at hand; and clear and orderly." Thus, those individuals who were able to meet the formal criteria of a concise, complete, and coherent narrative, were found to be the parents of children who were securely attached. Further, this result held even with parents whose narrative content demonstrated that they themselves had undergone dysfunctional childhoods (Fonagy, 2001, pp. 22–23).

Siegel's formulations are crucial indicators of the vital significance of the narrative work of psychoanalysis. In clinical terms, the importance of the ability to narrate one's subjective experience has been described and emphasized in many ways. Thus, the constructs of (among others) disavowal, dissociation, compartmentalization, posttraumatic stress, enactment, and, most significant, transference, have their roots in the failure of the capacity to reflect on experience and "put it into words."

In this regard, I can note, but not here do justice to, the work of Harry Stack Sullivan, who codified behavior in accordance with its semantic coherence, postulating prototaxic, paratoxic, and syntactic ways of being in the world, each of which represented the attainment, or lack thereof, of intrapsychic and interpersonal integrity (Mullahy, 1979).

The significance of the narrative function is also evident in Bion's (1992) prescient writings, which showed the ability to integrate Schore's emphasis on affect attunement with Siegel's emphasis on the construction of narrative, noting how the container function of the mother, manifested in her attuned "reverie," allows the affect-charged experiences of the child to be metabolized into assimilatable "alpha" particles consonant with coherent thought. When the mother's container function fails, emotions and experiences are doomed to a "beta particle" existence. Incapable of being incorporated by alpha functioning, they remain in the realm of what Bollas called the "unthought known," inchoate and unspeakable. As such, the only resolution for these experiences is extrusion through projective identification.

But Freud (1914, 1963) might have expressed it best, linking the failure of the capacity for verbal expression to the dynamics of acting out and repetition. Thus, he indicates that the symptomatic patient *"remembers* nothing of what is forgotten and repressed, but ... he expresses it in *action*. He reproduces it not in his memory, but in his behavior; he *repeats* it, without, of course, knowing that he is repeating it" (p. 160) [emphasis his].

Freud goes on to demonstrate that the "compulsion to repeat," which replaces the "impulsion to remember" (p. 161), finds its final home in the transference. Not insensible to the affective substrate that must be present for the work to be successful, he notes: "When the transference has developed to a sufficiently strong attachment, the treatment is in a position to prevent all the more important of the patient's repetition-actions and to make use of his intentions alone *in statu nascendi*, as material for the therapeutic work (pp. 163–164) [emphasis his]. Once the patient's destructive compulsion to repeat is bound firmly into the transference, Freud embraces it, saying: "We admit it into the transference as to a playground, in which it is allowed to let itself go in almost complete freedom and is required to display before us all the pathogenic impulses hidden in the depths of the patient's mind" (p. 164). Thus does "the talking cure" do its work.

In reviewing the complex interrelationships between the right and left hemispheres, verbal and nonverbal modes of expression, conscious and non-conscious ways of knowing, and ways of being, I am reminded of a singular morning. The patient talked of his mother. Unbidden, an image floated to my mind from a book I had read before my African summer, which described how poachers on the savannah would kill a mother elephant and tie her still-living calf to her dead body. I put the thought aside. Later, still talking of his mother, my patient said: "I just remembered that in Africa the pygmies would hunt elephants by coming up under them and spearing them in the heart." Coincidence? Co-creation? Contingent communication? Whichever — the resonance of our two images, converging to make the hunted animal and the orphaned/trapped baby animal one, became the subtext of a session filled with ambiguities surrounding questions of need and aggression, hunter and hunted. I interpreted his feelings of persecution by and enchainment to an emotionally cold, dead mother, so that he always felt trapped, terrified, and ultimately alone. With sorrow, he concurred, but also drew back as if I and my words were as sharply dangerous as a poison-tipped pygmy spear, or what he called his mother's "toxic breasts." In the sorting out of this as-yet-untamed and unnamed wilderness of feeling lies the work. But I am still left wondering: Who sang up all those elephants?

This is a true story.

References

Bion, W. (1992). *Cogitations*. London: Karnac.

Carroll, L. (1862). *Alice in Wonderland*. In *The Annotated Alice*. (1960). New York: Potter.

Chatwin, B. (1988). *The Songlines*. New York: Penguin.

Eliot, T. S. (1943/1971). *T. S. Eliot: Quartet*. New York: Harvest/HBJ Books.

Fine, R. (1973). *The Development of Freud's Thought*. New York: Jason Aronson.

Fonagy, P. (2001). *Attachment Theory and Psychoanalysis*. New York: Other Press.

Freud, S. (1914). Further recommendations in the technique of psychoanalysis: Recollection, repetition and working through (1963, pp. 157–160). In P. Rieff (Ed.), *Freud: Therapy and Technique*. New York: Macmillan.

Freud, S. (1917). Mourning and melancholia (1957, pp. 124–140). In J. Rickman (Ed.), *A General Selection From the Works of Sigmund Freud*. New York: Doubleday.

Freud, S. (1924). The economic problem in masochism (1963, pp. 190–201). In P. Rieff (Ed.), *Freud: General Psychological Theory*. New York: Macmillan.

Jaynes, J. (1976). *The Origin of Consciousness in the Breakdown of the Bicameral Mind*. Boston: Houghton Mifflin.

Mahler, M., Pine, F., & Bergman, A. (1975). *The Psychological Birth of the Human Infant*. New York: Basic Books.

Masterson, J. F. (1976). *The Psychotherapy of the Borderline Adult: A Developmental Approach.* New York: Brunner/Mazel.

Mitchell, S. (2000). *Relationality: From Attachment to Intersubjectivity.* Hillsdale, NJ: Analytic Press.

Mitchell, S., & Aron, L. (1999). *Relational Psychoanalysis: The Emergence of a Tradition.* Hillsdale, NJ: Analytic Press.

Moore, R. (1999). *The Creation of Reality in Psychoanalysis: A View of the Contributions of Donald Spence, Roy Schafer, Robert Stolorow, Irwin Z. Hoffman, and Beyond.* Hillsdale, NJ: Analytic Press.

Mullahy, P. (1970). *Psychoanalysis and Interpersonal Psychiatry: The Contributions of Harry Stack Sullivan.* New York: Science House.

Rieff, P. (1961). *Freud: The Mind of the Moralist.* Chicago: University of Chicago Press.

Schafer, R. (1983). *The Analytic Attitude.* New York: Basic Books.

Schore, A. (1997). Interdisciplinary research as a source of clinical models. In Moskowitz et al. (Eds.), *The Neurobiological and Developmental Basis for Clinical Intervention.* Northvale, NJ: Jason Aronson.

Siegel, D. (1999). *The Developing Mind.* New York: Guilford.

Spence, D. (1982). *Narrative Truth and Historical Truth Meaning and Interpretation in Psychoanalysis.* New York: Norton.

Stern, D. (1985). *The Interpersonal World of the Infant: A View From Psychoanalysis and Developmental Psychology.* New York: Basic Books.

Stern, D. (2004). *The Present Moment: In Psychotherapy and Everyday Life.* New York: Norton.

Stolorow, R. D., & Atwood, G. E. (1992/2000). *Contexts of Being.* Hillsdale, NJ: Analytic Press.

Stolorow, R. D., Brandchaft, B., & Atwood, G. E. (1987/2000). *Psychoanalytic Treatment: An Intersubjective Approach.* Hillsdale, NJ: Analytic Press.

Winnicott, D. W. (1960). The theory of the parent–infant relationship (p. 39). In *The Maturational Process and the Facilitating Environment.* New York: International Universities Press.

Index